W9-BLK-497

LILYVILLE

LILYVILLE

Mother, Daughter, and
Other Roles I've Played

Tovah Feldshuh

hachette
BOOKS

NEW YORK

Hachette Books
Hachette Book Group
1290 Avenue of the Americas
New York, NY 10104
HachetteBooks.com
Twitter.com/HachetteBooks
Instagram.com/HachetteBooks

First Edition: April 2021
Published by Hachette Books, an imprint of Perseus Books, LLC, a subsidiary of Hachette Book Group, Inc. The Hachette Books name and logo is a trademark of the Hachette Book Group.

The Hachette Speakers Bureau provides a wide range of authors for speaking events. To find out more, go to www.hachettespeakersbureau.com or call (866) 376-6591. The publisher is not responsible for websites (or their content) that are not owned by the publisher.

Print book interior design by Linda Mark.

Library of Congress Cataloging-in-Publication Data
Names: Feldshuh, Tovah, author.
Title: Lilyville: mother, daughter, and other roles I've played / Tovah Feldshuh.
Description: First Edition. | New York: Hachette Books, 2021.
Identifiers: LCCN 2020044346 | ISBN 9780306924026 (hardcover) | ISBN 9780306924033 (ebook)
Subjects: LCSH: Feldshuh, Tovah. | Actors—United States—Biography. | Singers—United States—Biography. | Mothers and daughters—United States—Biography.
Classification: LCC PN2287.F417 A3 2021 | DDC 792.02/8092 [B]—dc23
LC record available at https://lccn.loc.gov/2020044346

ISBNs: 978-0-306-92402-6 (hardcover), 978-0-306-92403-3 (ebook)

Printed in the United States of America

LSC-C

Printing 1, 2021

For my Forebears, my Afterbears,
for Andy and all who bear with me . . .
and for Momma Lily
Whose name will always be above the title in my heart.

Contents

Contents

Program Note

WHEN THE PUBLISHERS FIRST ASKED ME TO WRITE MY memoir, I could only imagine what they were envisioning: sparkling opening nights and backstage love affairs, long rehearsals, and triumphant curtain calls. There was plenty of that to be sure, but little did they know that the greatest role of my life has been the role of Lillian Kaplan Feldshuh's daughter—a part I never auditioned for, and I couldn't have been luckier to get. Since the death of my extraordinary mother, Lily, I have felt an urgent need to share her story—and mine—and our lifelong journey to understand one another.

During the more than six decades that Lily and I were figuring *us* out, expectations for women were transformed again and again by the women's movement, the sexual revolution, and the subsequent mandate for women to "have it all." My mother and I are emblematic of the way these changes created a divide between generations—and the way that it might be possible to bridge that divide through patience, compassion, and empathy. I believe that a branch, in order to bear fruit, must learn to bend. As my mother, Lily, endured these shifts, she put it more succinctly: "*Oy, my kishkes!*" (Yiddish for guts.)

Of course, I couldn't possibly envision my memoir in any format other than the one I know best: a theater piece. And thus, I invite you into the theater of my memories. There will be generations of family: the births, the deaths, the laughter, the sorrow, and even a *bris*.

Finally, in honor of my family's tradition, as well as in honor of the third of the Ten Commandments, this non-Kosher-keeping first-time author has chosen to refer to the Being Upstairs as *G-d*.

Lilyville

Preshow Announcement

O F *COURSE* I KNOW THIS IS A BOOK, BUT I'M ABOUT TO CON-jure for you the entire world of Lilyville, and nothing gives me the adrenaline I need like waiting in the wings for my entrance and hearing an announcement like this:

At this time, please silence your cell phones and turn off all electronic devices. As a courtesy to those around you, unwrap all hard candies *now*.

Please be advised that this production contains fog, haze, smoke, strobe effects, loud sudden noises, mature language, and nudity.

The taking of flash photography . . . is always a delight.

Thank you.

Places, everyone!

Overture

THE PHONE RINGS. THE CALLER ID SAYS "BARRY WEISSLER," and I say to myself, "*Broadway producer* Barry Weissler? I'll pick it up!"

"Tovah, we'd like you to do *Pippin* for us on Broadway at the Music Box Theatre. Can you come down to play on the trapeze? We want to see if trapeze is part of your world."

"Trapeze, part of my world?" I muse.

So I bike down to the Music Box Theatre at Forty-Fifth and Broadway. I enter the stage door, and that is my audition, mind you—playing on the trapeze. They hoist me at least thirty feet in the air: no net, no mat, and no insurance. And I am hanging from the rafters, and Barry yells up to me, "TOVAH, Tovah, tovah! ARE YOU SCARED, Scared, scared?" I take a deep breath and suddenly I realize I'm not and say, "NO, No, no! ARE YOU, You, you?!" Without singing a note or dancing a step, I won the role of Grandma Berthe in *Pippin*, because I could swing on a trapeze.

My mother, Lily, came to every show I ever did. . . . Well, almost. One day she called and said, "Tovah, I'm not coming to see you in the *'Virginia' Monologues*, I can't say the word! But three women in black dresses in front of three music stands talking about their chach-burgers—*forget it!* So, if you're pretty and there's movement and there's color, give me a call."

So I gave her a call to take her to *Pippin*. *Pippin* has unbelievable color and movement, and I looked darn good in that bustier with fish-net stockings. All the trapeze work had taken me down to 112 pounds, which is what I weighed in seventh grade. With joy, I took my mother, with her beloved aide Joyce, to the Wednesday matinee of our Tony Award–winning revival. Grandma Berthe sings the hit tune "No Time at All," which I performed while doing a full-out trapeze act. This num-ber brought down the house. Look, you put an old bird singing upside down on a trapeze and it engenders hope in everyone. So I go to my mother after the show, and I say, "Mommy, mommy, mommy." Sud-denly, I'm three years old, grasping for mother's milk. "Mommy, how did I do?"

Her voice took on the familiar tone of a strident coronet. "Tovah, that you should still have to earn a living like this, and on a *trapeze* yet!"

That was my mother. She didn't give an inch. Looking back at when I portrayed Prime Minister Golda Meir in *Golda's Balcony*—which be-came the longest-running one-woman play in Broadway history and won me my fourth Tony nomination—my mother's comment was: "Tovah, I rate your parts by how you look. Dolly Levi was a ten. Golda Meir? *Zero!*"

Once, still aiming to please, I took my mother to the Actors' Fund of America's benefit performance of *Hair*. It too had color, movement, and leading actor Will Swenson, who, in the finale of Act One, left the stage and straddled an audience member's armrests. He chose my mother's armrests. That boy was standing over my mother like the arch of St. Louis—in his loincloth! My mother, in her little Saint John knit, she looked up, she looked down, she looked up. As the house lights came up, I timidly asked, "Momma, how did you like Act One?"

She replied, "How did I *like* it? I haven't had sex like this since Daddy died!"

Welcome to Lilyville, where my mother Lily reigns. Lily, who gave birth to this adrenaline junkie, perfectionist daughter. Lilyville, where, when I wanted to go to Juilliard, my mother said, "You're not going to trade school!"

If you came looking for behind-the-scenes tales from *The Walking Dead* or the history-making miniseries *Holocaust* with TV's *Crazy Ex-Girlfriend* sprinkled in between, or if you're looking for secret anecdotes about my roles on Broadway in *Yentl, Pippin,* and *Golda's Balcony,* with classics like Juliet and Dolly Levi folded in—it's all here. Plus you'll find encounters with Barbra Streisand, Viggo Mortensen, Liev Schreiber, Cybill Shepherd, Patti LuPone, Ruth Gordon, Garson Kanin, Nobel Laureate Isaac Bashevis Singer, and Supreme Court Justice Ruth Bader Ginsburg.

And though all my career roles have happened on Broadway, in film, in television, and in concert, my longest run, and ultimately my most profound, was as the daughter of Lillian Kaplan Feldshuh. All these roles took place in Lilyville, witnessed by its monarch during her robust 103 years on this planet. (And in my mind's eye, eternally thereafter—for better or for exasperation.) So, come on in. I'm Jewish, we are all about schmoozing. Well, schmoozing and suffering. Well, schmoozing, suffering, and guilt. (Did you call your mother today?)

ACT I

How to Make an Entrance

L ITTLE SURPRISE: MAKING A MEMORABLE ENTRANCE IS IN MY DNA. My mother Lillian Kaplan Feldshuh was born on a dining room table in the Bronx on April 18, 1911. You may think the dining room table is what's remarkable about this story, but what's remarkable to me is the number 18. Eighteen is the numerical value of the letters in the Hebrew word *chai* for life. If ever a number suited a person, it was chai for my mother Lily!

My Russian grandfather Gershan and British grandmother Ada welcomed their third child with joy and excitement—and no doubt platefuls of *flanken* and *kneidlach* (think Jewish spare ribs and dim sum). My grandparents had a railroad apartment on one floor of a brownstone on Charlotte Street in the South Bronx. They moved there from Seventeenth Street and Second Avenue when their oldest daughter, Rose, got pneumonia. The doctors said, "To save little Rosie's life, you must move to the country." Yes, the Bucolic Bronx! Today the Bronx is just moving uptown, but in 1909, escape from the city to the country was exactly what they did.

Charlotte Street was originally a bridle path across the estate of the Quaker pioneer William Fox, who married Charlotte Leggett, a woman of Bronx pedigree dating back to 1661. Charlotte's brother, Samuel, founded the New York Gas Lighting Company that would illuminate Broadway for the very first time, earning the longest street in New York City the nickname The Great White Way.

When Lily was a child, Charlotte Street meandered through lazy countryside still covered in bridle paths that ran parallel to the elevated train lines: the old meeting the new in a way that was, and still is, uniquely New York. My mother often reminisced about the wildflowers growing in the vast patches of land she could see behind her home. For the first years of her life, beyond those wildflowers was nothing but horizon. When the eyes can see that far, the mind can dream big. In 1922, at the age of eleven, she witnessed the laying of the first bricks of Yankee Stadium. On April 18, 1923, her twelfth birthday, Yankee Stadium opened its gates for its first major league game—and beat the Red Sox 4–1. The Kaplans have been Yankee fans ever since!

My mother was one of four daughters. First, there was the glamorous, chic, and creative Rose, whose bout with pneumonia brought the family to the Bronx in the first place. Then there was Nancy: chubby, stalwart, kind, and generous. After Nancy was my quiet, modest mother, Lily, and twenty-one months later, Ada and Gershan had their fourth and last child, May. My grandfather had desperately wanted a boy, and so being a resourceful man as well as a master cutter of men's clothing, he designed knickers for his youngest daughter, which she wore with high socks, high spirits, and bobbed hair.

May and Lily were inseparable. They started out life practically sharing the same crib, then graduated to sleeping on the same pullout couch. Lily played the piano, May played the violin. Lily played tennis, May played tennis. I have a picture of May as a girl wearing boxing gloves and having a pretend prize fight with Lily in their Aunt Leah's small Boston backyard. Lily stands victorious with her foot resting gently on May's chest, her gloved fighter's fist proudly thrust up in the air. I treasure that picture, not because it was unusual to see my mother victorious, but because it was rare to see her visibly *proud*. She tended to understate her victories when I was growing up, and until my father died, she was extremely modest.

However, in those brief moments of her youth, she was a buoyant spirit of the Roaring Twenties, roller-skating over convention, with her cropped hair and her rolled-up skirts, gliding through the wilds of Crotona Park and navigating Indian Lake, which beckoned her to roller-skate around it in the warm months and ice-skate on it in the cold. Lily was in search of adventure, romance, self-improvement, poetry, and true and endless love. Even as I write this sentence, I see so much of myself in young Lily. Are these innate personality traits also passed along in our DNA?

The diaries my mother kept as a teenager reflect an adventure-filled youth, albeit one on a tight budget. They also reveal a deep, dark secret. Inside, Lily saw her personality as "beige," uninteresting. In one entry, she compared herself to wallpaper and wrote, "I've got to work on my character and my personality. I am determined to become vivid." Thus, fifteen- and sixteen-year-old Lily wrote about, and exalted in, her outings, her parties, her country excursions, and boys, boys, boys. Her diaries belied her shy personality; she wrote of unfettered experiences with wild flights of imagination. But while Lily was starring in a whimsical, Gatsby-inspired play in her own mind, in reality, she was a girl coming of age in a cataclysmic era of rapid, radical change. She would face the First World War, the Spanish Flu, the stock market crash, the Great Depression, and World War II—all before the age of thirty.

Her mother, Ada, a London girl, wanted to be an actress on the British music hall stage. Ada walked in to audition at the Theatre Royal Haymarket in 1900 ready to sing, ready to dance, and instead, the producers said to her: "Ada, show us your ankles." Reluctantly, she showed them her ankles. Then, delighted, they said, "Ada, show us your knees." That was the end of her theatrical career.

Nobody saw her knees except Grandpa—and even then, "Not so often!" she'd yell. Ada's dreams of being an actress faded to a mere echo when she became a wife and mother of four. For her, the New World did not hold the Palace Theatre, but rather a poker table with friends like Ceil Somack, whom she visited every afternoon after finishing her household chores. Kaplan family lore maintains that she, Ceil, and their poker ring were busted one night by the police. Did Grandma Ada have a rap sheet? That's one story she never revealed to me, much like her knees. Either way, Ada was considered somewhat of a *banditte* (Yiddish for bandit). For instance, she would give Grandpa Gershan a good shot of scotch, and as he dozed off in his armchair, she would sneak out for another round of cards.

The four children of Ada Kaplan were latchkey kids. When my mother and her sisters would return from school, Ada was never there. "I left the key by Sadie's windowsill," she would instruct. Evidently, this was Ada's version of home security.

Lily, like her mother, had a rich imagination. If Ada could dream of being an actress, Lily could dream of living the life of a movie star. She gave herself a secret stage name: Hortense. She only shared that name with her best friend, Gladys Loeb. Hortense played tennis in all whites. Hortense went to concerts and plays, bobbed her hair, played a mean piano, and danced the Charleston. Hortense was hopeful, gay, expressive, expansive, and searching for her Prince Charming. Hortense was teaching Lily how to vivify. In fact, Hortense reminded me of myself as a teenager. Perhaps that's why my mom and I rarely saw eye to eye for years; by the time I came into Lily's life, she wasn't anything like Hortense at all.

All four Kaplan girls went to Walton High School, which Mary Walton originally started as a "dame school" back in colonial times. Mary Walton's first classroom was in her home, where she taught little girls to read, write, and master household chores.

Walton High was still girls only when Mom and my aunts went there. It had an excellent academic reputation, and my mother excelled enough at her studies to be accepted into NYU's College of Arts and Sciences in 1927—at just sixteen years old! Ada and Gershan, like many immigrant families, couldn't afford to send Lily to college, so she decided to fund her own education. She secured a job after school and over the summers, working at the Bowery Savings Bank at Seventy-Second and Broadway to earn the four-hundred dollars a year she needed to attend the university.

My dad, Sidney Feldshuh, was wildly handsome. He was voted "Lady Killer" at Paterson High School in New Jersey in 1926. Back then, in the pre-OJ days, that was a compliment. Sidney was an eighteen-year-old sophomore at NYU when he met my mom, because Lily's locker happened to be next to his sister's. Sylvia Feldshuh was a senior with plans to enter NYU School of Law the following year.

"Have you seen my brother?" Sylvia asked Mom one day.

Lily replied, "Who's your brother?"

A few days later, she got her first glimpse of a fellow she thought was Rudolph-Valentino gorgeous. This *wow* was Sidney Feldshuh. Thanks to the divine providence otherwise known as Lily and Sylvia's adjacent lockers, Dad also got a glimpse of my beautiful mother. That was it. Shakespeare put it best:

No sooner did they meet but they looked, no sooner looked but they loved, no sooner loved but they sighed, no sooner sighed but they asked one another the reason, no sooner knew the reason but they sought the remedy.

—*As You Like It*, Act V, Scene 2

Forgive the dramatics, but I see my life as a theater piece, and this is one of my favorite theatrical moments in my family's history.

The name "Felt Shoe" only begins to capture how these two were a perfect fit. He danced like Fred Astaire, and she, like Ginger Rogers. He spoke fluent German, and German was her major. They were a match in their beauty and brains, but Dad told me it was Mom's common sense and modesty that won him over.

The trip from the Bronx to NYU was a trip between worlds. The trip from Paterson to Washington Square was the same. The young couple kept their romance private, but not secret. Ada and Gershan probably learned about Sidney by the end of 1928, but you didn't bring a boy home to meet your parents unless it was serious. In fact, my mother didn't meet Marion Feldshuh, Sidney's mom, until she and Dad were formally engaged.

Lily and Sidney courted throughout the spring, fall, and winter of 1928. Hortense was in love. By 1929, Lily was elected to student government, and Sidney was pulling straight A's. The couple studied downtown by day and popped up to the Harlem nightclubs on Saturday nights. They went to hear Bessie Smith, Eubie Blake, and Jelly Roll Morton. "Sidney Feldshuh!" my mother would tease, as my dad put his arm around her in Washington Square Park. "Do you realize you have your arm around the Vice President of the sophomore class?" They were in love, and unbeknownst to them, they were dancing on the razor's edge of history.

On Thursday, October 24, 1929, the stock market crashed and everything about New York City changed overnight: business closures, mass unemployment, and bank failures. The crash was not the sole cause of the Great Depression, but it did accelerate global economic collapse. Luckily, Mom had saved her pennies. She kept her job at Bowery Savings, where she worked under the name of Lillian Kaye to avoid the stain of anti-Semitism. And luckily Dad's family still had enough money to support his education until he graduated from NYU in 1930. Admidst this economic crisis, my father won a scholarship to Harvard Law School.

By 1932, Lily and Sidney had dated for nearly five years and reached a critical point in the relationship where they had to go one way or another. Either they would get married or my mother would have to break it off.

"Break it off?" said Sidney, "Are you out of your mind?"

They eloped on January 28, 1933.

Back to *As You Like It*, Act V, Scene 2:

. . . And in these degrees have they made a pair of stairs to marriage, which they will climb incontinent or else be incontinent before marriage.

(Note: In Shakespeare's time "incontinent" meant unrestrained. Thank goodness!)

A few months later, though they had already been sleeping together as man and wife for over two years, they officially announced their engagement. And on Flag Day, June 14, 1935, as far as family and friends knew (except for Ada, Gershan, and Lily's sisters), they got married for the first time on the rooftop of the St. Moritz.

My last *As You Like It* quote, I promise! Still Act V, Scene 2:

They are in the very wrath of love, and they will together. Clubs cannot part them.

(In Shakespeare's time, "will" meant carnal desire.)

My father kept the elopement a secret from his family his whole life. The truth is, Grandma Marion did not regard Lily as good enough for her one and only "sunny son," who was also her baby. Lily's origins were Russian and financially modest. Sidney's origins were Austrian and German, and financially rich. You draw your own conclusions. Two days before his death, I asked him if he had at least told his sisters that he had been married to my mother for sixty-three-and-a-half, not sixty-one, years. He shook his head and put his finger to his lips and said, "Shhh."

My parents sailed for Europe on the Cunard's SS *Rex* for their hon-eymoon. No one from my mother's background could afford that kind of a journey, but somehow, the pennies were saved, and Dad's mother, now a widow, supported the trip—as long as the honeymooning cou-ple took Sidney's sister, Sylvia, with them on the crossing. Can you imagine?

I discovered, according to the Paterson-Passaic census, Marion Feldshuh had owned a business since 1917, and she was generat-ing her own independent income that made this honeymoon all the more possible. Stop the ship: My grandmother owned her own business strapped in a corset before she had the vote? I'll take that bloodline!

When my parents returned to New York, they settled on Park Ave-nue and Eighty-Fourth Street, renting the living and dining rooms of what was once a single-family mansion. It was quite a step up from the railroad apartment at 1534 Charlotte Street in the Bronx. The living room, with a pullout couch, served as both their bedroom and enter-taining space. The dining room was for breakfast, lunch, and dinner, and the pantry was divided in two to provide a kitchen and a bathroom. They were in heaven.

They pursued the life they saw in the art-deco movie musicals. They were great ballroom dancers long before *Dancing with the Stars*. My father used to say to me, "The kids today know only two dances: fast and slow. But in my day, we danced a hundred dances: the Charleston, the Lindy, the Samba, the Mambo, the Tango, the Meren-gue, the Jitterbug, the Polka, the Waltz." My mother could follow ev-ery step. They cultivated being great dancers because it was a mark of breeding and class. Young Lily and Sidney, with their pals from NYU and Harvard, were living the life. Only one hiccup: Lily could not get pregnant.

After ten years of marriage, my mother went to have her whole reproductive area diagnosed. After blowing air into her fallopian tubes, the doctors reported they were closed. Then in 1943, childless, my father was drafted into the United States Army. With the specter of losing her husband to the war effort, a miracle took place; my brother David was conceived just days before Dad had to leave for boot camp. *Necessity is the mother of conception.*

At age thirty-three, Sidney was in training for the Army infantry at Fort Benning in Georgia, with soldiers more than ten years his junior. Mom left Park Avenue and moved back in with her parents, who now lived at 955 Walton Avenue in the Bronx. She was in her sixth month.

My father finished his basic training down south and was stationed in New Jersey at Fort Dix. He was granted a weekend pass the Saturday after Thanksgiving and was to meet my mother for the Columbia-Army football game at Columbia University's Baker Field.

It was November 27, 1943, and my mother was well into her third trimester. She was preparing their warm stadium lunch in the kitchen of 955 when a call came from the Red Cross.

"Are you Mrs. Sidney Feldshuh?" they said.

"Yes," she replied.

"This is the American Red Cross. Private Feldshuh will not be able to attend the game." My mother would not see my father or hear his voice for the next two and a half years.

Let it be noted that my grandfather David Feldshuh died November 27, 1926, and Sidney Feldshuh, his only son, was shipped away from American shores on November 27, 1943. There are no coincidences: odd or G-d?

Dad was shipped to England and stationed in Manchester Barracks, where he continued training for the infantry and begged his superior officer for an intelligence test. D-Day was five months away. The US Army finally granted him the test, and his ability to speak fluent German and French whisked him out of the infantry and into Army intelligence, under General Dwight David Eisenhower.

Dad went from holding rifles to running bulletins and intel, from carrying belts of ammunition to sticking pins in battle maps, all in the bowels of Knightsbridge Barracks. He went from taking orders from a staff sergeant to taking orders from the high command. He was promoted from private to warrant officer, and he would be one of one hundred men helping General Eisenhower plan D-Day.

My brother David Mark Feldshuh was born January 31, 1944. My mother said David's *bris* was one of the bittersweet moments of her life, because her sweetheart, or as she humorously called him in German, her *schmeerkate*, was fighting in Europe for a free world. The whole family—six aunts and six uncles, Grandma Marion Feldshuh, and "Papa and Mama" Kaplan—were all at the bris, and cried along with the infant David, who screamed bloody murder as his foreskin was snipped from his infant gherkin. Only Dad was missing, but thankfully not Missing in Action. My father wouldn't meet his son until David was two years old.

My cousin Lucille has a memory of my mother back in the Bronx, breastfeeding my brother David in those lonely early months of '44. Tears were dropping off her cheeks onto her breasts and the face of her baby boy. Was Sidney going to come home to her or was she going to be a widow?

Those years without my father left David reaching for my mother and my beloved Grandfather Gershan who, after four daughters, was delighted to have a grandson. My grandfather, still in the prime of his life, became the center of my brother's universe.

My father finally hit the shores of America in January of 1946 and immediately made his way from Fort Dix in New Jersey to 955 Walton Avenue. Mom was getting ready to go out with friends for the evening. The doorbell rang, she opened the door, and there stood my father in full uniform.

"Sidney!" Mom screamed, then cried, then laughed. Ada and Gershan came running, and so did Aunt May and Uncle Harold, who charged up the stairs from their apartment. Joy that transcended language abounded. "He's home, he's actually home!" my mother cried in disbelief.

My father entered the nursery and carefully walked up to David's crib to see his son for the very first time. David, with eyes like saucers, brunette ringlets in his hair, and a bit of a sniffle, looked up at Sidney curiously.

"David, I'm your daddy," my father said gently.

"You're not my daddy. That's my daddy," my brother replied, and pointed to a picture of my father with his officer's hat on. My father carefully returned his military hat to his head, held the picture next to his face, and said, "That's me in the picture, David. I'm your daddy." And so the process of getting my brother to understand who his father was, and forging a bond with him, officially began. Then everybody sat down and ate. Jews and food—no family celebration was complete without being consummated with an embarrassment of food.

The easiest route for Dad to reacclimate to the US and restart his civilian life with his wife and young son was to stay in the Bronx near Mom's family. So they rented their own apartment in the building at 955 Walton. They lived on the sixth floor, my grandparents lived on the fifth floor, and my Aunt May, Uncle Harold, and cousins Jonny and Peter lived on the fourth floor.

———

Now, LEST YOU THINK I made my entrance in the Bronx, have no fear. Innately, and apparently in utero, I timed my debut so that it could happen on Manhattan's Upper East Side. My parents were invited to a wedding on December 26 at the Waldorf Astoria on Park Avenue. My mother started to have labor pains after she ate stuffed derma (who wouldn't?). Dad said, "Why go home? Why don't we just go to Beth David?" Two hours later on December 27, I was born, happy-go-lucky Terri Sue Feldshuh on Lexington Avenue. . . . Well, not actually *on* the avenue, rather in the pristine Beth David Hospital.

My first visual memory is my Grandpa Gershan's big dining room table at 955 Walton Avenue. My crib was positioned in the corner of that dining room for all family gatherings. Maybe that's why, to this day, I love to eat. I can still hear the Kaplan clan shouting *"PASS THE BRISKET!"* with desperation, as if a famine were about to descend upon the entire tribe, rendering us extinct from starvation. Eating and extended family imprinted themselves boldly on the beginning of my life. I remember how warm the air felt from all that nourishment. I remember the smells of eating "Jewish," from *gefilte* to *kreplach*. (Think fish mousse to wontons.) There were mounds of food; "portion control" was a phrase that never entered our consciousness. An abundance of food was a clear symbol of success and security in this gorgeous, new *Amerika*. Food was more than food. Eating was integral to a heightened sense of family, comfort, and celebration. We all dressed properly for dinner. Well, everyone except me; I was still in my Dr. Dentons.

From the beginning, family *l'dor v'dor*—from generation to generation—was part of who I was. It was the blood in my veins. My intimate family *was* my extended family, and home was a cast of dozens. It's no wonder I wound up in the theater. A good cast in a good play is akin to an extended family. Everybody fundamentally helps each other. They exchange dialogue across a long table called a stage, and each actor gives the spotlight to the next actor when it is their turn. The more the sharing, the better the story. Every member is committed to the same goal. They want the play to be a hit, just as our family wanted our lives to be a hit. No actor or family member leaves the play until they've taken the final curtain call.

My home was full of stories. From the time I was two, my Papa Gershan would tell me tales of *Minsk Gubernia* in Belarus, with its dirt roads and yearly pogroms. I could taste his distaste for the *shtetl* and the constant strain of uncertainty living in a part of the world that had state-sponsored anti-Semitism. The word "Cossacks" sent shivers up my little spine, for it was the Cossacks who took the life of Great Grandmother Shifra.

By the time I was three and we had moved to Scarsdale, my father would put me to sleep by regaling me with war stories about his involvement in the invasion of Normandy and the Battle of the Bulge. How I ever got to sleep, I'll never know. My father would finish his story, turn out the lights, give me a gentle kiss on the forehead, tell me how much he loved me, and wish me sweet dreams. I would shut my eyes and have nightmares of armed men in trench coats coming out of my closet.

My first years of life in the Bronx were warm and safe, maybe the warmest and safest of my life. My playground was three apartments, two staircases, and one vast lobby where we could roller-skate on rainy days, and the treasured outdoor courtyard where I could ride David's hand-me-down tricycle in clockwise circles around the bayberry bushes in the middle of the deep red, oval "racetrack."

We lived literally on top of one another. How could I be lonely? If Mom were busy, I'd go to Papa and Grandma Ada's. If my grandparents were busy, I'd play with my cousin Jonny. Happily, Papa, who was retired, seemed forever available. As the Kaplan women were running around housekeeping, cooking, and cleaning, and in the case of Grandma Ada, gambling, Papa would be sewing, mending the family's clothes whenever they needed it: a button, a zipper, a hem that sagged, or a waistband that lost its elastic. In between stitches, he would sneak me Bartons milk chocolate–covered raisins and almonds. Yum!

Then he would take me for long walks in Joyce Kilmer Park and point out the natural treasures of each season. To bundle up with Papa in the dead of a Bronx winter was a dream come true. He never missed the beauty of a leaf or a fresh snowfall. Each blade of grass, each branch of a tree meant something to him. He never skipped over the opportunity for us to play in nature and to see and appreciate, in a child's rhythm, the beauty of the natural world—right in the middle of the Bronx!

Growing up surrounded by my grandparents, aunts, uncles, and cousins ingrained some very strong core values that have stayed with me to this day. Here now are the Kaplan Ten Commandments:

Never hold a grudge—it gives you gas.
No shady money deals—you'll get an ulcer.
No getting drunk—Schnapps fine; *shikker* (drunk) not fine.
Eat, Mamele, Eat!—only the skinny die young. (Oy, I was skinny!)

The age of reason for the Jews is three—so get going!

There's honor in work—so get busy!

Always be ready to travel—the Cossacks are coming!

Always keep hope—wherever there's shit, there must be a pony.

Honor thy father and mother—and grandparents and aunts and uncles and cousins and great-grandparents—*and* the super.

Don't suck your thumb, don't wet your bed, don't bite your nails—I did all three.

But these anxious inclinations only started when the rug was pulled out from under me and we moved to Scarsdale.

Lily on Mothering

Lily often said to me, "Women from my generation didn't feel we were good mothers unless we were correcting our children. So Terri, when you get chubby, I say, 'You're fat! Lose weight.' When you get thin, I say, 'You're gaunt! Would it kill you to eat a *schnecken*?' And when you go shopping, I say, 'You're at Chanel, I'm still at Loehmann's, what's wrong with this picture?'"

You Are What You Wear

"*I*, *AS YOUR MOTHER, GAVE YOU YOUR LIFE, AND* I *HAVE THE right to feel comfortable when I am with you. I've already given the spotlight to Sidney, so I'm already operating at half-mast when I'm with your father. But you are my child. I have the right to feel at ease with you. When you do wacky things that feel unfamiliar, it makes me tense. It makes me frightened, and it makes me ashamed.*"

Did my mother ever speak these words? No. But the message was clear even before the age of four.

The curtain came down on the Bronx and rose on sunny Scarsdale and, in the words of George M. Cohan, "Only forty-five minutes from Broadway, oh what a difference it makes." What an understatement. Here came the first big scene change of my life. Looking back on that seismic move, there was much expected of me, and much for which I wasn't prepared. I was recast in a new community with a mother who believed, "You are what you wear." This was no superficial consideration; this had to do with identity, arriving firm-footed as an American family and discarding any traces of the old *shtetl* roots. But who under-stands this at three years old? All I knew was that I liked to hang upside down from Dr. Clark's apple trees next door—there were no apple trees in the Bronx. Call me a tomboy at heart.

Actually, I was so much more than a tomboy at heart. I was a free spirit, and I was being plucked out of a community that was vibrant and cozy, that resonated with an energy that made me feel alive. Now I was in a setting where I was being reined in to conform to something I didn't quite grasp. It looked more like a magazine photo spread come to life, an image that you gazed at, but never lived in. What followed were two trajectories. On the surface, Scarsdale was lovely. It had space, and it was so green. But underneath it all was the muffled whimper of a lonely soul being tamped down. What three-year-old is interested in being in *House Beautiful?* Outside the house, there was plenty of space for me to run around, but inside the house, no matter how big it was, it felt closed in yet not at all cozy. I was lonely.

We moved to Scarsdale in November 1952, the day Eisenhower was elected President of the United States. My father was thrilled. He loved Eisenhower. Ever since he was invited to join the Commander's G-2 intelligence unit as one of the one hundred young men who helped Eisenhower plan D-Day, Dad credited the general with saving his life. On top of this, Sidney was awarded the Bronze Star Medal from Ike himself, who cited Dad's heroic achievement and meritorious service to the Allied forces. The commemorative photo is proudly mounted in my brother's home to this day. Sidney knew Eisenhower was a supe-rior commander and also felt he was an outstanding human being. He thought it was an auspicious omen that we moved into our very own dream house on the day the nation chose Ike as the thirty-fourth Pres-ident of the United States.

The house at 47 Penn Boulevard marked my mother's clear entry into the upper middle class and my father's return to it. Building 47 Penn gave my parents the opportunity to thank their parents for bravely crossing the Atlantic to create for their children a better life. My father was very generous, and Ada and Gershan were often weekend guests in our home. My mother was thrilled to have them, for Scarsdale gave them a closer alternative to Rose and Albert's beautiful Willow Downs estate, which was much farther away in Croton-on-Hudson. In one generation, Grandpa Gershan had gone from experiencing the pogroms of Russia to enjoying the sixteen-acre estate of his oldest daughter and now the fourteen-room Scarsdale ranch house of Lily's, all in verdant Westchester County.

My father wrote Mother in one of his love letters, "I will build you a house on a hill, and you will never have to wonder whether you'll be able to afford a new pair of shoes." Here was the house. The shoes would follow. In the two and a half years it took to build 47 Penn, my mother handpicked every detail: the aged brick for the outside walls, every stick of furniture, every precious antique. She wisely hired Rose's savvy decorator, Beatrice Small. Aunt Rose had briefly attended Parsons School of Design after Walton High School. It was there she met "Bea," who graduated with a degree in interior design.

With Willow Downs as Lily's inspiration and Bea Small by her side, much like a theater scenic designer, my mother built the sets where the formative years of my life would unfold. Meanwhile, Aunt Rose, who had purchased Willow Downs with her husband Albert the minute the war ended, soon opened an antique shop in neighboring Ossining. With her exquisite taste, she was able to accumulate myriad priceless pieces that my mother later bought. The house was Lily's promise to her parents that the East End of London and the dirt roads of Minsk Gubernia were experiences never to be revisited and left long behind. It was also the brick-by-brick proof of my father's upwardly mobile success.

What I loved about 47 Penn was that it was flat and long, and to my three-year-old eyes, it looked perfect for roller-skating. I was often firmly reminded, "This house is not a roller rink." Pity. Our home was adorned with irreplaceable antiques plus wondrous carpets from Persia, as well as custom-made rugs from Stark, whose showrooms glistened on New York's posh Upper East Side. Not even four years old, I had no idea these were costly items. Yes, they were different than my wooden crib in Grandpa Gershan's dining room, but whatever Mom put in that ranch house, I regarded as "the new normal."

"Not so fast," said Lily. "These things are precious and one of a kind. Be careful!" In other words, roller-skate in the driveway. I did— and even made it out of the driveway, sailing along Haverford Avenue toward Swarthmore like the wind. I loved to roller-skate as much as I loved climbing the forest green street poles marking one Quaker street from another. The whole neighborhood was my playground. The streets outside my home were suburban-silent, just like my mother. It was a new world, but the quietness of it seemed to echo the silence inside our home. Gone was my extended, boisterous, chubby Kaplan clan. That loveable cacophony was replaced by the hush of the suburbs and a reticent mom.

On my very first day of kindergarten, I waited for an enormous yellow school bus to pick me up. I was so excited. I had a new "back-to-school" dress and brand-spanking-new red Keds. I held my mother's soft white hand at the corner of Penn Boulevard and Swarthmore Road. She wore the colors of fall: a beautiful beige-and-olive shirtwaist with pumpkin accents. She finished the outfit off with her favorite pearls and the smell of Arpège perfume.

As the bus pulled up, my mother simply said, "You sit with Sam Houston on the bus," and pointed to a young boy sitting toward the back.

So, I did what my Mommy said. I sat with Sam Houston on the bus every day for the entire year of kindergarten.

Sam Houston was the only Black child in my grade and one of only three Black children in our town. In one sentence, a decent mother drastically diminished the specter of prejudice. Lily's silence belied her open heart. Every day, I walked down the long aisle of that yellow bus and in the second-to-last seat on the left, I sat next to Sam Houston. I remember teaching him cat's cradle.

Forty-five years later, I was in San Francisco playing *Golda's Balcony* at the American Conservatory Theater. I received a letter backstage that read:

> *Dearest Terri Sue,*
>
> *I don't know if you remember me, but my name is Sam Houston. From day one of kindergarten, you sat next to me on the bus. You were my very first friend. Thank you for keeping me company.*
>
> *May I come backstage to see you?*
>
> *—Sincerely, Sam*

Ours was a tearful and profound reunion.

———◆———

BY SEVEN YEARS OLD, I figured that if I wasn't allowed to roller-skate in the house, I could at least jump rope, and I decided to do that on the sea-green slate floor of our entry foyer. I didn't notice the Josef Inwald Opalescent Barolac art-deco tulip vase that was proudly centered on the French polished-mahogany breakfront. My jump rope noticed it, however, and grabbed it. Crash, bam, smash! The vase shattered. My mother screamed.

"How dare you jump rope in our home?! Does this look like a playground to you?"

She grabbed my jump rope and said, "You're going to be punished. You can forget about jumping rope for a while. I'm putting it away. Plus, one full week of no television."

As terrified as I was to displease my mother, I was more upset by the punishment. My little world was imploding, so I started pleading hysterically, "Take anything, but don't take my television time! Please, please don't take my television time! What about Walt Disney?! Please, Mommy, please!"

Lily stood firm, and that was the last precious antique I broke and the last episodes of *Walt Disney*, *Leave it to Beaver*, and *Howdy Doody* I missed.

Scarsdale in the late fifties was a sleepy Quaker township built on a pre-Revolutionary fox meadow, settled in 1701. In the 1950s, it read primarily WASP. However, we moved into a new section called Quaker Ridge, which was primarily Jewish. I guess the 3 percent Jewish population of the town must have congregated in our neighborhood right off Weaver Street. Nonetheless, the fifties stood for conformity. We had just come out of World War II, and now we were involved in Korea. We needed to stand together as a nation. Who doesn't remember the morning pledge? "I pledge allegiance to the flag of the United States of America . . ."

In uniformly constructed Scarsdale, assimilated white, Christian, and Jewish businessmen boarded the train to New York every morning while their wives stayed home and took care of their 2.4 children. *Father Knows Best* was on the television, and the Scarsdale mothers all seemed to look like Jane Wyatt, who played Margaret Anderson, Robert Young's wife—except the Scarsdale wives had full-time help. Shirtwaists and pearls were *de rigueur* as my mother and dozens of other mothers managed to model themselves after the perfect fifties housewife in a perfect fifties upscale village and manage it all with grace and without breaking a nail—and certainly without smashing a vase.

Simple, right? I don't think so. And I know. I was there.

Once Mother had finished the construction of 47 Penn, her next task was to cast the supporting players. Like a talent scout, Mom watched what people wore, how they talked, and what they talked about. Her intelligence influenced her taste in friends. She reached out to the many other women who, like herself, had gone to university and were JWAs and JWPs: Jews Without Accents and Jews Who Pass.

Now it was time for the wardrobe, hair, and makeup team. She made friends with Lord & Taylor and Saks Fifth Avenue. She had her hair meticulously done every Friday, first at Macy's, then at Très Jolie, the crown jewel of the new Golden Horseshoe Shopping Center on Wilmot Road. Like a great wardrobe mistress, Lily sent my father's suits and our clothes to be cleaned at the *esteemed* Wilmot Dry Cleaners, which picked up and delivered. Now that I look back at the aspirational Très Jolie beauty parlor, which sought to echo the great salons of Paris, I remember how it abutted the Golden Horseshoe Delicatessen. We'd order pastrami sandwiches that were so thick they looked like a jungle, spilling over with Russian dressing and coleslaw, and we savored every bite, dressed in our preppy Viyella plaid bermuda shorts and blouses with Peter Pan collars. The highbrow couldn't quite eradicate all the lowbrow in our backgrounds—most of the grandparents in Quaker Ridge had Eastern European accents after all.

The next addition to the Scarsdale cast of characters was a dressmaker, a warm Italian woman named Faust, who custom-fit Lily's clothing and, eventually, custom-made dresses for both of us. That was quite a leap forward for Mom, whose beloved mother Ada sat at the sewing machine with a broken dream making dresses for her four daughters.

When I think of my mother in those days, I also remember her gliding like the beautiful horses on a carousel, smooth as silk but never stopping. Marketing at Gristedes for the best meat, stopping at the jeweler's, then the shoemaker's, filling the Chrysler up with gas, and preparing dinner, in addition to stealing an hour while David was at school to exercise *in the nude* to Jack LaLanne and his "trimnastics" coming out of the DuMont television. I remember some mornings when I was very young being mesmerized watching Mommy doing leg lifts and stretches in the buff. I could not reconcile her quietness and modesty with her willingness to be naked in the family room. Somewhere, Mother must've loved her body and longed to climb her own proverbial apple tree.

She certainly loved Scarsdale. She loved the expanse of her house, the expanse of the lawns, and the safety of knowing her children were going to be well-educated in a public school system upon which she could depend. Lily stood back and breathed it all in.

I have to marvel at how my mother sprang into action given the challenges of such a profoundly new universe. In this pre-computer age, she built her personal World Wide Web from a reservoir of local talent. Lily may have been quiet, but she was capable! Knowledge is power, and she accumulated a wealth of information about artisans and workmen who could help her, giving them explicit instructions. To us, however, her own feelings remained unspoken.

The one place my mother seemed to fully express herself in my young life was at the piano. Through the piano, she entered another world: emotional, melodious, and expansive. For as long as I can remember, my mother spoke to me through music. She emoted through Mozart, she rocked through Rachmaninoff, she beamed through Beethoven. This passion to express the repressed through music was innate in me too. Music is, and always has been, one of the direct portals to my soul. I was also learning an equally important lesson about presentation. My mother was costumed for these most intimate recitals. There she would sit on the antique mahogany chair with the petite point seat cushion in her meticulous, pink, polished cotton shirtwaist dress, cinched at the waist with a red leather belt and a beautiful double-strand of cultured pearls around her neck with matching cultured pearl earrings. As I imagined her transported out of our living room and onto a concert stage, I intuitively grasped that "you never get a second chance to make a first impression." Suiting up is as important as showing up.

Since I wanted so desperately to be near her, I too became a classical pianist. The Mozart "Rondo," the Rachmaninoff "Prelude in C-Sharp Minor, Opus 3, Movement 2," and my favorite, Chopin's "Polonaise"—these were the first melodies that wove their way into the tapestry of my childhood. They were gifts from my mother. These were her sounds: sensitive, disciplined, beautiful—just like her outfits.

Broadway showtunes, though beloved, were a sidebar. The musical priority was the classics.

With all the years that we shared the same musical instrument and related musical repertoire, it's revealing that my mother and I never sat side by side and played a four-handed piece, something for which I deeply longed. The single mahogany piano chair sent a clear message.

I continued to be lonely for her warmth and long for her verbal expression of love. We never even practiced together. I don't remember her helping me through a difficult passage or showing me a fingering sequence. Her support only manifested after a piece was mastered, and then she would ask me to "play for the company." Maybe it was I who shut her out, again afraid of her being critical of my abilities. Finally, perhaps part of the reason we never sat down at the piano together is that she didn't want to intrude.

I don't remember ever relaxing with my mother as a child, except when she permitted me to lie on her lap in the master bedroom as she reclined on the pale petal-pink silk chaise lounge. She would invariably be talking on the phone with one of her sisters, or another relative, or one of her close friends. I would lie beside her with my thumb in my mouth and my beige, soft wool blankie under my nose, held up by the arch of my right index finger. I loved smelling my blankie because it always smelled like Tide: fresh and clean, just the way Momma kept her house. I remember the comforting softness of her lap. I remember the beauty of her pale white skin. I remember loving her perfume. Still do!

Scarsdale was luxurious; Scarsdale was class, but for me, Scarsdale was ultimately lonely. I could not feel my mother in the quiet of my custom-made corner room; the air always seemed cold. There was never enough heat, and my bedroom was too far away from the kitchen to catch the delicious smells of Jewish cooking. My mother was spectacular at all of it, from her matzah balls to the walnut cake with homemade whipped cream and bananas inside; from *flanken* to silver dollar pancakes; from rich chicken soup that was a meal in itself to chocolate chip cookies. We were as American as we were Jewish. The warmth of the stove at 955 Walton that spilled over with dishes from the old country seemed as distant as Minsk Gubernia itself. The hugs that once came from my mother's Bronx family came only from my father now—and even then, only when he came home from a long day at work.

Before I was even four, I would look into the full-length mirror on the back of my bedroom door and fascinated ask, "Are you real? Do you really exist?" I pondered those questions. I was not sad, I was simply asking if I existed or if my image was a dream, a mirage. To my child's mind, my reflection was proof that I *did* exist. I loved performing for the mirror: singing, dancing, making faces. It was my private time with my second self. I made up simple monologues, and after much rehearsal, bursting with enthusiasm, I toured my show to the bathroom. There I stood on my yellow step stool and continued working my routines in privacy and safety. There were no rules, no adults telling me what I could and could not do. No brother waiting to roughhouse. I felt content and safe to keep myself company. This was the beginning of creating my artificial universe. Some children have imaginary friends; I had imaginary scenes swirling in my head.

As I grew older and more confident, I took the big step of touring my show from the bathroom to the living room. There, two reliables awaited me: my mother and my father. My father always made a fuss; he was an easy mark. My mother, not so much.

In July of 1953, Mother sent me to the Heathcote School Summer Program. I had not yet entered kindergarten. On costume day, I was dressed as a bunny. The summer program finished at noon as it always did, and Mom was not there to pick me up. All the other children were met by their mothers, and they were on their way. Slightly panicked, I waited for what seemed an eternity in the enormous glassed-in vestibule outside the large oak-doored auditorium of Heathcote School. *Where was my mother? Where was the blue Chrysler?* Even as a little boy, David would say, "Mom loves us because Mom is always there." When she failed to show up, it was so out of character that I assumed she had left forever. And this was her choice. Gone, Baby, Gone.

This was long before my bike-riding days when my two-wheeler Western Flyer would take me from Penn Boulevard to Heathcote Five Corners and back, long before the Heathcote School down the road became a familiar landmark. At four years old, nothing was familiar but my own backyard. Waiting for my mother, I was a stranger in a strange land.

To this day, my body feels the terror of my mother's momentary no-show. I'm sure that's one of the seminal reasons I tend to be a few minutes late: to avoid the agony of waiting for someone who might never show up. That day waiting for Mommy is engraved on the cells of my soul. I remember crying in panic, afraid of being heard. I must have looked like Edvard Munch's *The Scream*.

I was briefly comforted by an anonymous adult who soon left. I was alone, just waiting, waiting for my mother. I became so nervous that I started to jump in the air in my bunny costume like a frog, knees to my ears, trying to release the panic. When Mom arrived, I was like a bubble that burst. Mammoth tears fell down my burning cheeks. My grief poured forth with relief, but lurking in the back of my mind was this nagging suspicion that my mother didn't really want to be my mother.

This was the first time I vividly remember her saying, "Don't be ridiculous." "Don't be ridiculous," in a voice that could cut glass, showed up a great deal in my young life, followed by, "Don't be selfish." Soon, I began to wonder if the sun would ever come out around my mother, or whether there would just be a clouded sky of correction filled with the subconscious, lingering thought, "Terri Sue, let me fix you."

In the evenings, during the school year, Mother would serve dinner in two shifts: double the time, double the effort. She would first feed David and me at 6:30 p.m. After our dinner, we would clear our plates and return to our rooms to continue our homework. Then she would prepare Dad's plate, clean the kitchen, and lovingly pour his double shot of Jack Daniel's in a Thermos with ice. Dad's portable cocktail hour was completed with a plate of Ritz crackers generously spread with Velveeta cheese and carefully wrapped with Reynolds aluminum foil. After a quick mirror check of her hair and makeup, she would grab the Thermos and plate and slip into the blue Chrysler to pick up my father at Larchmont Train Station for the 8:02.

Sometimes Dad was so tired from his day of verbal jousting as a litigator that he would sleep through his train stop, and Mom would have to drive to Harrison to get him. I never heard her complain. She was like Patience on a monument, just as beautiful—but perhaps better dressed. She greeted Dad with a smile on her face and his favorite hors d'oeuvres and libation, her signature Lilyville Happy Hour.

Mom and Dad would then have dinner, just the two of them. Of course, we would greet our father every night and he would regale us with a story or two of his exciting day as a defense attorney, then David and I would hurry back to our desks in pursuit of straight A's. Until bedtime, my mother looked flawless. It was as miraculous as it was mysterious, and I thought to myself, "How does she do this?" Lily was constantly fulfilling the selfless, seamless role of the ideal 1950s wife.

Sometimes Dad would call Mom around 6:00 p.m. and say he had to have a legal brief in by the morning, and would take the last train to Larchmont, then grab a cab to 47 Penn. When that happened, his dinner went in the fridge with handwritten instructions in perfect script attached to the ever-useful Reynolds wrap, her strawberry-blonde hair went into brush rollers, the makeup came off with Pond's Cold Cream, the nightgown and satin robe went on, and Lily would put her children, and then herself, to bed.

My mother basically spent a good deal of her life waiting for Sidney to show up from his demanding work that he loved so much. I watched this, and I swore that when I grew up, I would wait for no man. This vision was bolstered by my father's uniquely progressive advice to me when I was five. "Terri Sue," he said, "Always remember: Never beg a man for a hat." I quickly came to understand that this was a metaphor for, "Terri Sue, always have your own money and earn your own living," because financial independence in a marriage meant freedom. From the beginning, my father was my ticket to gender equality long before its time.

Born in 1911, my mother came from the generation that believed a woman's fate was inextricably linked to the match she made, and to her husband's success. A great match meant a husband who was incredibly intelligent, ambitious, and able to provide. Plus, it didn't hurt if he were handsome, but for our bunch, intelligence always trumped looks (Democrats, please excuse the verb). Lily knew her husband had to bring home enough bacon (Jews, please excuse the noun) for her to spend her days caring for their children. Then there were book clubs, walking clubs, Jewish charities, and local politics. She participated in all of them, mostly as an observer-learner. I don't ever remember her taking the floor at meetings. Nonetheless, Mother was in the full swing of upper-middle-class life. Point of fact: 47 Penn didn't own a sewing machine. Point of fact: 47 Penn *did* have live-in help, six days a week.

I was being raised to be a lady from a fine family, so I was *dressed* as a little lady from a fine family. In reality, I would have been just as happy hanging upside down from the metal trapeze on my swing set in my brother's hand-me-down dungarees.

My mother felt a young lady needed a coat for three out of the four seasons. After all, who needs a coat in summer? A cashmere sweater will do. However, for fall, winter, and spring, different coats were a necessity, along with three different matching hats—a beret for the High Holidays and cool fall weather, a fur cap to keep me warm in the winter while I played in the snow, and a flowered spring bonnet to celebrate the buds of April and Passover. My mother called this spring millinery confection an "Easter Bonnet," even though we never celebrated Easter. Well, truth to tell, one spring afternoon Peggy Schwarz and Edith Banks, the mothers of David's best friends Eddie and Harold, joined Lily Feldshuh in our kitchen and dyed Easter eggs. We put bunny decals on them, and then our mothers hid them in our back lawn, and we had an Easter egg hunt. I have no doubt this came from my mother's British-Jewish side of the family. Please don't tell Daddy!

Besides my Easter bonnet, I also perpetually had patent leather Mary Janes so shiny you could see your reflection and, of course, those white lace anklets. Top it off with wee matching purses and white gloves, and my ensemble was complete. Before I was allowed to put these garments on, my mother would perfectly coif my hair. She then taught me how to step into a dress, so as not to muss my hairdo.

If you were looking into my closet back then, what would you have learned about me? Well, first you would have learned that my closet and the clothes therein meant a great deal to my mother. My hangers were custom-made, navy-blue cross-stitched polished cotton, with navy plastic heads and a white bow around the neck. Yup, no wire hangers. There were coordinated outfits in colors that fit the season: olive green, burnt orange, and taupe for fall; navy blue and forest green with a touch of red (but not too Christmas) for winter; and pastels for spring: pinks and yellows and the palest greens. Summer brought white, and woe unto you if you wore white past Labor Day weekend. It was a clear message from my mother that clothes were not just clothes; clothes were the message to the world that my father and mother, children of immigrants, could pass "for Scarsdale." I looked like I had just walked out of *Seventeen* magazine, and David looked like he had just walked out of a catalog for preppy sexy fashions. My brother and I both knew that when it came to fashion, Mother's aesthetic was developed and spot-on, just as her older sister Rose had developed a discerning eye for priceless antiques. These girls looked, learned, and launched.

One morning, when I was four, I remember my brother David coming to the dinette table in his pajama top. He finished his breakfast, got up, and Mom said, "Where are you going?" He replied, "To school."

"David, you're not going to school in your flannel pajama top," Lily said.

"But Mom, please," my brother pleaded. "I love it. It's so comfortable."

"You can love it at home," Mom said, "but you're not going out of this house dressed like that. In this house, we dress like respectable human beings, especially when we go to school. We do not dress like *vilda chayas*." (Yiddish for wild animals.) "Now go change, please."

Courageous, imprudent David made a mad dash for the utility room side door, his school books tucked under his arm to minimize wind shear. My mother did not even look up from her *New York Times*. As he passed her, she extended her right index finger, effortlessly caught a small hole in the seam of his pajama top, and ripped it right off his back in one fell swoop. David was speechless. He was also topless and without options. He howled in grief. I hid under the dinette table. He had no choice but to surrender and slink back into his bedroom to change.

"Remember what Papa Gershan said: 'If you dress like a bum, you *are* a bum.'" Now yelling down the hall as David took cover in his bedroom: "Your grandparents did not escape the pogroms of Russia and the anti-Semitism of Victorian England for their grandchildren to dress like a *chazzer*." (A pig.)

One morning in the fourth grade, I put together a fabulous outfit I believed deserved to be in the display windows of Saks Fifth Avenue: a pink polka-dotted blouse, a pink striped belt, and a brown-and-pink flowered skirt. None of these three garments were related in design, but they all were related in color. At the time, I thought I was the bee's knees. I walked into the kitchen like a runway model on a catwalk, waiting for my mom to notice me. I thought for sure she would compliment me on my impeccable sense of style.

Remember, this was the '50s—coordinated outfits were a must. Madonna wasn't born yet. Lady Gaga wasn't even a zygote. My mother took one look at me and said, "Terri Sue, you cannot go to school wearing that outfit. The belt doesn't go with the skirt and the blouse doesn't go with either. People will look at you and get dizzy and then they'll think *you're* dizzy, *mishuganah*!" (Yiddish for crazy person.) "Don't embarrass us."

"Mom," I said, "This looks great! I mean, it's 1958!"

She replied, "Exactly, it's 1958. When have you ever seen a concoction like the one you're wearing?"

"Mommy, c'mon," I implored.

She came back quicker than a flying matzah ball: "Your grandparents did not escape—"

"I know. . . ." I yelled, "The pogroms of Russia and the anti-Semitism of Victorian England—"

Then together: "For their grandchildren to dress like a *chazzer*."

"OK, OK!" I burst, "What can I keep on?"

Mom said, "Take your pick, but I would go with the skirt. Now go get your solid-pink blouse that matches those flowers and your solid-brown belt. At least then the outfit makes sense." In that moment, a potential Saks Fifth Avenue fashionista died.

My mother being involved in every aspect of my early fashion choices at least gave me contact with her. Dressing properly and with style was one of the pillars of Lily's mothering, which I yearned for in those years. I craved my mother's time and her touch, so when she spent the time and focus to straighten each ruffle and tame each ringlet, it felt like heaven to me. It bridged the gap. For a moment, it penetrated the silence.

In addition, through her role as my chief fashion advisor, my mother and I finally had a forum in which I was the object of her attention. Even though as an actress, my process is not from "out to in," when it came to the Lily Feldshuh Costume Department, we soared. Fashion was our lightning rod of connection. It was in Lily's blood. After all, her mother's immigration papers read "Ada Kaplan, Hebrew Tailoress, London, England." And Gershan's read, "Hebrew Tailor, Belarus, Russia."

How I loved those shopping forays! Daddy gave us a $200 budget for my fall wardrobe, which I would carefully select with Mom. He was generous. In those days, $200 went a long way. I also loved my mother's shopping rules. We only bought underpants and "quiet" garments at Alexander's Department Store. Our good clothes had to come from Saks

Fifth Avenue or Lord & Taylor. My mother loved American designers: Bill Blass, Anne Klein, and Geoffrey Beene. She would buy her own clothes mainly from Saks or the upper-crust boutique Schulman's on Main Street in White Plains, New York. She always went into New York City with white gloves, a custom-made hat, and matching purse.

Daddy wore perfectly pressed suits and elegant silk ties to his New York law office. On weekends, when he wasn't in his jodhpurs and hacking jacket, he wore a Brooks Brothers blazer that I'm sure Lily picked out for him. Sidney was right out of Ralph Lauren before there was Ralph Lauren. On formal occasions, he wore this superb white dinner jacket that reminded me of Desi Arnaz. Mother wore taffeta cocktail dresses in jewel colors with a crinoline underneath that swished as she walked.

After our shopping trips, I put on fashion shows for my father— clearly, this was the precursor to *Project Runway* and, for these moments, I was *America's Next Top Model*! Dad: he loved seeing his all-American girl, and I loved modeling my fall wardrobe for him.

One Thanksgiving, Mother even took me to Signora Faust in Yonkers and asked her to attach a white ermine necklet to my new winter coat. The genuine little ermine was a gift from Mom's furrier. *Quel faux pas!* Today it would be faux fur. Still, I felt like a Disney princess.

Then of course, there were the outfits for *shul* (synagogue) that had to be respectful and refined, especially on the High Holidays. From my Mary-Janed feet to my white-gloved hands to my felt beret, I looked like I was ready for my first communion in Paris, but I felt fabulous!

When I was seven years old, my mom was taking David and me to the original Metropolitan Opera House on Broadway and West Thirty-Ninth Street to see a performance of the Young People's Concerts, conducted by the great Leonard Bernstein. My mom was driving the 1956 blue Chrysler, which looked more like a boat than a car. We left early, hoping to find a parking space that was big enough on the street so that we wouldn't have to pay the astronomical garage charges. My mother's credo regarding money was, "Love to spend, hate to waste." She wasn't cheap, but could be frugal. This I realized fully when she discovered Loehmann's designer discount store. It was like watching a hunter seek out its prey.

I was in a Saks taffeta plaid party dress, my fall coat, my beret, my Mary Janes, and my white anklets with their usual delicate lace trim. I was filled with anticipation as I quickly entered the car and we drove down Penn Boulevard toward Weaver Street on our way to the Hutchinson River Parkway. I loved when my mom took us into Manhattan. It was the center of all our cultural expeditions, and it was loud, colorful, and alive—not unlike my Bronx family.

Driving down Penn Boulevard, I realized in my haste that my hands were bare. *Where are my gloves? Where are my gloves?! I forgot my gloves!* Dread instantly eclipsed my excitement.

Do I tell her? Do I not? Do I tell her? Do I not? cycled furiously in my brain. Finally, I said sheepishly, "Mommy, I forgot my white gloves."

She repeated, "You forgot your white gloves?!" then immediately hit the brakes, whipped a U-turn, and sailed back into the driveway of 47 Penn. Over her shoulder, she said, "Terri Sue! We do not go to New York City without our white gloves." I ran inside and grabbed my delicate, white wristlet gloves from the kitchen counter. *Aye-yai-yai* and aye aye, captain!

To this day, you don't want to be near me when, with the specificity of a scientist, I check and recheck my costume details so as not to have a repeat of that terror: not having the proverbial *white gloves* while I'm onstage.

Mom must have felt that her love manifested through her principle of "Preserve and protect my young." She also felt she showed her love through her mitzvahs, or good deeds. "Who carpools you everywhere, witnesses your lessons, attends your sports games?" These choices were supposed to communicate, "Of course I love you." That message failed to get through to me for the first twenty-five years of my life because it was never verbally expressed, and a mind reader I was not. That is why to this day, if there's one thing my children, and now grandchildren, know, it's that I love them because they breathe.

Being so reliably present in our lives was Lily's way of showing love, but for me, the temperature of her presence was cold—even though her dependability was like Fort Knox. This wasn't love, this was silent devotion—except when she was fixing us. Her love almost felt like an eleventh Commandment she was obligated to obey: "A mother *shall* love her children." I also couldn't shake the idea that she was far more bonded to David than to me. Together they had weathered the absence of my Dad, not to mention World War II.

Time has given me one insight into this void I felt from my mother. Perhaps it was my father's attachment to me that drove my mother away. I was his one infant born after the war. Dad was so grateful to witness my mother's pregnancy, my birth, and his newborn baby girl. He didn't have that with David—war robbed him of that primal experience. In homage to Dad's survival, perhaps Mother gave him the space to be Daddy Supreme to Daddy's little girl.

BY THE BEGINNING OF SEVENTH grade, I was preparing for my Bat Mitzvah, scheduled to take place on December 8, 1961. A point of interest: in 1978, December 8 would become Prime Minister Golda Meir's *yahrzeit*, the date of her death. The Bat Mitzvah is a monumental milestone in a Jewish family's history and thus, for my mother, another opportunity to step into the role of theatrical producer. A Feldshuh big production number was in the works. My mother's work ethic and great attention to detail would later inspire me in my own career, from first rehearsal to opening night.

I had been sent to "Sunday School" from 9:00 a.m. to 11:00 a.m. at Temple Israel Center in White Plains since I was five and a half years old. It was a Conservative synagogue, headed by Rabbi Max Gelb and Cantor William Wolf. By the time I was nine, I was attending religious school eight hours a week: Tuesdays and Thursdays from four to six and Sundays from nine to one. Very few other Scarsdale families went to Temple Israel Center, so my temple friends mostly came from White

Plains. In fact, I was the only girl in my grade at Quaker Ridge who went to Hebrew School—excuse me, Sunday School—at all.

The anticipation for this production was sublime because I knew from my brother's Bar Mitzvah what an extravaganza looked like. Only this time, I would be the star! At my side would be my personal dresser, Momma Lily, with the taste and acumen of an Edith Head. While my first task was to learn my lines (in Hebrew and without vowels), Mother wisely knew all of her decisions would stem from the selection of *the dress*. At last we joined forces, our shared vision of perfection aimed in the same direction.

After striking out at Saks Fifth Avenue and Lord & Taylor, we went to Bonwit Teller and found what we were searching for. The dress was white satin brocade with a deep-kelly-green cummerbund. It came with a matching white bolero jacket, which I would wear in the synagogue and then take off for the party (and the cover of this book). Then we went to Miles Shoe Store on Main Street in White Plains to have satin heels dyed to exactly match the green of my cummerbund. Dyed pumps were the way to go in 1961.

Since we were required to cover our heads in synagogue, Mother had a hat made for me. It was a green satin pillbox with a dainty green veil that I wore angled toward the back of my head just like Jackie Kennedy. The Kennedys were in the White House, and my hat reminded me of the pillbox hats Halston made for our gorgeous First Lady. I felt Camelot elegant. Mother even lent me one of her own coats. It was brown tweed with a mink collar, just modest enough for a young girl who was about to become a woman in the eyes of her community. I felt so grown up and thrilled that my mother trusted me—the notorious vase breaker of 47 Penn—to wear one of her fine coats with that fur collar. I had been well trained by Mother to appreciate such fur finery since the day she had Faust attach the ermine necklet to my winter coat so many years before.

Bat Mitzvahs were held in those days at the Friday-evening service. Bar Mitzvahs were held on Saturday mornings. In 1961, it was still very rare for girls to even have a Bat Mitzvah. Temple Israel, bless its Jewish star, was quite progressive.

Every girl, who was also referred to as a Bat Mitzvah, was paired up with another girl for the ceremony. I was with my friend Nancy Kardon. I wondered, even back then, why was I *sharing* my Bat Mitzvah when I remembered the boys going solo?

Nancy and I would be called up to the *bimah* (altar) to sing our Shabbat blessings, which took about 60 seconds, since it was only the blessing over the candles. Mr. Kardon handled the blessing over the wine and Dad made the blessing over the challah bread. Then, Nancy and I were asked to chant a portion of the *Haftorah*, also known as The Prophets. This is the part of the Hebrew Bible that is adjacent to the Torah. Historically, the Jews chanted the Haftorah when they were forbidden to chant the Torah at all. Women were still forbidden to chant from the Torah in 1961, *or* hold it, *or* touch it for that matter! My Bat Mitzvah was *Torah lite.*

I was coached in my study by the wife of the senior cantor, Mrs. Leah Rabinowitz. She was chubby and squishy like Grandma Ada, and I immediately adored her. We mastered my Haftorah portion in no time. There would be no *D'var Torah*, or speech, commenting on the passages I chanted. David was required to do a *D'var Torah* because he was actually permitted to read from the Torah. I was just expected to give a thank-you speech to my parents and the synagogue. It was meant to be heartfelt, short, and sweet, but not nearly as intellectually challenging as my brother's. Never mind! I was asleep to any concept of gender equality and was just thrilled to get a Bat Mitzvah at all. All the kids at school had little thirteen-year-old birthday parties with twenty people, a cake, and some dancing. Compared to that, this was a Broadway show!

My Bat Mitzvah sailed forth on a cold but clear December night. No snow. We left for synagogue early Friday afternoon to take the obligatory formal pictures. Even my demure Bat Mitzvah album was miniature next to my brother's full-sized dark-green leather-bound tome. Nancy and I both recited our Haftorah portions well. The synagogue gave us our own pair of Shabbat candlesticks and dainty little prayer books engraved with our names in gold in the lower right corner of the white leather cover. These were to last us the rest of our lives.

Now here's a question: What's open at ten o'clock on a Friday night in Scarsdale in 1961? I'll tell you what. Nothing. After the ceremony, our guests were invited back to a reception in the basement of our home, where brown crêpe paper had been carefully wrapped around the ugly, gray metal pillars that supported the house. The brown-wrapped pillars led up to kelly-green palm fronds also made of crêpe paper but shaped and supported by wires at the top, so that each pillar looked like a palm tree in the Côte D'Azur. I didn't quite understand why Mom had chosen the south of France for my decorations, but I thought the basement looked magical. Madame Lily Cannes do! Even the enormous boulder that protruded up from the floor in one of its corners, which was too cumbersome to bulldoze out during construction, was painted gold.

My Bat Mitzvah was a big success, but it wasn't lost on me that David's celebration was at a country club and mine was in the basement of our home. But the most important fact is that my parents fought to have my Bat Mitzvah happen in the first place. They didn't know they were fighting for gender equality, but frontline warriors they were. And indeed, they were on the right side of history.

My thank-you notes were pale pink, engraved with my name in shocking pink using elegant Monsieur La Doulaise Script. I wrote thank-you notes all through Hanukkah and finally finished on New Year's Eve. A thank-you note from our house was supposed to be written within twenty-four hours of being gifted, but in the case of my Bat Mitzvah, there were so many to write that I was given a month. I knew I shouldn't miss this deadline, and I didn't. I understood implicitly that when I was behaving within the parameters of my mother's rulebook,

I could receive a little applause. These rules were not in place to intimidate David and me; they were in place to take care of the community, to teach us that treating another person with care was important.

That is why to this day, I learn the names of everyone I possibly can, on every production, in every new venue, and have opening-night gifts for everyone from the leading players to the brand-new interns, from the stage doorman to the lead producer. I take time to handwrite cards of gratitude to those who are part of the network of talent it takes to make the show a success and bring me to my best.

I learned so much from those early Scarsdale years that continues to serve me as an actress today, including the importance of getting the sets right, casting the most supportive players, and never missing a cue. Oh, and I learned one huge insight about costuming: while my mother worked from the outside in, I needed to work from the inside out.

But the larger Lilyville life lesson was clear: when you were on the accepted, time-honored, traditional track, you would be acknowledged by Lily. There would be attention paid. That attention, whether she was aware of it or not, could often be tone-deaf in the delivery and more bulldozer than whisperer, but the attention was paid. Conformity was the expectation, and I could do it. I could do it! "Look at me Mommy, I can do exactly what you want, and then you will love me."

How could I ever tell her that the role she wanted me to play was too confining to my young heart? How could I ever let her know that all I craved in life was to color outside the lines? How could she know how wildly I was going to miss the mark of her limited expectations for me?

Her message was, "I love you, Terri Sue, but I only love you fully when you stay on track—*my* track."

Lilyism

Mother and I went to JFK Airport to pick up my daughter, Amanda, who was returning from her summer program in La Coruña, Spain. Amanda, like Lily, has size-C bosoms. Amanda came through the gate, and Mother took one look at her and one look at me with my A-cup acorns and said, "Well, I guess it skips a generation!"

Don't You Have to Be Born with a Voice?

H OW BRILLIANT WAS BARBRA STREISAND DURING THE OSCARS "Year of the Woman" telecast in 1993 when she stated plainly, "I look forward to the time when tributes like this will no longer be necessary. They won't be necessary because women will have the same opportunities as men in all fields and will be honored without regard to gender but simply for the excellence of their work."

I was indoctrinated into this gender struggle early in my life. Through Judaism, it occurred to me that girls were not treated as equals to boys. It didn't make me angry, but I did start searching for a path out of that inequity. My parents were very helpful in this search because at thirteen-and-a-half, the year of my Bat Mitzvah and entry into Jewish womanhood, they sent me to the South of France for the summer. I was about to become a woman of the world, and I still had six months left in the eighth grade!

In June, it was time to say goodbye to the Quaker Ridge School that had cradled, sheltered, nurtured, and enlightened me. I was about to make the leap from community theater to the big time—Scarsdale High where there were four hundred kids in each grade, and most of them Christians.

In 1961, the year of my Bat Mitzvah, there was a most unsavory incident that occurred when the Scarsdale Country Club, headed by Charles McCallister, refused to allow a young man who converted from Judaism to the Episcopal Church to escort a young lady to her debutante debut at the club. It was the club's policy to prohibit Jews from the premises. To his credit, Reverend George French Kempsell of the Church of St. James the Less announced that he would ban any supporters of the club's decision from receiving Holy Communion. The event thankfully marked a turning point toward the decline of anti-Semitism in Scarsdale.

A few months after that incident, it was time for my junior high graduation. For the final assembly, I was asked to play Gershwin's *Rhapsody in Blue*—the entire, unabridged version. I practiced as any aspiring professional would: long hours with focus, relentless attention to detail, and enough repetitions to make the piece seem effortless. Mastery was a new tool for me at that young age but one that is the very foundation of my work today and is only achieved through the gifts of time, vision, and relentless practice. I can hear the Greek chorus of my costars and directors chanting, "Yes, Tovah, we know thy process well."

It was during this period I had a revelation. I shared it with my mother: "Momma, if you're good to the piano, the piano is good to you, but people you can never depend on. You can be nice to them, but you never know what you're going to get back." Was that really my worldview in the eighth grade? Lily, certainly not seeing her part in this statement, immediately shot me down: "Terri, don't be ridiculous!"

If my children said such a thing, I would stop everything and ask them, "What would make you see the world this way?" More than ever, I had discovered that music in and of itself was a G-dsend and could be a comforting and reliable companion.

As it happens, when my father was fourteen years old, he had the good fortune to hear Gershwin himself play the *Rhapsody* at Aeolian Hall in NYC with Paul Whiteman conducting. Dad was so moved that he never got over it. I loved my father and he loved Gershwin, thus I loved Gershwin. Naturally, I aspired to master the piece for Dad's sake as well.

English art critic Walter Pater said that "all art should aspire to the condition of music." Music soars beyond words and actions. It was the one ancient art form that Plato salvaged in his *Republic*. I feel there is a primal connection between the musical beat and our heartbeat.

The hand-eye coordination for mastery of any advanced piece kept my mind quick and sharp. Studying music taught me how to study all academics. First, one masters a note, then a phrase, a measure, a system, a passage, a movement, and finally the whole opus. There is no mystery when one hits a wrong note: one needs to go back to practice it. One must practice the great works for piano until they are accurate, excellent, and effortless. I agree with Shakespeare that music is the food of love, and indeed, we should play on! Ultimately, the piano brought people toward me as it had brought people to Lily before me. To master it, however, I had to forge the path alone.

On graduation day in June of 1962, I performed *Rhapsody in Blue* for the eighth-grade graduates, their parents, our teachers, and all the kids at QRS. It was my very first standing-room-only crowd. Granted, I didn't have top billing, but I did bring down the house. I stood and took a bow, and as the audience came to their feet, clapping, I caught the eyes of my father beaming with unequivocal love. I would never forget that gaze.

"Terri Sue, you're going places!" shouted Eileen Terner's mother, who had come rushing up as soon as I stepped off the stage. Mildred Terner was as emotionally expansive as she was beautiful. I loved that about her and secretly hoped she was right. The only place I knew I was going that day for sure was home to change into the fancy white eyelet dress with the pink velvet sash that my mom and I had picked out for the diploma ceremony. Still, the experience of playing *Rhapsody* for a sea of people kept me flying high. Music was a language with wings. I felt alive at the piano, and I discovered the marvelous pastime of accompanying myself on Broadway tunes. Singing touched deep parts of me. When I have had the honor of teaching in New Haven, I have often told the students, "When words can no longer contain our feelings, we burst forth into song." I know. I can't control myself around my grandson Rafael or my granddaughter Sidney Mei. I'm a singing fool!

When I grew up in the '50s and '60s we collected LPs or long-playing records, which were groundbreaking technology at the time. My parents had all the Broadway records stacked vertically in the golden wire record rack next to the Philips stereo in the living room. By the time I attended Camp Taconic, my first sleepaway camp in the Berkshires, I was singing up a storm. Every morning, this camp celebrated each new day with thirty minutes of "morning sing." I was nine years old, and singing elated me, from Woody Guthrie to Rodgers and Hammerstein.

Seven years later, I was "sweet sixteen" and vocalizing in the living room, standing at the beautiful 1935 Steinway grand piano. I was singing arpeggios and chromatic scales, even trills with *crescendi, decrescendi*, in two tempi, *lento* and *allegretto*.

Why? I had begun to take lessons with the first of a select lineage of life-changing voice teachers. At my fervent request, my mother consented to take me to study with renowned voice teacher Madame Olga Eisner at her glorious apartment in The Ansonia Hotel. The Ansonia was situated in Manhattan on Seventy-Second and Broadway, right across from the Bowery Savings Bank where my mother had worked as a sixteen-year-old to earn money to attend NYU.

The Ansonia was a grand, iconic old palace, a French hotel in the classic sense, built beginning in 1899 and across the turn of the century. I could almost see the ladies with their bustles and parasols coming and going in the lobby. The Ansonia had been designed as a sustainable community before anyone had ever conceived of such a thing and originally had a real working farm on the roof, complete with cows and chickens and even an apiary with honeybees. The guests would receive fresh eggs and milk at their doors every morning. Oh, for that tradition today! It soon became home to stars like Chaplin, Stravinsky, Caruso, and even Babe Ruth.

Madame Olga Eisner was a master of opera and lieder singing, and when I was in the room with her, I was one degree of separation from Albert Einstein! That's right, when her hearing began to fail, Einstein invented one of the very first hearing aids expressly for Olga so that she could continue her storied career. Her husband Bruno, a renowned professor of piano, known from Berlin's Stern Conservatory to Bloomington's University of Indiana, was also Einstein's accompanist when the math genius wanted to play his violin. Pictures of Einstein with Olga and Bruno dotted her salon.

I would visit Madame Olga every Wednesday afternoon for my lesson. I was practicing for that lesson when Lily walked into the living room, and after a pause, simply asked, "Don't you have to be born with a voice?"

You could have blown me over with a feather. It never occurred to me that my voice wasn't absolutely lovely and a gift to share with others. Her comment shattered all my confidence. I'm not sure why I allowed it to dismantle me for decades to come, but from that moment on, I felt I had to work twice as hard as anyone else to get a job as a singer because I had a terrible secret to hide: *I was not born with a voice.* Maybe with endless effort, no one would find out.

Over the years, I have tried to rationalize what was to me a devastating comment. Instead of embracing the self-lacerating idea that I had no vocal talent, I pursued the question from my mother's point of view. Perhaps she felt *she* was never born with a voice—verbal or musical. Even with her considerable pianistic abilities, she accompanied others and remained vocally silent. Was she wondering whether she too might have had an opportunity to cultivate her voice? Was she asking the question rhetorically? Was Ada's voice singing "I'm only a bird in a gilded cage" echoing in her aural memory in that minute?

With that simple sentence: "Don't you have to be born with a voice?" it was as if my mother had cast a spell on me that I spent a lifetime trying to break. It also marked a downward turn in my connection with my mother; I felt she couldn't be trusted, and I must proceed with caution.

My trip to the south of France would be my first taste of using distance to buffer myself from my mother's critical eye. I was leaving for the Côte d'Azur for six whole glorious, independent weeks. By the 1960s, Dad was meeting and representing many of the Iranian Jews in America. Many of the families had been close to the Shah, but left Iran because they could see the writing on the wall. With the rise of Ayatollah Khomeini, Iran was about to become incredibly anti-Semitic.

Through a Persian business acquaintance named Robert Rokhsar, Dad developed an international network of Iranian clients. The one who affected my life most was Monsieur Jean Mikaeloff. Jean and his wife Fernande left Tehran for Lyons, France, by the end of World War II. Their children Philippe, Jean-Serge, Yves, and Leilà were brought up in Lyons, living on Avenue de Foch. Very Posh! Monsieur Mikaeloff had a thriving Persian-tapestry-and-rug business. The family summered in Cap Martin on the Côte D'Azur near the Italian border.

In early spring, with David finishing his freshman year at Dartmouth College and my graduating from Quaker Ridge, the Mikaeloffs invited us to join their family in their summer apartment from June 23 to August 5. Perhaps they wanted their children to learn English. Perhaps they wanted to make a match between David and their lovely daughter Leilà. Whatever the reason, my father was surprised and thrilled. My mother was not. "Sidney, she can't go, she's only thirteen." "Lily," Dad answered, "she's getting on the plane." It was a heated disagreement, but Dad prevailed.

While flying as Peter Pan in 1978 was an unforgettable thrill, nothing will surpass the experience of my first plane ride on Air France, the gold standard of air travel at the time. Will we ever see those days again? We dressed to travel. I remember my mother leaving for the airport to go to Cuba in 1952 when I was four. She wore foxes around her neck (to go to Cuba!) and a black suit with a matching black, felt cloche hat, black suede gloves to the elbow, black pumps, silk stockings, and Arpège. She carried a green leather train case with ivory leather trim and the initials LKF engraved in gold block letters on the top.

Now it was my turn. I wore a linen navy-blue, yellow, and white outfit. The skirt on the dress was A-line, the coordinated jacket was yellow with blue trim, and the blouse on top was white. No woman is complete without white gloves, stockings, navy blue Cuban heels (I should've given them to Mother!), and a blue pillbox hat with yellow trim. The secret stowaway in my matching leather purse was Mother's Revlon lipstick. Tell no one. With house gift in hand, we boarded the plane.

This would be my brother's and my first experience in Europe. My parents couldn't give me a more meaningful gift to reward my coming of age than a trip abroad. I had been studying French for two years and loved it. David had studied Spanish, so good luck to him! We left JFK on Friday, June 22, 1962, and there was food on the plane! Every morsel to me was a miracle! Though looking back, I want to shout to myself, "Terri Sue! That food was terrible, oversalted, and dehydrating! You must hydrate, girl—think of your voice, think of your skin!"

People smoked in the cabin. In those days, it was considered cool. But in my upbringing, smoking, drinking, riding motorcycles, and not studying were definitely considered *not* cool. Those were the emblems of hoodlums, and I needed a bad boy like I needed a *luchen kop*. (Yiddish for hole in the head.) The Jews had enough to contend with—why would they choose to be hoodlums?

Exhausted but still euphoric, we arrived in Nice two planes and many hours later. The Mikaeloffs' Portuguese driver picked us up at the Nice airport in a gorgeous big black Jaguar with custom maroon side stripes, and we were driven to Les Appartements à Cap Martin on the Côte D'Azur. I had landed in Wonderland. My bedroom had a beautiful antique bureau with inlaid wood, and my window looked out upon the Mediterranean Sea. The bathroom was *en suite*, and it had a bidet, which I thought was a footbath. Madame Mikaeloff explained that it was for *other* purposes. After that visit, having a bidet would forever signal an aspirational level of sophistication and elegance. And yes, I have achieved that pinnacle of comfort in my home today. Too much information? Use it as subtext!

In the six weeks I was with the Mikaeloffs, I became a citizen of the world. I played tennis with a girl from Milan named Donatella. We spoke only in French, which was our *lingua franca*, our common tongue. I also spoke only in French to the Mikaeloffs. I mean, it was either that or Farsi, and who knew Farsi? I became fluent in French in short order, and that ability would influence the rest of my academic career. I fell in love with foreign languages. I went on to study Spanish and Italian and became fluent in those as well. Yes, I'm a language triple threat! And that's not including Hebrew, which, while not fluent, passes at Passover.

My mother's trepidation about the trip was calmed by my father's assessment that "the Mikaeloffs will be far stricter with the children than we are." He certainly was correct when it came to me. When it came to David, once again, it was gender inequality. Gender inequality *and* ageism. David was five years older, and I suppose, to be fair, that was a significant divide in our maturity. Today we are *ten* years apart in age. That's my story, and I'm sticking to it!

David disappeared for three days with Jean's third son, Yves Mikaeloff, to seek ecstasy in the arms of some Scandinavian beauties. David's squeeze was an oo là-là named Oola. He returned with a smile from ear to ear. I was not thrilled about being left alone so soon after our arrival.

I corresponded regularly with my mother on these convenient, little blue aerograms which we folded in threes making an efficient envelope that was light as a feather because international postage was so expensive. Mom told me of her summer days in Westchester, going to the Saxon Woods public pool and golf course, and often just relaxing in the garden. Dad rarely wrote because he was so busy with work, but I have a few letters from him as well, and he always said things were "great!"—the eternal optimist. Thankfully, the Mikaeloffs had an Iranian cousin in Britain, a young girl named Janice Haskell. She was flown in, and for a brief respite, I had an English-speaking cohort to disrupt the solitude and my burgeoning French fluency. Then I was on my own once again—so I made new friends.

Having seen my parents French-kiss in the foyer at 47 Penn, I thought I would try it myself with a boy named Jean-Serge. He was tall and handsome and chased me around the lobby Ping-Pong table to get that kiss. When he left for Paris with his family, I tried the same ping-pong chase with a boy named François. The lobby game room became the home base of my adolescent infatuations. All these romances were carried on in French. Ping-Pong, kisses, and French—oh my! My head swirled with the sophistication of these new adventures.

Other highlights included Saturday nights when the whole family piled into the Jaguar and a Citroën, and we went dancing in Juan-les-Pins, at Le Vieux Moulin. I went shopping in the neighboring town of Menton with Madame Mikaeloff to buy my first bikini. It was white and, I realized once I was in the Mediterranean, wildly revealing. *Beach Blanket Tovah* . . . who knew? David and I were often taken in the Mikaeloff yacht to Italy to lunch in San Remo. I had never experienced this kind of a lifestyle. It was thrilling.

Once, we went to visit Jean's brother Simon at Saint-Jean-Cap-Ferrat, where he was staying at the beyond-belief Grand-Hôtel-du-Cap. We had lunch there, and I had my first Île Flottante (floating island), comprised of crème anglaise, thick cream, vanilla bean, whipped egg whites, and a touch of cognac. Four words: Out. Of. This. World! It's telling that this vivid sense memory of food exists so much more vibrantly in my mind than any of those Ping-Pong kisses. Jews and food—what can I say?

In her adolescence, my mother dreamed of living like Hortense. Now, in *my* adolescence, thanks to my parents, I *was* living like Hortense. For six magnificent weeks, I was in a fantasy world fit for Noël

Coward. As a matter of fact, I met him on the Caravelle jet flying from Nice to Paris on August 5 on my way back to the States.

Boarding just ahead of me, there was a very dapper man with a camel cashmere coat draped over his shoulders being wheeled slowly onto the plane. On his lap, he had a train case as beautiful as my mother's but in camel leather with a sparkling gold monogram. He looked so familiar, I was compelled to speak. I said "Excuse me sir, but don't I know you? Are you a friend of my Uncle Harold's from the Bronx?"

He replied archly in a perfect, clipped British accent, "No, I do not know your Uncle Harold and I *certainly* don't know the Bronx."

"Are you sure, sir? *Judge* Harold Silbermann? I mean, I know I know you!"

"Young lady, you do not know me, and I do *not* know your Uncle Harold."

I then saw the initials on the top of his posh train case: NC for Noël Coward. "Oh my G-d. Mr. Coward, forgive me." By this time I was turning bright red—pinker than my already sunburned face. "I'm a pianist and your songbook with your picture on the cover sits on our Steinway at home in New York. That's why you look so familiar."

He brightened up, "At home in the Bronx?"

"No, Mr. Coward, in Scarsdale."

"Ah, Scarsdale. I *know* Scarsdale. Liz Taylor is living there with her husband Eddie Fisher."

I thought, *She was?*

By the time I returned home, I had been transformed by all these experiences. I had gone international and my vistas were bursting open. With Lily's strict rules still in place, there was even more ground for conflict. Instead of rejoicing in my growth, she again tried to rein me in to the safety of the familiar.

For the last two weeks of summer, I begged to visit my trusty old Camp Taconic. Lily said, "Haven't you had enough adventure for one summer?"

"Mom," I said, "it's only August seventh! There's still three weeks of summer left." Dad said, "I have an idea. You, Mom, and I will drive up to camp in the Chrysler. We'll drop you off at Taconic and then attend some great concerts at Tanglewood and Jacob's Pillow. How about it, Lily?"

Mom glowed. "Perfect," she whispered.

I arrived at camp in Hinsdale, Massachusetts, and the senior bunk, which I would have been in, was filled with old allies who were not as welcoming as expected. I was surprised and hurt, but then again, perhaps I was horning in on an already set rhythm. My beloved Camp Taconic became a lost cause. Then again, how could you compare Senior Banquet in Hinsdale, Massachusetts, to L'île Flottante on the Côte D'Azur?

That fall, I entered the ninth grade at Scarsdale High, and the following summer I applied to go to National Music Camp in Interlochen, Michigan. I dove into music and musical theater with an appetite that was voracious. Even at thirteen, I sensed that a life on the stage was my ticket to gender equality, to never begging a man for a hat, and to the big wide world I had discovered by traveling to France.

Mother said "no" to me a great deal growing up, and I dealt with that, but once I arrived in high school, her strict rules, based on fear, became harder and harder to accept. I soon figured it was better to be forgiven than denied. I would show up on time for the 12:30 a.m. curfew with my date at the door but remain talking with him for at least another half hour. I was lucky, because most of the time, my parents were asleep. I have to admit, her judgments were wise in the long run. She would say, "What good can come of a sixteen-year-old being out at one in the morning?" A lot of good kissing, Ma. In the short run, however, I felt caged and over-monitored.

I kept my dreams of becoming a singer and an actress secret. I knew that wasn't the direction my mother wanted me to go. Surprisingly, she said, "Terri Sue, why don't you consider becoming a doctor, or lawyer, or professor? You want women's lib, Terri Sue? Here are three roads to it." These were the "high-end professions" favored by the Jewish people. They were the professions that required erudition, expertise, and a sharpened mind. They were also stable and they *used* to be reserved only for men. I think it was quite progressive of Mother to think these careers were possibilities for her baby girl.

I entertained law school because my father was a litigator, and I only wanted to go to Harvard, his alma mater. Thank G-d I only made the waiting list. The closest I would get to a law degree was several seasons on NBC's *Law & Order*, which frankly, was better: there was catering.

My greatest pleasure was being onstage. Performing never felt like a job, it felt like a privilege. But to my mother, the theater was a "trade," not an art. If I wanted to pursue it, I was on my own. She was not going to lift a finger.

The reason for her attitude, I now understand, was the uncertainty that theater brought with it. Whether it was the Côte D'Azur or life on the stage, it was all unnecessary risk to her. For a first-generation child of Jewish immigrants who built their way up from Seventeenth Street and Second Avenue to a floor-through in the countrified Bronx, Lily had quantum leaped to a large, opulent house in Scarsdale that she created. Funny that she thought venturing "out of the box" was dangerous and foolish. Surely, she had done the same. Everyone has dreams. Did she not remember that her mother, Ada, wanted to be an actress on the British music hall stage?

Standing on my own two feet and going it alone was a pattern I was used to from my early days at 47 Penn. I think this is one big reason I gravitated to the stage. In the theater, I was never alone. The theater is communal to its core. The theater reminded me of the Bronx. When I was in a play, it was like a second home to which I could escape, and because I knew the beginning, middle, and end of the story, the stage felt safer than real life. In a play, you knew what was going to happen and when. You carefully rehearsed every scene, so you could fling yourself into the center of these plots with abandon. It felt like flying.

Inside those fantastical tales were other peoples' travails and im-possible challenges. They were separate and different from my own, but if I went deep enough, if I mined the gold of the universal through the characters I portrayed, I could give the audience a great gift. I could give them insight into their own lives. Bringing these stories to life gave me a purpose to which I could dedicate myself, a path that was greater than myself, and took me above and beyond my small adolescent con-cerns. These journeys were sacred and wonderful and, at their best, fundamentally connected to a deep common human experience. The stage may not have had the delicious smells of Jewish cooking, but the theater was as close as I had ever come to re-creating the warm, nour-ishing feeling of the family around my grandparents' dining room ta-ble. On the stage, the cast was my family.

In my last year of high school, Indira Gandhi was elected the third prime minister of India. Simon and Garfunkel hit the charts with *The Sound of Silence*, and the Vietnam War was raging on in the distance. The United States Selective Service System drafted 382,010 men into the armed forces in just one year, but I still didn't know anybody from Scarsdale who had died over there. That would change, and soon.

When it was time to think about college, I longed to get into the heart of the city because it was the heart of Broadway. All the arts were happening there—avant-garde theater, off-off-Broadway, off-Broadway, and Broadway. And because I wanted to pursue music and theater, I told my mom I wanted to go to Juilliard.

Without a moment's hesitation she replied, "You are not going to a trade school." "But, Ma, it's *Juilliard*!" I knew that my mother set high standards that had nothing to do with a conservatory. Her values were wedded to a full-out liberal arts education, and I knew her high standards well because, in my mind, I was one of the people who never quite measured up to them.

I was accepted at several colleges. Vassar was my first choice be-cause I thought the grounds of the campus and the crimson Victorian velvet and mahogany decor in Main Hall were exquisite. I liked the way it looked. . . . Deep, huh? Also, Jackie Kennedy had attended Vassar. Plus, the college was a full two hours away from Scarsdale, so I would be "away" for my college experience. Perfect, yes? "Don't be ridiculous," Lily said.

Seven of us from Scarsdale High were accepted at Vassar, but only two of us were accepted at Sarah Lawrence. We were still in the heyday of women's colleges, and these particular schools were very difficult to get into. Dean Fitzgerald at Scarsdale High thought I should definitely go to Sarah Lawrence because I was "so creative." My heart sunk a bit, but my mother enthusiastically agreed with the dean that I should go to Sarah Lawrence. Sarah Lawrence was only seventeen minutes from 47 Penn.

"Bronxville is not Poughkeepsie," she said to me, arguing her case like she was in front of a jury. "If you go to Sarah Lawrence, you'll be close to the city, Terri Sue, so maybe Sarah Lawrence will give you credit for studying acting in New York while you are at college. Maybe you can get admitted to one of those well-known studios." So began my once-in-a-lifetime relationship with my first professional acting teacher, the legendary Uta Hagen.

The message was clear. Go away, but not too far. Mother said, "Have you seen the Taconic Parkway? They have the highest mortality rate for car accidents in New York State. How do you get to Vassar? The Taconic Parkway. Forget it!" Sarah Lawrence it was.

Lily on Sitting *Shiva*

By the time her best friend Gladys Loeb died, Mom was close to one hundred. I gently told her, "Mom, I'm so sorry. Gladys Loeb has passed away." She wailed, "Gladys? Dead? That's terrible, terrible," then on a dime, "What's for lunch?" I said, "What's for lunch?!" She replied, "Tovah, I've got ten seconds to mourn, that's it at this point. Make me a tuna on rye."

Instincts-Schminstincts

AN ACTOR IN A SCENE ALWAYS HAS AN INTENTION: IT'S THE through-line underneath every spoken line, gesture, or action. In the following scene about my college years, I have two intentions, two takeaways for you, the reader. One: trust your instincts (I did not). And two: if you make a misstep, you can still transmute it into gold. Here's what happened.

I was not convinced that I should go to Sarah Lawrence. My instincts were telegraphing me a message loudly that, sadly, I was to squelch in order to please others. This instinct is vital to me as an actress when I'm contemplating projects. I need to feel in my gut that I am stepping into a cast, crew, and company where I can thrive. When I look back at my career, it's the moments where I acquiesced instead of trusting my gut instincts that I found myself in a setting where I couldn't flourish. In this instance, I took a leap of faith based on the advice and enthusiasm of my high school college counselor, Dean Fitzgerald, and my mother. I entered the college in the fall of 1966. Beautiful, bucolic Bronxville was a big step up from Grandpa's beautiful, bucolic Bronx! Maybe it considered itself so because it would not sell real estate to Jews or people of color. Brace yourself, Bronxville, here we come!

In my very soul, I wanted to major in theater. Instead, my major was . . . philosophy. Doctor? Lawyer? Philosopher! Thank you, Lily!

Sarah Lawrence was originally founded under the umbrella of Vassar College. Its curriculum was based on the Oxford-Cambridge system: three courses per semester explored in depth through plenty of reading, class discussions, papers, and in rare instances, quizzes and tests. However, there were no grades. *No grades?!* I felt like I was on Mars. How would I know if I achieved excellence? I had come from high-powered, structured Scarsdale High; I was accustomed to enjoying the pressure of studying. To me, no grades were like no feedback and zero gravity. I was floating aimlessly, and as such, I'd rather go to Yale to see my boyfriend and get tonsillitis. So I did.

Sarah Lawrence did have one great advantage, however: proximity to New York City. It was twenty minutes by car or train from Bronxville to Broadway. New York had just been crowned "The Big Apple" by handsome Mayor John V. Lindsay, another American aristocrat who was just as dreamy as the Kennedys. There were free concerts in Sheep Meadow in Central Park. I got to hear Judy Collins and Barbra Streisand. Little did I realize, as a seventeen-year-old, that I would become a friend of Ms. Streisand once I starred in *Yentl* on Broadway, as she starred in *Yentl* on film. Back in Bronxville, there were great professors. I heard the lectures of Joseph Campbell, Grace Paley, and Ada Boseman, and in classes of ten was directly exposed to Ilja Wachs, Gerda Lerner, André Singer, and Harold Aks. Those were priceless opportunities.

I found my way to what ultimately proved useful to me at Sarah Lawrence—this was a place that celebrated taking chances. Here was a haven where I was encouraged to take a risk and there wasn't a, "Don't be ridiculous!" waiting for me on the other side. As Anaïs Nin said, "Life shrinks or expands in proportion to one's courage," and courage and curiosity are critical ingredients as an actor—and a human being. I sowed the seeds of these invaluable qualities during my years at SLC.

In my classes, I was encouraged to be fearless and intellectually adventuresome. The A was no longer the target. The insight was. On the journey of courageous self-discovery, the faculty understood that missteps were inevitable. They taught us that we can fall in public and simply get up again without an overlay of humiliation or shame.

I did some of my most tasteless work in college—and some of my best. Both were met with reassuring encouragement, and the suggestion to reach further and deeper. Thus, today in my rehearsal process, I aspire to be fearless with my choices, fearless with the direction I'm given, and work at 100 percent, however the chips may fall. I love rehearsing. I love exploring. I love taking chances. I love the respite from my own self-judgment. I love the work so much I forget to look at my watch. Thank G-d for this school that allowed me to finally turn the volume down on the incessant chatter of Lily's disdain for my unbridled imagination.

As she had advised in Dean Fitzgerald's office, Mother's vision that I might be able to study in New York, as well as frequent it, proved right. Sarah Lawrence granted me credit for studying acting with one of the master teachers in Manhattan: the great Uta Hagen. At barely eighteen, I was being taught by the Tony Award winner who had originated the leading roles in Broadway's *Who's Afraid of Virginia Woolf?*, *The Country Girl*, and *Saint Joan*, as well as starring in renowned productions of *The Cherry Orchard*, *A Streetcar Named Desire*, and *Mrs. Klein*. She played Ophelia to Eva Le Gallienne's Hamlet, Nina opposite the Lunts in *The Seagull*, and Desdemona opposite Paul Robeson in *Othello*.

I auditioned for Ms. Hagen with a friend from Sarah Lawrence. We performed a short excerpt from *The Stronger* by August Strindberg. I started the audition as Mrs. X, the talkative one, and then we switched roles, and I played Mrs. Y, who doesn't speak but with deep, clever work can make quite an impression through focused listening and subtle reactions, using a look, or a twist of the body, or the use of a prop. When we finished, Ms. Hagen simply said, "Thank you." I said to myself, *Thank you? What does that mean?* Little did I know, there would be fifty more years of asking myself the same question after each audition.

A week later, both of us were accepted to the Hagen Berghof Studio! We were ecstatic.

Entering Ms. Hagen's class in the spring of 1967 was artistic nirvana. Talk about being empowered by a teacher; she was a transformative force in my life. For one, Ms. Hagen never criticized, but instead, redirected her students. This was utterly epiphanous to me. I knew who should be auditing this class: my mother!

If our scene work missed the mark, Ms. Hagen would simply say, "How interesting. You've mastered this point of view, so now, why don't we try it another way?" No judgment. She knew well enough we would all face plenty of that later. For now, in her class, it was time to explore and soar in the craft we loved most. In the absence of grades, what I often earned upon finishing a scene was the joyful nod of my mentor saying, "Very good, Ms. Feldshuh. Very, very good."

What Ms. Hagen really gave me was a piece of gold. Whenever the chips were down, I always remembered that Uta Hagen believed in me. When I arrived on Broadway, I wrote her: "You were a treasure to me. The first nurturer of my work. Your wisdom and support meant everything."

I was her youngest student, and like everyone else, I happily worked with the brilliant Bill Hickey for six months until I was permitted to transfer into her class. The HB Studio was at 11 Bank Street in the West Village. Oh, the Village in 1967! What a wonderful carnival it was! I would frequent Ellen Stewart's La MaMa Experimental Theatre Club, where some of my classmates performed a piece called *Camilla*. I would trek out to Brooklyn to see *Paradise Now* created by The Living Theatre with Julian Beck and Judith Malina. Soon after, I saw the work of The Open Theater headed by Joseph Chaikin, who would become my teacher at Sarah Lawrence. Again, Lily's logic held true. I don't know who was teaching acting up in Poughkeepsie at Vassar, but we had some of the greats at Sarah Lawrence because it was a hop, skip, and a jump from New York City.

Finally, in the fall of my sophomore year, I was given the opportunity to perform in New York myself at the Judson Memorial Church on West Fourth Street. To me, this was my New York debut! I was hitting the big time! I had a supporting role in *The Good Woman of Szechuan* (now *The Good Person of Szechuan*) by Bertolt Brecht. I was over the moon. I remember I was about to make my entrance from the back of the long aisle of the church; I had on my Chinese mask and my do-it-yourself costume. Just as I was about to enter the play, there was a tap on my shoulder. It was my mother. "Terri, here! I brought you a sweater!" she barked. "I thought you might be cold." I thought I was going to fall through the floorboards.

Outside in the world, we were *all* falling through the floorboards. The Vietnam War was in full and tragic swing. The My Lai massacre was just months away. The *Evénéments de Mai* in Paris upended the Sorbonne and this social tsunami spread waves of upheaval across university campuses in the US from Columbia to Berkeley. The spring of 1968 was volcanic. Reverend Dr. Martin Luther King Jr. had just been assassinated. Columbia students from SDS (Students for a Democratic Society) took over the Low Memorial Library, including the president's office, to protest the university's affiliation with the US Department of Defense and the war in Vietnam. The Student Afro-American Society was protesting a racially segregated gym that was about to be built for the university. "No peace without justice" was the slogan of the day on any number of fronts.

Sarah Lawrence, a bastion of liberal thought and courage, soon followed Columbia. A core of politicized students took over Westlands, our main administrative center for the college, as well as the president's office. Westlands was the heart of our campus. Our president, Esther Raushenbush, was the prototypical kind, intellectual Jewish mother (she could have been related to Golda Meir). My best friend Alicia Fleissig and I could not imagine why the radicals were giving this elegant, wise grandma such trouble.

Alicia and I would sit in Bates Hall and have tea together and try to figure out what the heck was going on. The college was already loosey-goosey in its educational methods. What more did they want?

With the takeover of Westlands, the college spiraled into orbit. The war careened along, and then a boy from Scarsdale was killed. I heard from my mother, who had clipped the article out of *The Scarsdale Inquirer* to show me. A month later, she was marching with us in Washington against the war. Now that it had touched the boys in Scarsdale, normally quiet Lily wasn't going to be silent about that, no matter what.

Although I lived on campus, and participated as fully as I could in campus activities—which weren't many—I went home to see my parents at least once a week. How do you rebel when someone is waiting to do your laundry at 47 Penn and fold it meticulously in two piles, being sure not to mix prints and stripes? When Mother's delicious cooking is a much greater temptation than the food at Bates? When the school you go to is so individuated that you are lonely, but the minute you step over the threshold at 47 Penn, your parents delight in seeing you?

I thought I went home to ease the sting of the empty nest for my folks, but perhaps it was just as comforting for me to revisit my home plate, which was actually emotionally warmer than the college I was attending. Now *that's* saying something. Inside the classroom, I was fine. Outside the classroom, I found it hard to connect.

The breakdown of society in 1968 fomented a time of expansion and creative experimentation in my life. It was the first time I was given my own car, a red Toyota Corona, and lived in a dorm. I went to my first mixer (WASP for a *simcha*). I traveled to Yale and Princeton for the first time for weekend dates, and thanks to those amazing weeks in the south of France and to my father's sense of adventure and my mother's common sense, I knew I could, I knew I should, and I knew I would.

In my freshman year, I joined the all-women Sarah Lawrence Chorus under Maestro Harold Aks. With Professor Aks, we sang all over Europe. We even went to Russia over Christmas break to sing in Moscow, Kiev, and Leningrad in the depths of the Cold War of 1968. Nobody went to Russia then except the Beatles! I bought a long, gray maxi coat with huge, gray mouton collar and cuffs, and fell briefly in love with a Russian general's son who was a full foot taller than I (which actually isn't saying much when you're five foot two). He could literally sweep me off my feet and often did.

In Kiev, we were taken on our first midnight sleigh ride pulled by four horses as white as a Siberian winter. That image has stayed with me through every Chekhov play I've seen or done. Russia was passionate and dramatic, hardy, full of heart . . . and vodka. For the last song of each concert, Professor Aks put his hands behind his back and conducted us with just his eyes. I thought the audience was going to go mad. We were young, we were beautiful, and we were astonishingly musical. We yelled to our Russian sold-out house, *"MY VAS LYUBIM!"* ("We love you!") "And we love your stamping feet and standing ovations!" And here was an odd sensation: I wanted my mother to be here in the country that spat upon my grandparents and great-grandparents to witness this miracle.

In sophomore year, my suitemates were Francesca Draper, whose father was the portrait artist to the Shah of Iran; Wendy Baker, who was Senator William Proxmire's niece; and Anne Baker, a radical from Chicago who for an American, was quite European. I remember vividly she didn't shave under her arms. She wouldn't have even been able to cross the threshold of 47 Penn without Lily saying, "Hello! You want a shirt or a razor?"

It was an eclectic and inspiring collection of young females. With my suitemates that year, we traveled to Yale to hear The Jimi Hendrix Experience at Woolsey Hall. From Anne Baker, I learned details about SDS, which was at the forefront of the fight for labor and civil rights, who screamed for an end to the Vietnam War, who used anarchy when necessary, and who sometimes responded with violence when treated with violence by the police. From Wendy Baker and Francesca Draper, I learned what New York City wealth looked like up close—and often through bleary eyes because it was they who introduced me to pot (yes, Lily, I did inhale).

When I visited Francesca's stately brownstone on New York's Upper East Side or the Yale Club for drinks with Wendy Baker and her dad, I felt like I was living the life of a debutante in a Hollywood movie. Only it wasn't a movie; these were vignettes Lily could only dream of. Look at me now, Hortense!

Having completed a year of Italian, I was accepted into the Sarah Lawrence summer program in Florence. I had the good fortune to live in *Il Torre di Bellosguardo*, a grand hotel perched on the verdant hills outside of Florence that looked down upon this magnificent renaissance city, which bloomed under the Medicis. We read Dante under flowering wisteria trellises and gazed upon the streets where he met his beautiful Beatrice and waxed poetic about her in *La Vita Nuova* (1294 CE). In the bedroom that I shared with my best friend Alicia, there was a little chapel sculpted into the thick plaster walls over my four-poster mahogany double bed. If I needed to pray to Jesus, he was right there.

One weekend, we went on a wild viaggio to Venice. Getting to Venice alone was a major adventure. We took the train and stopped at the Scrovegni Chapel to view the extraordinary frescoes by Giotto. So entranced were we by Giotto's bravura sense of naturalism and the disciplined beauty of the chapel, that we ended up missing the last train. It didn't hurt that we had a picnic outside of the chapel and imbibed a full bottle of Chianti. Relaxed and giggling, we thought, "Un bel giorno"—until it hit us: *how do we get to Venice tonight?*

How did eighteen- and nineteen-year-old women get anywhere in Western Europe in the late 1960s? By sticking out their thumbs on the main road and being picked up by two young men on their way to Viareggio. I could hear my mother's scorn: "Hitchhiking. This is exactly why I don't want you venturing abroad. Where's your judgment?"

These young men ended up being decent fellows, and we made it to our destination safe and sound. Even though we were innocent, we had some common sense and good survival instincts. I can see my mother shaking her head: "You were lucky as hell."

The first thing I noticed in Venice were the masks. Beautiful hand-painted masks adorning the doorways and windows of shops, luring this aspiring actress to enter. These magical masks were reminding me that I had to soak in all these sights, sounds, and textures for my actor's reservoir of experience. I may need to draw upon them later. Indeed I did. When I played Juliet at The Old Globe Theatre in San Diego for famed director Jack O'Brien ten years later, I had the sights, the sounds, and even the smells of Verona, Venice, Florence, Rome, and San Gimignano wafting through my mind.

In Venice, we were staying near the Ponte dell'Accademia in a little *albergo* (hotel) that had no air conditioning. Following the example of Major League Baseball players of the fifties in the US, we decided to shower ourselves in cold water, exit the shower soaking wet, and sleep with the ceiling fan blowing on our wet, naked bodies in order to cool ourselves enough to fall asleep in the unfathomable night heat. Tennessee Williams's hot tin roof didn't hold a candle to this torpor.

In the morning, we hopped to the nearby Galleria dell'Accademia, then a ferry to the Basilico di San Giorgio Maggiore to see Tintoretto's *The Last Supper*, then to the art and architecture of the Palazzo Ducale, and finally caught our breath with a delicious espresso in the Piazza San Marco, where there are more pigeons than people. We took our first gondola ride on the Grand Canal, feeling like Italian royalty. We bought Murano glass, and a salesman named Gianni wanted to take us out on the town—boy, do I remember him. We walked on the Rialto Bridge and thought of *The Merchant of Venice*, and sighed on the Bridge of Sighs. I also knew that I was on the location where Katharine Hepburn did her own stunts in the film *Summertime*, falling into the Venice Canal, and I can hear Lily filling in: "And got an incurable eye infection that lasted the rest of her life!"

In the fall of my junior year of college, I returned to Sarah Lawrence and was cast in the co-ed production of *The Crucible* that we did with the boys of Wesleyan University. During that production, I met a senior who was documenting the show with a fancy still camera called a Hasselblad, and I thought that camera was terribly sexy. I thought the cameraman was even sexier. I was smitten on sight. And apparently for him, when my image came into focus in that Hasselblad, the feeling was mutual, and the sparks flew. His name was Michael Fairchild.

By the spring of my junior year, I was officially in love. I was so taken with Michael's beauty, manners, and kindness, not to mention his exquisite photography that always captured the soul of his subjects, that he easily captured my heart. If I'm honest, part of his allure was that Michael was foreign territory for me. Blond, blue-eyed, quietly expressive, and incredibly WASPy, with parents who had forsaken the United States for the island of St. John's and some great cocktails. Michael was an artist, and his family had come to America in the 1600s.

When not on campus, Michael resided with his remarkable grandmother, Julia Fairchild, in the family house in Cold Spring Harbor, a marvelous hamlet on Long Island's North Shore that vibrated with history. Michael's grandfather had attended Yale, transported to New Haven each fall by horse and carriage. *My* grandfather had "attended" pogroms, running each spring from the horses of the Cossacks.

Julia Fairchild was a member of the elite Colony Club on Park Avenue, an establishment I imagined was far older than the Daughters of the American Revolution. I figured the club's title stood for the lineage of the women who were allowed membership. I thought these ladies had to have great-great-grandmothers who settled in America when there were just thirteen colonies, long before the Revolutionary War. Indeed, between The Chandler Dukes, The Harrimans, The Morgans, The Astors, The Vanderbilts, and The Rockefellers, the Colony Club enjoyed an extraordinary social roster—even if it *was* founded as late as 1903 as the first social and cultural club founded by and for women only. I loved that. Not a bad achievement considering gender equality was as unknown to their husbands as life on another planet. I learned that The Club and the street in front of it were often the site of large suffrage rallies sponsored by the Equal Franchise Society, to which many women of the Colony Club belonged.

My grandmother Ada was a member of a ladies' poker club. Their social circle was busted in the Bronx for illegal gambling. I was pretty sure I wouldn't qualify for Colony Club membership.

After lunch at the Colony Club, Julia and I would often walk down the brownstone blocks between Park and Madison in the East Sixties, and she would name every family who lived in each dwelling. She remembered when the land of Rockefeller Center was farmland for the Rockefeller family. This was a new world for a Jewish girl from Scarsdale and I wanted in. I wanted to see inside "The Restricted World," the world I often heard my parents whisper about beneath their breath. The other America, the America of debutantes, hunt balls, and cotillions. These we never had, and it all left me breathless.

The summer between junior and senior year, I was hired to play the ingenue leads at Theatre By The Sea in Matunuck, Rhode Island, made famous by Tallulah Bankhead, Marlon Brando, and Carol Channing during the golden age of summer stock. Tommy Brent, the managing producer, asked me if I had a stage name.

After only a moment's thought, I blurted out, "Of course. Terri Fairchild."

Michael was delighted that I wanted to take his last name, and I was delighted that he was delighted. In the words of Noël Coward, I was "Mad About the Boy," and during one of our forehead-to-forehead moments at Theatre By The Sea, Michael said, "Terri Sue?! What kind of a name is that for a girl like you? Were you ever called anything else?"

I thought for a moment, then said, "Tovah. I was called Tovah in ... Sunday school." (Well, Hebrew school, but I was too embarrassed to say Hebrew School, because it sounded too Jewish.)

"Tovah!" Michael repeated, making a meal out of the vowels.

His face lit up. "Now *that's* a name."

For years, the boys in my class were named Terry; my godfather's collie was named Terry. When I lived in France for a summer, "Thierry" was, again, a boy's name. In my foreign language classes I was called either "Thérèse" or "Teresa." "Terri" simply didn't translate on the international scene, and I was now an international woman of adventure! International women of adventure are not named Terri Sue.

To boot, my name sounded harsh to me—too many Rs—and it was a perennially juvenile name, doomed to be forever diminutive. I was now becoming a woman, and I didn't want a moniker that was "cute." I felt like I couldn't grow into a name like Terri Sue. In fact, I was busting out of it. The Debbies became Deborahs, the Barbies became Barbaras, the Terris became . . . *Terri*. Well, no thank you.

"Tovah" began as a love name between just Michael and me. The name Tovah originates from Hebrew, the ancient holy language of the Torah, and it means *good*. Not bad! To pronounce Tovah, the mouth soars into an open cathedral for the OH and then spreads generously wide for the AH . . . TO-VAH: mysterious yet melodious—and it was authentic to my history. Tovah was the Hebrew name of my mother's beloved Aunt Tilly. I carry her namesake. Tovah has an H at the end which stands for the covenant with G-d. It's a name that has gravitas. People would certainly take a Tovah more seriously than they would take a Terri Sue.

My mother was understandably concerned about my name change.

"What's in a name?
     . . . A rose by any other name would smell as sweet."
     (*Romeo and Juliet*, Act II, Scene 2)

Everything's in a name!

"We didn't come to this country for you to call yourself *Tovah*," she barked at me. "Sidney! Terri wants to call herself 'Tovah'! You already have an unpronounceable last name and now you're going to take

'Tovah' as your first name? Do I have to tell you what confusion you're creating? And do I really have to call you that??!"

Now, as a mother and a grandmother, I can understand Lily being upset. Rejecting Terri was rejecting Mom's America—the America of Debbies, Bonnies, Pattys, Susies—the "cute" nicknames that embodied the American girl. Post–World War II America was the land of the open heart. America was the great welcomer. Once you hit her shores, you were family, but my mom felt even as *mishpucha* (Yiddish for family), you had an obligation to blend in for patriotic and practical reasons. She felt this obligation in almost every arena of her life. It was built into her first-generation American DNA. It was her job. Regarding "Tovah," Mom's judgment, not surprisingly, was on the money. The name change was huge. The name change changed the landscape of my life.

I was the second generation, and I didn't need to blend in. Sarah Lawrence, in fact, trained me *not* to blend in. I now felt safe enough to stand out, to embrace my old-world heritage with pride. "Tovah" prevailed and ushered me into my womanhood. At a time when most people in the entertainment world were Anglicizing their names to *not* sound Jewish, I reclaimed my Hebrew namesake. Michael and I eventually went our separate ways, but "Tovah" remained, though it would be years before the name would find its way to my mother's lips in her everyday lexicon.

Now, without any romantic strings attached to my wings, Sarah Lawrence allowed me to apply to The Experiment in International Living, and I was accepted to go to France for a semester. I would study French culture, language, and even mime with the great Jacques Lecoq. I studied three months in Besançon to polish my language and history skills, and then my plan was to go to Paris and enroll in École Jacques Lecoq until I returned to Sarah Lawrence for my last semester.

My father had told me that I could stay in Paris with his French clients, the Mikaeloffs, with whom I'd lived during that wonderful summer of 1962. My father logically reasoned that if I had lived with them for an entire summer as a thirteen-year-old, there was no reason they wouldn't welcome me for at least that time as a twenty-year-old. One problem was that the head of the household, Jean Mikaeloff, lived in Lyon. Only his sons, Yves, Philippe, and Jean-Serge, lived with their wives and young families in Paris. None of them wanted me moving in. Dad was delusionally optimistic, and despite his efforts, he could not work out a homestay for me. He lived in such hope that he didn't tell me the bad news until three days before my departure. It was shocking for me, and I remember this as the first time my father ever seriously disappointed me. It was from this experience I learned not to make promises I couldn't keep.

My father did come up with a Plan B. I was to take the train from Besançon to Paris and a Monsieur Mayer would meet me at the platform at the Gare de Lyon. My father, an intelligence officer in the US Army during World War II, had helped Monsieur Mayer reconnect with his French family after the war. He was a rotund, kindly gentleman, and indeed he did meet me at the Gare de Lyon. He drove me to a small *pension* on the left bank, gave me the *International Herald Tribune*, and said in French, "Read the rooms-for-rent ads and follow through on them first thing in the morning." I was a newbie in a new city, but the newspaper was in my native language, and necessity pushed me forward.

I found a small room in an apartment at 18 Rue Xavier-Privas in the *5ème Arrondissement* near the Boulevard Saint-Michel. It was owned by a Missouri farmer named Gardner Smith, who said he had come to Paris to "regain his virility." *Oy*. Not on my watch.

The Palace of Versailles this apartment was not. In fact, my room was so small that to enter it, the bed had to be folded up against the wall. Once inside, you could pull the bed down, and it would take up the entire room. That bed was my platform on which to eat, to sleep, to study, and to dream. I called this space the "mouse hole." It had a sliver of a window where if I craned my neck, I could see the moon. Through that sliver, like the French, I created my own cold-air refrigerator by hanging my favorite *fromage et beurre*. Of course, this meant that my window had to stay open all winter, but I would rather freeze to death than let my butter and cheese spoil. This too is very French. I found my Bohemian existence quirky yet exhilarating. Lily would've found it un-acceptable. "No fridge?! How can you live without a fridge? And in a mousetrap, yet!"

Every morning, I would take the Metro to the *15ème Arrondissement* with my student carnet and study with Lecoq: circus techniques, clown skills, and the very basics of mime, which were more profound than I ever imagined. Lecoq taught us about *le point neutre*, or the neutral point. It's the "everyman starting point" from which an artist begins to create their characters. It's the delicious *zero*. He taught us stillness, focus, Zen (blank) mind, and the precision of 120 movements to get in and out of an imaginary bathtub. Just 120 movements, mind you, not 119 and not 121!

Lecoq was a serious, dedicated teacher. He lived in the metaphor, something I love. He saw mime as a pathway to the human condition. In silence, we created vivid situations with only the help of our hands and our bodies. One needed to be flexible, specific, trained, and precise in order to dig down into the river of common human experience and achieve a depiction of "Everyman," which is, at its heart, all of us.

In 1969 and '70, life in Paris was simple. Money was tight, posses-sions were few, and classes took up only half the day. By two in the af-ternoon, we Lecoq students would eat lunch together, deciding whether we had enough *argent* (money) to order what we really wanted: steak frites. Then, I would set out to discover Paris. I particularly loved the Rodin Museum. As a budding actress, I would stand in front of Rodin's extraordinary larger-than-life sculptures and physically mirror their body positions. *The Thinker*, *The Burghers of Calais*, and my favorite of favorites, *The Kiss*. *The Kiss* was hard to imitate solo, unless you were a contortionist.

Living in France truly pushed me out on my own for the first time. In addition to culture, I acquired the domestic skills of independence: cooking, cleaning, laundering, and even entertaining. I also began fully managing my own money. I paid tuition to the École Lecoq and lived within the budget of the allowance given to me by my father, who, as always, did not spoil me, but was generous enough that I didn't have to worry. One of my father's greatest virtues is that he didn't covet money. To him, it was a symbol of empowerment, and as Dolly Levi said in *Hello, Dolly!*, "Money . . . is like manure; it's not worth a thing unless it's spread around encouraging young things to grow."

My mother was noticeably absent from my life during that time. Of course, I would get the occasional little blue prestamped aerogram from her. Her penmanship swept smoothly and meticulously across the page with detailed descriptions of her winter days in Westchester County— the snowstorms, my father's cases, the responsibilities at 47 Penn, the parties, and the loneliness at Hanukkah. By now, Mom was a stalwart Democrat and Dad remained a Republican because of his enduring loyalty to Eisenhower. The political poles in our house gave some added spice to Mom and Dad's relationship. He'd leave for the office, and Mom would throw a luncheon for Nita Lowy, our Democratic representative in the House. Nita later introduced Lily to Hillary Clinton. I have the picture. My parents' divergent politics didn't seem to bother either one of them. Ah, the good old days!

In her letters, my mother did not ask me about my life in Paris or what my plans were for the future. I'm not sure to this day if she was giving me my space to discover myself or if she was just too afraid to hear my answers. At any rate, I volunteered very little, especially the fact that I was having a love affair with the son of the Moroccan ambassador. Such a thing would have never even occurred to Lily. This was a good thing. I never lied to Mom, but as Golda Meir would say, "Don't lie, just don't speak."

I returned to Sarah Lawrence in late February 1970 filled with new experiences. I was now fully fluent in French and could boast a mastery of rudimentary circus techniques, clown skills, and mime. Where I was going to use these, I wasn't sure, but I knew having these circus skills might distinguish me in the future. Isn't luck when opportunity meets excellence? I kept practicing my juggling, acrobatics, and mime, thinking, *Mom didn't want me to go to a conservatory, so I ended up creating one on my own.*

I was also emerging as a responsible adult, molting my adolescent skin. I now spoke passably in four languages, five if you count mime, my go-to whenever I hit a speedbump in the other four. I traveled to Europe on a regular basis and knew Manhattan and Paris like the back of my hand. I truly felt like a citizen of the world. I burned my bras and read Betty Friedan and Eldridge Cleaver. I was awakened to the depth of racism in America and the strength of the plateglass ceiling women had to break through.

Back at school, besides the philosophy of science and women's studies with the godmother of modern gender studies, Gerda Lerner, I threw myself headlong into the SLC theater program with *Renard* by Stravinsky (my first title role—I played the fox!); *A Midsummer Night's Dream*, where I played Bottom the weaver—a traditionally male role (the first of what were to be many of my "trouser" roles); and best of all, song study with John Braswell. I immersed myself in my craft with vigor and single-minded devotion. My artistic passion was my escape hatch from loneliness and silence. My artistic passion was my attentive, ever-present lover. Success was ecstasy; struggles and failures were devastation, but I knew that just like with the piano, *if I was good to my artistic life, my artistic life would be good to me.*

They say it takes twenty years to learn how to act—and then twenty more years to learn how *not* to. It took me decades to understand that great acting is a *beingness.* Just as I had learned years before as a classical pianist, the actor also strives to become accurate, excellent, and finally, effortless. How? Through thousands of hours of exploration, which we call rehearsal. An actor at his best can climb inside the soul of another human being and tell that person's story effortlessly and often brilliantly. With the great actor, there is a seamless relationship between the actor and the character. At your best, when you're onstage, it feels like improv, like a cadenza by Mozart. The actor educates himself to know everything about his character so that he can walk onstage and *know nothing*. Then it will appear as if he is making up the lines on the spot, in that second, just for that audience.

I graduated from Sarah Lawrence in June of 1970, all of us wearing black dresses in mourning for the massacre at Kent State. Mother said, "This looks like a *shiva!*" It was the right thing to do, but I have to confess, I missed my cap and gown.

My Sarah Lawrence College diploma was my last legal document with "Terri Sue Feldshuh" on it. I felt that final salvo was the least I could do for my parents, who so generously paid for my education. As I pulled away from the sheltered, refined, suburban cupola of Scarsdale, I realized my European education was something my father cheered and my mother, despite her trepidation, allowed in silence to happen. How ironic that this push-away from my parents was actually sponsored by my parents. Lucky break. But from this time on, it was up to me to carve my own path.

It's one thing to fly from the nest when you're flying in the direction your parents have chosen for you. It's quite another when you're setting off on your own against the winds of your background. This demanded that I power my wings with conviction and a keen sense of direction and purpose. Mother had made me strong for the world, but her vision outside her nest was a bleak one. I was flying toward azure skies. I knew they were there, waiting for me. *Oh, please G-d,* let them be there waiting for me.

Lilyism on 54 Below

When I was making my debut at Michael Feinstein's prestigious supper club, 54 Below in New York City, my mother said, "54 Below? That's not a theater, that's a temperature! My daughter, the Broadway star, now performing in an *igloo*!"

What Other People Think of Me Is None of My Business

"HELLO, MOM? PUT DOWN *HOUSE BEAUTIFUL*," I SAID, holding a payphone. "I'm standing in the lobby of the Guthrie Theater. I just auditioned in the finals for the McKnight Fellowship, and as I was walking up the aisle, they stopped me before I could even exit the theater and said 'You've won!'"

(Lily on the other end of the phone.) "Two kids in the theater? What did I do wrong?" I'm sure she was pressing the receiver to her breast, but I could clearly hear her *kvetching* to heaven, "Papa, I'm glad you're not alive to see this. *This* would kill you."

The "this" was the McKnight Fellowship in acting, which meant 3M (Minnesota Mining and Manufacturing—forgive me, environmentalists) would pay for my master's degree at the University of Minnesota, and I would become a journeyman in the prestigious classical acting company of the Guthrie Theater in Minneapolis. Because my brother David had won the same fellowship five years before and was still at the Guthrie as an actor and associate artistic director, it felt a bit like a second home—only the Minnesotans had a wild accent and ate a lot of pork products.

Neil Armstrong had just walked on the moon, Courrèges go-go boots and miniskirts were all the rage, and so, outfitted in my stylish regalia, I arrived in the Twin Cities as the "New York Sophisticate." Really, I was a bright-eyed and bushy-tailed kid straight off the boat from Scarsdale with a dollar and a dream of becoming a professional actress. I can still remember the thrill I felt when I was given my first Equity card as a professional member of the Tyrone Guthrie Theater Repertory Company. I had arrived!

The season opened with a welcome speech from Artistic Director Michael Langham, a Shakespearean purist who had come straight to the Northwest from Stratford, Canada, and before that, from a slew of prestigious theaters including the West End and The Old Vic in London. He was elegant and dapper, with piercing blue eyes and an equally piercing intelligence. He was *veddy* British.

I had heard through the grapevine that Mr. Langham had honed his extraordinary focus on the words of the Bard while directing plays in a German prisoner of war camp, and his intensity bore that out. Langham seemed almost mythical to me, and in that little world of the Guthrie, he was like G-d himself. If he liked you, Mr. Langham was witty, kind, insightful, and generous. You could understand why Christopher Plummer had famously said that he owed his career to Michael Langham. If Michael didn't like you, well, as Shakespeare would've said, *Woe unto you!*

In that first season, I was cast as an actress, a poet, and a nun in the new adaptation of Rostand's *Cyrano* by Anthony Burgess, most famous for his book *A Clockwork Orange.* I was also cast in the ensemble of *Taming of the Shrew*, and I was assigned to understudy the incomparable Roberta Maxwell as Bianca. Long story short? I never went on for my leading lady, which meant I delivered one line onstage during the whole season. It was in *Cyrano*, Act I, Scene 1:

But a hundred men against one poor poet—why?

Quite a mouthful, right? Short, I know, but it packs a wallop. Listen, it was my only line, and I was a professional actress now. I needed to make the most of the crumbs I had been given. That's how it works at the beginning. "You work with what you've got," Uta Hagen would say to me. I must have rehearsed that line a hundred thousand times with my brother David. With each read, he would give me a new direction so I could give the line a fresh acting beat and a different emphasis, until he finally said, "Enough, Tovah! It's only nine words." Poor David, he's probably still repeating those nine words in his sleep.

Finally, rehearsal day one arrived. The whole cast was assembled at the theater. After a read through of the play, the production stage manager officially asked us to get up on our feet for Act I, Scene 1 of *Cyrano*. "Oh, my G-d," I thought. "This is the scene that contains my line!" I could hardly bear the electricity of the moment. I stood on that majestic Guthrie thrust stage for the first time in my life, and with movie star sincerity, uttered my nine words.

"But a hundred men against one poor poet—why?"

"Can't hear you!" Director Michael Langham shouted from the middle of the house.

"*But a hundred men against one poor poet—why?*" I said again, this time projecting my voice from my diaphragm the way my voice teacher Madame Olga Eisner had taught me.

"Louder!" Langham shouted once more, and I felt my stomach drop to somewhere around my ankles.

"BUT A HUNDRED MEN AGAINST ONE POOR POET—WHY?" Yelling at the top of my lungs, all of my thoughtful, nuanced inflection; all of my rich subtext—gone! Now I was going for pure volume.

"Now I can hear you," Langham said, "but I can't understand you."

That sentence felt painfully familiar. I thought to myself: *My mother can't hear me, and when she does, she can't understand me. Now Michael*

Langham can't hear me, and when he does, he can't understand me. Langham's humiliating remark teleported me back to an earlier similar feeling born out of my mother's silence. How did this nightmare get on a plane and follow me over a thousand miles from Scarsdale to Minneapolis?

So yes, I had a rough go of it that first season at the Guthrie, but like my dad always said, "If you work hard, if you strive for excellence, you will master skills that nobody can take away from you." So I dove into my singing lessons, tap lessons, ballet lessons, Shakespeare lessons; I "lessoned" myself into oblivion. Did this make Michael Langham like my work any better? No, it did not. And as I learned from Lily and now emphatically from Langham, you only get one chance to make a first impression. Langham's impression was that I was a poor actor, and he stuck to it.

In between seasons, I fared surprisingly well. I got hired to play the baker's wife Lise and the Mother Superior in the Bucks County Playhouse's production of *Cyrano* opposite the delightfully funny Tom Posten. I also understudied Roxane. Just getting hired to say more than nine words was encouraging. I figured Bucks County must not have found out my big secret: that according to Langham, you can't hear me and you can't understand me. Bucks County Playhouse heard and understood me just fine. Maybe I wasn't as bad as Langham thought. Maybe.

I returned to the Guthrie in April, astonished to have been rehired but ready to master my new assignments, whatever those might be. The second season at the Guthrie mercifully brought me more visibility. I was cast in my first "big" speaking role in Shakespeare's *A Midsummer Night's Dream* as Peaseblossom, the first fairy. I played a maid in *The Relapse* and a leper in *Oedipus the King*.

"You're playing a *what*?! A *lepuh*?!" squawked Lily.

"Yes, Mom, in *Oedipus* I play a mother who has lost her child to leprosy."

"*Oy.* Don't look for me on opening night."

The direction in the script said I had to "scream in despair," at the loss of my child, so I did. I literally howled from the depth of my soul.

"You're not going to do that are you?" Michael Langham's disapproval rang out loud and clear from the cheap seats.

"What adjustment would you like me to make, sir?" I asked, taking my life in my hands and daring to question the god of the Guthrie himself.

"I'd like to believe you," Langham said with stentorian disdain. "Try it again, only this time, make it credible."

I let out a howl that I think was more about my deep upset about being at the Guthrie under the baton of "Let's-Bully-the-Young-Ones-Langham" than it was about the character's despair. Thank goodness I had Uta Hagen's voice in my head saying, "Great substitution. Yes, use that subtext!"

"Oh my G-d," Langham huffed. "If you're going to do that, just turn your back to the house. If I have to hear you, at least I don't have to see you." I didn't speak a word at his rehearsals for the rest of the season. Didn't he understand that "if you're good to the piano, the piano will be good to you"? That you get more with honey than with vinegar?

Finally, rehearsals started for *A Midsummer Night's Dream*, which was being directed by John Hirsch, *not* Michael Langham. Hirsch was a Holocaust survivor with legendary status in classical theater, and the whole company was in awe of him before rehearsals even began. I was keeping my fingers crossed that this experience would be a little more amicable. I was Dianne Wiest's understudy. Dianne was a brilliantly vulnerable, fluttery Hermia who, like Roberta Maxwell, never missed a performance. This season though, I didn't just have one line of my very own, I had an entire speech! I think my brother was nervous.

On that first day of *Midsummer* rehearsal, I took a deep breath and full throttle, grabbed opportunity by the fairy bells to begin my speech:

"Over hill, over dale,
Thorough bush, thorough briar,
Over park, over pale,

Thorough flood, thorough fire,
I do wander everywhere . . ."

"Just vat deh hell do you tink yaw do-ink?" John Hirsch interrupted in his heavy, Hungarian accent.

"I'm reciting my speech, Mr. Hirsch," I said. I mean, really? Again with this? What was I doing wrong? Was I that terrible as to drive these Shakespearean masters purple with rage?

Now, in measured tones, Hirsch said, "So, you vant to be an actreeece?"

I'm thinking, *Umm, yes, I vant to be an actreeece. Why else do you think I'm standing on this stage half naked playing a pea flower?* But I merely nodded silently.

"Hmm, I see. Vell in zat case, I suggest you *act!*" said Hirsch. "Othervise, be an accountant. Yes, maybe you should be an accountant."

I was mortified.

And was that the specter of Lily sitting behind him, shaking her head saying, "Are you hearing this? Are you listening to this man?"

All the air went out of the room. For me, time stopped, and once again I felt deeply humiliated. I was the youngest, the littlest, the least powerful new member of the Guthrie and I was being singled out, for what? I realized I was going to have to persevere on my own, without encouragement, a skill I had honed at 47 Penn, or take Hirsch's advice and become an accountant. And I hated math.

I didn't let anybody see me break. I doubled down from that point forward. I showed up to learn at every opportunity that was available to me. I listened to all the directions given to other actors to see if they could show me how to handle a director's request. I watched rehearsals of plays I wasn't in. And privately, I sobbed a lot. While Lily may not have approved of my choice to be an actress, she had taught me how to steel myself with resolve when facing a challenge.

In the productions in which I was cast, in every tangible way, I showed up professionally. I said my lines, picked up my cues, and never missed a performance. I was determined that unless they fired me, they were stuck with me. With the shadow of Langham looming over me like Hamlet's ghost, I adopted a policy of mouth shut, eyes open—a policy of compliance. But in secret I labored, perfecting my skills, preparing for a time when the clouds would part, and the spotlight would shine. I was born under the sign of the goat. I just kept walking up that hill, hoof by hoof by hoof because I knew that if I did, my moment would arrive. Every goat has her day.

Daybreak began when my beloved brother David was given the opportunity to cast me in the supporting role of the bride in Eugène Labiche and Marc-Michel's *An Italian Straw Hat*, which he was directing on the mainstage. Langham gave him pushback because he preferred another actress in the role, but my brother stood firm. Working with my brother was truly liberating. All of a sudden, the criticism and the public humiliation stopped, and I started to feel free to simply *be* onstage. I could breathe.

At the end of the 1972 season, Langham went into rehearsals on a musical version of *Cyrano*, which he had commissioned from Anthony Burgess and would star his good friend Christopher Plummer. I was crossing all appendages to be cast. I could sing, I could dance. "Maybe he'd see the light," I prayed.

He didn't.

Instead, I was offered the now familiar three bit parts: actress, poet, nun. The parts were so small that I'd exit as one character, do a quick change, and come on as the next character. I reconciled myself to the fact that I would once again be assigned to the shadows of the show. Then lightning struck.

Michele Shay, one of the Guthrie's premier leading ladies who was playing the food seller in *Cyrano*, dropped out of the production. She had been hired to star in New York in the Negro Ensemble Company's production of *Home*, which ultimately wound up at the Cort Theatre on Broadway. This left Michele's role open, and Michael Langham, for some reason, found it in his heart to give it to me. My only guess, to this day, is that somebody forgot to tell him the food seller had more than one line.

Mind you, this wasn't by any stretch of the imagination a starring role, but the character had not just one, but *fourteen* lines and an entire scene alone with Christopher Plummer. And the topper? I had the opening lines of the show! They are emblazoned in my memory: "Oranges, pomegranates, lemonade!" Pure poetry!

Desmond Heeley, the Tony Award–winning costume designer, made me a red velvet dress that was, in a word, sensational. "Send me a picture!" Mother exclaimed. "You know how I love velvet."

Cyrano the musical opened in Minneapolis, then left the Guthrie *forever* for the greener pastures of the Royal Alexandra Theatre in Toronto. The Royal Alex was a gorgeous heritage house built in 1907 that was carefully painted in gold leaf and regal red to go perfectly with my red velvet dress.

"You know you're important when they paint the theater to match your costume, Tovah!" Lily cooed. "But tell me about the décolletage! You *know* you're gonna need breast pads!"

Next stop was the Colonial Theatre in Boston, where shows like *Porgy and Bess, Carousel*, and *Annie Get Your Gun* had their pre-Broadway runs. Then we were booked to come into the one and only Palace Theatre in New York. My theatrical debut in the city of my birth was slated to take place at the most historic theater on the Great White Way. The Palace still stood as the top rung Vaudeville house in America, where Fanny Brice, Ethel Barrymore, Sarah Bernhardt, Sophie Tucker, and Judy Garland had trod the boards. This goat had reached the summit of her first hill! Even Lily, always restrained regarding my career, cheered, "My daughter . . . my daughter's playing the Palace!" This was news that merited a call to everyone in her address book, including the painter, the cleaners, the shoemaker, the beauty salon, the synagogue, and best of all, *The Scarsdale Inquirer*.

As rehearsals progressed though, *Cyrano*, under Langham, was having a good deal of trouble acquiring the spit and polish it needed for

Broadway. Producer Richard Gregson began to worry. Unbeknownst to the cast, there was a heated debate in the executive offices of the Guthrie between the higher-ups about whether *Cyrano* was a musical drama or a musical comedy. This decision was pivotal to the success of the production. One morning, right during the Minneapolis previews, we all showed up for rehearsal, all that is, except Michael Langham. In his stead, Gregson came out to say that both the director and the choreographer had resigned from the production and they would be replaced immediately by Hollywood director and choreographer Michael Kidd.

Michael Langham had been fired?! It was as if the Pharaoh of Egypt had fallen off the tip of the pyramid, as if the sun god Ra had tumbled from the sky. A day later, Michael Kidd, famed choreographer of such movie musicals as *Seven Brides for Seven Brothers*, *Guys and Dolls*, and *Hello, Dolly!*, arrived from Hollywood to shine up the show to Broadway standards. One by one, everyone who could not sing or dance was let go.

During rehearsals in Toronto, trying to solve the finale of Act I, Scene 1, Mr. Kidd called out, "Who knows how to do cartwheels?"

My hand shot up. "I can do cartwheels, sir."

"Great," he said. "I need two cartwheels stage left to stage right, end of scene one. You good with that?"

"I'm perfect with that, sir," I said.

Who knew those cartwheels would turn into my job security?

We opened on Broadway at the Palace on May 9, 1973. The opening-night party at Sardi's was star-studded and extravagant; Natalie Wood, Lauren Bacall, and Stratford greats such as Roberta Maxwell, Len Cariou, Zoe Caldwell—they were all there. My parents, of course, also attended. Fishing for a compliment, I asked Mom, "What'd you think of my Broadway debut?"

She replied, "I was sitting next to Natalie Wood. What's not to love?"

Hoping for a little more, I said, "And me?"

"You? If I blinked I would've missed you, but you were very good. *And that dress was fabulous. Fabulous!*"

"Thanks, Mom," I said with a sigh, ego balloon punctured. *But this was my first opening night on Broadway, damn it! So buck up and turn the page, Tovah! Turn the page!*

Unfortunately, the show ran for only forty-nine performances, but for every one of those performances, I was on stage left in my fantastic red velvet dress, waiting for Cyrano to come my way. And he did—eight times a week. Christopher Plummer, actor extraordinaire and soon to be Tony Award winner, kissed my hand from Minneapolis to Broadway.

Between the fourteen lines, the red dress, and my youth, agents began knocking on my door. I thought of the Chinese proverb: "Change your place, change your luck." Who knew, "Oranges, pomegranates, lemonade!" would be the matchstick to the flame of my life on the Broadway stage, and then on to television and film?!

I learned four things during those difficult years at the Guthrie: don't worship at the altar of other people's opinions; show up at every opportunity to learn; overprepare to go with the flow; and best of all, in this topsy-turvy world, you're ahead of the game if you can do cartwheels.

Lilyism Regarding *Miss Saigon*

"Isn't the point of theater *not* to have the helicopter?"

Oy, She's Playing a Hasidic Boy!

*"A leper, cartwheels, and a Hasidic Jewish boy?
These are the options?! This is not going well."*

—LILY FELDSHUH, 1974

I HAD SOME REAL CAREER MOMENTUM GOING AFTER *CYRANO* AND that amazing red dress. It was enough to land me offers from Judy Abbot, an agent at the William Morris Agency, and an ambitious boutique agent named Gary Leaverton. Leaverton was known for his hard work. James Richardson, my then-boyfriend, was also represented by Mr. Leaverton, and so I chose to throw my fate in with him as well. Before *Cyrano* even closed, I was offered the ingenue leads for the 1973–1974 season at the Cleveland Play House and StageWest in Springfield, Massachusetts. The roles in Cleveland, starting with Eugene O'Neill's *A Touch of the Poet*, seemed richer and more challenging.

I mean, it was O'Neill after all; it doesn't get richer or more challenging than that. Also, the Cleveland Play House season was longer. I could hear Lily saying: "More weeks of paid work and health insurance."

"Not on your life," Gary squawked, leaving little room for argument. "I mean, Cleveland? Really, Tovah? I'm going to tell you what you are going to do. You're going to accept the StageWest offer, and every Monday on your day off, you're driving down to New York and auditioning for Broadway shows. You're not going to Cleveland. End of discussion."

"Aye, aye, sir," I replied.

So, every frigid New England winter Sunday, after the StageWest matinee of Chekhov's *The Cherry Orchard* or the musical *The Drunkard* by a little-known composer named Barry Manilow, I pulled on the maxi coat that had kept me warm across two continents, and wrapped blankets around my legs to keep me from freezing to death in my now heatless red Toyota Corona. Then I drove the 150 miles one way from Springfield to New York City to audition all Monday, and drove back to Springfield in time for the half-hour call on Tuesday. What better way for a twenty-three-year-old starting out in the theater to spend her day off? It was exciting, exhilarating, and exhausting. I *loved* it.

By the end of January 1974, and while I still had some circulation left in my feet, I won the title role in the Broadway-bound musical *Brainchild*. This was an experimental musical all taking place inside the head of one woman: me. Sound confusing? That's what the critics thought too. The music was by Michel Legrand, and the lyrics were by Hal David, a winning combination that delivered to me some fabulous numbers, many with a delicious Brazilian samba beat. It was produced by the glamorous Adela Holzer. She was great to her actors, paying them generously and on time—unfortunately with other people's money. She would be indicted for a Ponzi scheme a few years later. That's how I met the infamous Roy Cohn, her defense attorney. I had to show up downtown at the New York State Supreme Court near

Foley Square with none other than the head of the Shubert Organization, Gerald Schoenfeld. We were both cross-examined by Cohn. Yikes!

Brainchild closed at the Forrest Theatre in Philadelphia before ever making it to New York. That show, however, ignited my thrilling life-long friendships with Michel and Hal. I remember the Passover when Lily and Sidney had to be out of the country and I was "Seder-less." Michel and Hal swooped in to take me out to dinner. They even asked for matzah to be put on the table at the posh Petrossian Restaurant. Imagine being politely served matzah at the most famous Russian Caviar restaurant, when just two generations back my Grandpa Gershan ran like hell from the Cossacks. Just the three of us at a table for four; the fourth seat was for Elijah.

By April of 1974, I was back to three of my favorite pastimes: auditioning, auditioning, auditioning. David Merrick was producing *Mack and Mabel*, a new Broadway musical about the silent movie king Mack Sennett and his main squeeze, Mabel Normand. I auditioned and got to the finals. The part went to Bernadette Peters. It's hard to feel bad about losing to Bernadette Peters—she had been in New York far longer than I, had paid her dues, and what's more, she was marvelous. From my father I learned, "Never begrudge talent." From Lily I learned, "There's always room for more cream on the top." (I think she meant that literally as well as figuratively.) Losing to another skilled performer was understandable and pretty much the system in New York because we are in the business of *live* entertainment. When I arrived in Hollywood, losing roles to people not nearly as skilled as myself because of their look, or the size of their breasts, or the shape of their derrière, was emotionally much rougher. But New York was still bound by the obsession with excellence. This, I understood completely.

The day after my audition, Merrick and his director and choreographer, the legendary Gower Champion, who had done everything from Broadway's *Bye Bye Birdie* to *Hello, Dolly!*, called me to come down to the theater. Heart pounding with anticipation, down I went. When we met, they offered me the small role of the piano player in *Mack and Mabel*, plus the chance to understudy Ms. Peters. During a long, confidential walk with Champion, and a fabulous lunch with Merrick at Sardi's, I almost said yes—twice. They were very persuasive.

"Look, Ms. Feldshuh," said David Merrick, "You'll get a double salary. One as the piano player, and one as the understudy. You'll be in a big Broadway musical. And if you don't want to understudy, I can even offer you the standby for Bernadette. Then you don't have to play the piano and you don't have to leave your apartment. Just call the theater every afternoon to see if you are on that night." I flashed back to my two years at the Guthrie as an understudy to actresses who never missed a performance. I hated the job of understudying. It left me playing small roles while having the huge responsibility of being ready to take over a lead at a moment's notice without enough rehearsal.

"Mr. Merrick, I love that you asked me," I said very, very gently. "And I'm thrilled to be offered any job by the great David Merrick. But I'm afraid I'm going to have to turn you down. I understudied at the Guthrie for two years of my life that I'll never get back. I never went on once. Even at best, it's a short-notice, high-stress assignment. One is under-rehearsed, yet has to always be overprepared for that last-minute call—'YOU'RE GOING ON!' If you ever have a good role for me in one of your productions that is *not* an understudy, I'll take it."

"You're making a big mistake, Ms. Feldshuh," David Merrick said. And I worried that he might be right. It was one thing to be brave when my own mother said, "You're making a big mistake," regarding my career choice. Here I was sitting across from one of the giants of Broadway hearing those same words. But this time I listened to my instincts. As it turned out, it wasn't a big mistake. *Mack and Mabel* closed in eight weeks.

Not long after, Mr. Merrick decided to produce Jean-Claude Grumberg's play *Dreyfus in Rehearsal*, starring my soon-to-be dear friend Ruth Gordon and directed by Ruth's husband, Garson Kanin. Garson Kanin wrote the award-winning play *Born Yesterday* and, with Ms.

Gordon, wrote *Adam's Rib* and *Pat and Mike* for Hepburn and Tracy. He also directed Barbra Streisand in *Funny Girl*, so he was amassing an amazing lineup of actors for his cast.

David Merrick, to his credit, said to Garson, "I've got this new actress I really believe in. Her name is Tovah Feldshuh. I think she'd be perfect to play the Polish actress Miriam Poladnik in *Dreyfus*."

"*Tovah Feldshuh? Miriam Poladnik?* With a name like that, she's gotta be right!" Garson said. "She doesn't have to audition. Just have her come in to meet me." And so I did.

I entered David Merrick's office to meet Garson in my Victorian best, since actress Poladnik plays Lucie Dreyfus in the 1894 play-within-the-play. I had been given the high-necked lace blouse that Jessica Tandy wore in the Guthrie production of *The Cherry Orchard*. I had taken it to StageWest with me when I played Anya in *The Cherry Orchard* and wore it throughout rehearsals. It was my good luck Victorian talisman. I wore it with a black skirt that came down to mid-calf and high black lace-up leather boots. I wore my hair half up and half down in what we used to call a "carousel." I swear I looked like the nineteenth century had hitched a ride to the St. James Theatre and walked through David Merrick's office door. I walked out twenty minutes later with the role in my pocket. On October 17, 1974, I made my dramatic Broadway debut at the Ethel Barrymore Theatre in *Dreyfus in Rehearsal*. We closed in ten days.

OK, so I wasn't landing a hit yet, but I *was* making a splash in the Broadway community. David Merrick and Gower Champion still wanted to work with me. Ruth Gordon and Garson Kanin became my Broadway grandparents, and Ted Mann, head of the Circle in the Square Theatre on Fiftieth Street, flat out offered me the lead role of Amy in the Broadway revival of *Where's Charley?* (Amy, as in the show's hit song "Once in Love with Amy.") The show was set to star Raúl Julia, whom I adored. I was ecstatic with the offer, the song, and the leading man, and said yes without thinking twice. The day I accepted the offer, a script arrived at the Ethel Barrymore stage door from director Robert Kalfin. It was a play called *Yentl the Yeshiva Boy*, which was set for a limited run in the black box theater of the Brooklyn Academy of Music (BAM).

I couldn't audition for *Yentl* if I'd already accepted Ted Mann's offer to play Amy in *Where's Charley?* So I took the 104 bus from my Upper West Side apartment to return the script to my new agent, Stark Hesseltine, at 119 West Fifty-Seventh Street. By the time I arrived at his office I had read it and I had a dilemma: I had fallen in love with the play.

Yentl the Yeshiva Boy is Isaac Bashevis Singer's moving story about a young woman who is driven to sacrifice her feminine identity in order to follow her passion to study Torah. At her father's knee, and although forbidden by the ultra-Orthodox Jewish society in which she lives, Yentl secretly learns the intricacies of the Torah and the Talmud. How could a woman be in the kitchen and raise a family if she were studying the Holy Books? Well, she couldn't. That right was strictly reserved for men—by men.

After her father's death, Yentl proceeds to cut her hair, don her father's clothing, and leave her Polish shtetl to enroll in a Yeshiva (an Orthodox Jewish Seminary), cloaked in her new male identity.

In other words, Yentl is a motherless girl/boy who is forced to leave home and find her own way in the world, driven by a passion for learning and a devotion to her father's legacy. Does that sound like a part I can relate to? Are you kidding me? And the funny thing is: I almost turned down the audition.

"Stark, I've accepted Amy in *Where's Charley?* What should I do?" I asked.

"If *Yentl* speaks to you, then you should audition," he replied.

I said, "But how are we going to handle Ted Mann? I mean, he is handing me another Broadway offer, and we've said 'yes.'"

"If this role speaks to you, then you should audition," Stark repeated.

Then my commercial agent, Marje Fields, chimed in emphatically. "Tovah dear, this is Isaac Bashevis Singer we are talking about. It's a brand-new play, not a revival like *Where's Charley?* This new piece could lead you anywhere and it's the title role. If you land *Yentl*, it would be your play. But you haven't gotten the part yet. So, for starters, get out there and audition." It was as if Lily's common-sense voice, had she been a stage mother, was speaking to me through Marje Fields.

I charged back to my apartment at 160 West Seventy-First to pick up a pair of combat boots, my yellow terry cloth robe, and a little boy's cap like one might wear in *Oliver!* or *Fiddler*. I took the long subway ride from the Upper West Side to the Brooklyn Academy of Music, and I auditioned for *Yentl*, shoving my hair up under my cap and pulling swatches of my brown locks forward to create makeshift *peyos* (forelocks). In this wild getup—thank you, Sarah Lawrence—I landed the role. I was now in what Laurence Olivier and Vivian Lee called "the house of beautiful troubles." Too many offers converging at once. What to do? Thankfully, Stark Hesseltine took the helm.

"Tovah, this is your first title role in New York. It is the chance of a lifetime. I will handle Ted and he will get over it; he's not the first producer this has happened to. He knows it's part of the business. But if you don't take this role, you might regret it for the rest of your life." I reluctantly bowed out of *Where's Charley?* And just as I expected, Ted Mann was quite put out—so put out, he didn't offer me another part for ten years. Payback is a bitch.

I remember the rehearsal period for that first run of *Yentl* at BAM as a time of pure immersion and joy in my craft. John V. Shea, who played my male study partner Avigdor, and I threw ourselves into our roles with abandon. I studied every nuance of my character. I ate, slept, and drank the role, submerging into the quintessence of "Yentlism." I wrote diaries as Yentl, filling in the backstory of Yentl's family history, how I lost my mother at birth and how my father, a Talmud teacher, had always wanted a boy and quietly tested the waters to teach me what he would have taught his son.

I wrote about my unexpected love for Avigdor. I even convinced a Hasidic rabbi to sneak me into a Yeshiva in Borough Park dressed as a modern Orthodox boy so I could witness firsthand the passion these teenage boys had for studying Torah. I wore a short *sheitel* (wig) that belonged to the rabbi's wife, a modern dark fedora hat, the rabbi's son's coat, shoes, and even gloves. I had to protect the Yeshiva boys from committing the sin of touching a woman without realizing it.

I conjured up the exercises Bill Hickey taught me, about how to allow myself to be sideswiped by emotion in performance by committing to fresh, new, overwhelming images. In scene two, when little Yentl tries to say Kaddish for her father, I dug down to my primal feelings of loss. Onstage, eight times a week, I said Kaddish for my grandfather Gershan. When that image dried up for me, I switched to secretly saying Kaddish for my living parent, my father Sidney. And let me tell you, I was sideswiped at the mere thought of losing my dad. It felt like cutting off my arm.

I was going home every night and rehearsing scenes with my boyfriend, Harold. Harold was an entertainment attorney, almost fourteen years my senior, who had much to recommend him, not the least of which were his air conditioners in his apartment on Riverside Drive. Harold's apartment was an oasis. You know that song that goes, "Hot town, summer in the city / Back of my neck getting dirty and gritty"? New York City was brutal in August.

Harold was not only a lovely and kind man, he was a lawyer who took tremendous interest in my work. He was always happy to run lines with me, offer interpretations of a scene, and make suggestions of acting beats; he made me feel safe, valued, and loved. I soon became creatively reliant on Harold. After all, he offered a protective umbrella from the struggles of living an artist's life in New York, plus he was steadfast in his belief in my abilities. After the Langham/Hirsch experience, I blossomed with Harold's support.

Harold also checked off all the boxes. He was Jewish. He was a lawyer. He was loyal and sincerely wanted to get married. I took him home to meet my parents, figuring Mom would be delighted with my safe and sensible choice of a potential husband. I wasn't nervous at all about the encounter. I'd figured, "What's not to like? He's a shoo-in." So, we all gathered for lunch in my parents' large, glorious yellow-and-white marble-floored solarium; the room they used to embrace all their guests with its disarming warmth.

As I was helping Mom clear the table, she pulled me into the utility room and looked me straight in the eye.

"You're not going to marry that old stick-in-the-mud, are you?" Lily said. "At best, you'll wind up as a nurse with a purse, and at worst, you'll be a young widow." I have to admit, I was flabbergasted.

"Mom, I thought Harold would be a choice that would please you, a choice you would encourage," I said, "Harold is kind, safe, and successful." *And did I mention the air conditioners?*

"That's not the point. Marriage is the hardest thing you'll ever do. Make sure you're the same race, religion, and social class. And make sure you're *crazy* in love. If you're serious about Harold, run, don't walk, to his home and meet his parents. If it doesn't feel like a warm bath, it's a red flag." I met Harold's parents in Miami, where they were living. It was a red flag.

Marriage was a serious undertaking in my family. We marry like Jews, *but divorce like Catholics.* Meaning: *we don't.* There hasn't been a divorce in our direct line in almost two hundred years. "My advice," said Mother, "is choose wisely. And I can see, *Tovahleh* (this was the first time she ever used this endearing diminutive form with my new name), you're not crazy in love. Don't marry Harold for our sake. You're so full of life, he'll forever be asking you to calm down."

Lily touched my cheek with her hand and went back to serve dessert. "I hope you like nutcake, Harold," my mother chirped on her way into the solarium, perky as ever, as if she hadn't just convinced me to dump Harold. I stood in the utility room, still stunned. Thank you, Momma.

In December of 1974, *Yentl* debuted in the small theater at BAM. From the very first night we went into previews, there were lines out the door and around the block. We were, as they say in the business, an overnight sensation. We played to standing-room-only crowds for the full run, and before closing night, Cheryl Crawford, one of the heads of The Actors Studio, put together a group of investors to take us to Broadway. Stark had been right: *Yentl* had turned out to be the chance of a lifetime. We ran in Brooklyn for just about six weeks, and when *Yentl* finished its run in January, we were told that the show was going to move to the Great White Way for the 1975 Broadway season.

The summer of 1975 before *Yentl* went to Broadway, Harold and I went to England, where I had been offered the title role in *Mademoiselle Colombe*, a musical that was supposed to open in London but sadly never did. Richard Rodgers had also offered me the Broadway musical *Rex* to play Anne Boleyn in the first act and young Princess Elizabeth in the second. That created another reason to go to the UK. From Hampton Court, to the Tower of London, to the Cliffs of Dover, Harold never left my side as I enthusiastically followed Anne Boleyn to her beheading and the young Elizabeth to her coronation. It was a spectacular trip.

When I returned home in late August, I prepared to go into rehearsals for *Yentl*, which was set to open in Philadelphia at the Walnut Street Theatre before moving to Broadway. I was to spend six weeks in Philly and I began to consider moving out of Harold's apartment and, to paraphrase Virginia Woolf, into a room of my own. Harold was understandably upset. He questioned me: "Why are you pulling away now?" And then he began searching for reasons.

He came across my diaries for *Yentl*, read them without my knowledge or permission, and became convinced that I was in love with my costar, John Shea. He thought that the pages I wrote exploring Yentl's growing love for her study partner Avigdor were in fact about John Shea and me. He hit the ceiling, and all for nothing, because while John Shea was, and remains, a treasured friend, we never touched each other. Not even once.

Finally, on October 23, 1975, we opened in New York at the Eugene O'Neill, and Glory to G-d, *Yentl* was a hit. Headlines read: "Feldshuh Brilliant as Yentl" (*New York Post*), "A Star Is Born" (*The Star-Ledger*), and in the *New York Times*: "Ms. Feldshuh was lovely in Brooklyn, but she is far more touching on Broadway." You get the idea. I thought I was dreaming. I will never forget walking into Sardi's on opening night and watching a room full of people that I had admired, some since I was a child, stand up and applaud as I walked through the door. My father, and even my mother, beamed from the banquette. From that night on, my mother didn't mind calling me Tovah. Bless you, Momma.

Uncomfortable moments with Harold began to grow more frequent and intense. One terrible night after we opened on Broadway, Harold barged into my dressing room unannounced during the sacred half hour before a performance, when an actor is transitioning to go onstage as their character. One never intrudes on an actor once half hour is called. Harold knew this, but nonetheless, he walked in and saw me topless in front of my beloved male dresser, Howard Rodney. Harold called me a whore, ran out of the theater, and threw up on Forty-Ninth Street. For me, this was the beginning of the end.

There is a climax moment toward the end of the play when Yentl is supposed to show her naked breasts to Avigdor to prove she is a young woman and not a little Yeshiva boy. Obviously, this is a big turning point in the story, in which my breasts figured prominently. Both the director and Isaac Singer wanted the audience to actually see my naked breasts. They wanted to shock the audience with the reveal. Harold very loudly disagreed. He demanded that I refuse to do nudity onstage and told me the climax of the play would be reduced to eleven hundred people staring at my nipples. I secretly agreed and thought, *my breasts are not actresses*. I listened to Harold and refused. The director was ready to fire me. I only kept my job because the creative producer, the visionary Cheryl Crawford, stood up for me and threatened to pull the play if I were replaced. We finally worked out a compromise where I would wear a false set of latex breasts over my own, made by our acclaimed costume designer Carrie Robbins. (Can you imagine the fitting?!) They were newly glued over my own breasts before every performance. And they worked, although Isaac and the director were never very happy about it. In the end, I was not replaced, but my nipples were, and so, ultimately, was Harold.

I still had *Rex* waiting in the wings for me, and everybody advised me to leave the role of Yentl to work for Mr. Rodgers six weeks into the *Yentl* Broadway run. Playing Anne Boleyn followed by Princess Elizabeth would clearly help me avoid becoming typecast in Jewish roles. Ruth Gordon was adamant that I should do *Rex*, but her husband Garson took me out to lunch soon after for a tête-à-tête.

"Tovah," Garson told me affectionately, and put a grandfatherly hand on my shoulder, "This is your play, and it's a big success. Never leave a hit, darling. Never ever leave a hit . . . and don't tell Ruth I told you."

To keep me in *Yentl*, although I had an out clause by December for *Rex*, the producers offered to double my salary and put my name up there with the title of the show on the marquee of the Eugene O'Neill Theatre:

Yentl
Starring
Tovah Feldshuh

Yes!

My salary leapt from $500 to $1,000 a week, and what did I do with this windfall? While I was starring on Broadway at night, I created my own "conservatory" during the day. I used my funds as tuition to pay for teachers: Edith Worman-Skinner, the head of the speech department at Juilliard; Judith Leibowitz, head of the Alexander technique at Juilliard; and Shakespeare coach supreme, Diana Maddox from Los Angeles.

I stayed with *Yentl* for the entire run, and was nominated for my first Tony. I won the Obie, Theatre World, Drama Desk, and Outer Critics Circle Awards that season. It was a golden year.

I did achieve another first with *Yentl*. I joined the ranks of Broadway performers who bowed to the more famous when their roles went to Hollywood. Barbra Streisand brought *Yentl* to the silver screen. I can only say this about that: everyone should have the magnificence of a Barbra Streisand in their lives. I met her through our common affiliation with *Yentl*. When she gave me the LP from her movie, she wrote, "To Tovah, who did such a beautiful job as Yentl. Too bad your show didn't have songs as well. With admiration, Barbra."

She phoned me after I did a picture called *Kissing Jessica Stein* because she was very moved by my character's relationship with her daughter, particularly in the porch scene. She talked to me about her son, Jason. What a kindness to call. Then, when she was moving out of her apartment at the Ardsley on Central Park West, she called again and said, "I'm moving out. Do you want any of my *chazerei* (crap)?"

I said, "Barbra, I'm arriving with a truck."

And thus, we remain fond friends, and her shower curtain remains in my guest bathroom. And my feet remain in her Donna Karan sneakers. I wrote: "If I wear your sneakers, will it improve my voice?"

She wrote back, "You don't need improvement."

Fate had one more thing in store for me that year that I never could have predicted. It might never have happened at all if it weren't for the marvelous run of *Yentl* and those ridiculous rubber nipples.

Lilyism Regarding Escorts

In honor of her one hundredth birthday, her alma mater, NYU, invited Lily to walk down the aisle of the enormous Javits Center as part of the commencement ceremony. Her reply?

"I can only tell you I had better be flanked by two handsome male graduates, 'cause I ain't using no walker!"

How Finger Painting Touched My Heart

T HERE I WAS, STARRING ON BROADWAY IN *YENTL*, WHILE LILY was lighting the Shabbos candles every Friday night, praying I would find a husband. Just not Harold! On Presidents' Day 1976, Andrew Harris Levy, a handsome, polished, Harvard-educated lawyer from Washington, DC, came to see the 3:00 p.m. holiday matinee of *Yentl*. Andrew was the older brother of Laurie Levy, my best friend from the National Music Camp in Interlochen, Michigan.

The first time I laid eyes on Andy, I was thirteen and I thought he was the cat's meow. He sported a crew cut, a yellow Lacoste shirt, Chino pants, and white bucks—he was white shoe even back then. He must have been on his way to Harvard by that point, and seemed so much older, wiser, and cooler than I was. He was also very preppy-sexy, which, for those of you who may not remember, was the pinnacle of attractiveness in the early sixties.

It was Laurie who suggested that Andrew, now a practicing attorney in DC, should "check out my friend Tovah in her show on Broadway." On Monday, February 16, Andrew had to travel to Connecticut to see a client. Laurie figured he'd have to catch the train at Penn Station anyway to get back to DC, so why not first stop at the Eugene O'Neill Theatre? She may have had an ulterior motive. That whole scenario seemed a bit of a stretch to me.

Indeed, Andy came to that 3:00 p.m. matinee at the O'Neill and asked to come backstage afterward. Now, not everyone is allowed backstage after a performance, let alone dressing room number one to see the leading lady. Broadway is constructed so that you have to jump through hoops to get to the actors. But he was Laurie Levy's older brother, and she was my best friend from camp, so I told the stage doorman, "Send him up."

After the show, he gently knocked on my door. My dresser, Howard Rodney, opened it and Andrew Levy swept into the dressing room, tall, handsome, and chic in a Burberry coat, Paul Stewart suit, and Hermès tie. I was a little worried about *my* appearance, however. I was dressed as an Orthodox Jewish boy, with peyos dangling in front of my ears and a short razor-cut wig. From the front, I looked like Lillian Gish; from the back, I looked like Larry Tisch. As long as we were eyeball to eyeball, we were fine.

"You were fantastic!" Andrew beamed. His crew cut had been replaced by much longer thick brown hair and a stunning auburn mustache.

"May I take you out for coffee?" Andrew asked politely.

Summoning my best Lily, I retorted, "Not on your life. I can't go out for coffee with you. You're Clarice Levy's son." Then, in the imperative, the way Lily always spoke to me: "You go back to Harvard and marry a Radcliffe teacher."

"Marry?" Andrew replied, "I'm just asking you out for coffee!" Not wanting to be impolite, I cautiously agreed. We decided to try the Eclair

Bakery, one of Isaac Bashevis Singer's favorite haunts. I'd been there with my playwright many times. This venerable old Viennese café on Seventy-Second Street between Broadway and Amsterdam was conveniently just one block from my home at 160 West Seventy-First Street. The Eclair served as the gathering place for many of the Upper West Side literati of the day, and the pastry was so delectable, the place was always insanely busy. You could never get in without waiting on line for what seemed an eternity, even if you knew the maître d'. We arrived at the Eclair and sure enough, there was that huge line. I expected to wait twenty minutes chatting with Andrew, but my new friend had other plans. He excused himself, calmly went to the head of the line, quietly whispered something to the maître d', and we were immediately escorted to a little corner table behind one of the doors. I never saw him reach into his pocket, so there wasn't even a tip involved.

"How did you manage that?" I asked him, very impressed. I was already well-known at the café because of Bashevis Singer, and not even I could have pulled that one off.

"All I did was ask," Andy said modestly. "Apparently nobody wanted the table." Understated, strategic, and so incredibly polite, he seemed a man of magic to me right out of the starting gate from that very first unexpected date.

Washington, DC, was Andrew's hometown. It's where he grew up and where his family resided. He was on the verge of becoming a partner at the firm of Arent Fox. As busy and as far away as he was, we started talking on the phone almost daily after that. He was a new color in my life: sunny, witty, and gallant. I have to say, he caught my attention.

The day I met Andrew prompted me to end my relationship with Harold. It took Anaïs Nin courage, but I followed my instincts—instincts, in this instance, that were in tandem with Lily's. It was a painful parting. Harold was truly a very good man, but broader horizons were beckoning. For the month that followed, I dated like crazy, trying to avoid the Cupid who was pounding on my door. I thought at first I was just celebrating being single again after almost two years with Harold. In hindsight, I was running away from the fact that I was falling in love with Clarice Levy's son.

During that month, I was out on a date with a lyricist of note (pun intended), and while walking down Restaurant Row on Forty-Sixth Street between Eighth and Ninth Avenues, I thought I saw Andy ahead of us.

"Andy?" I blurted out, right in front of my date. A stranger turned around. It wasn't Andy, but from that night on, I started seeing Andy everywhere, whether he was there or not. Months later I asked him, "How could you possibly be stalking me in New York City all the way from the Washington Monument? I'm seeing you around every corner." Andrew Harris Levy had invaded my consciousness within a month, and I suddenly realized this is what my mother was talking about. My heart sped, and in a flash of light, I realized Andy Levy was becoming my world.

Never mind. I held my tongue. Lily rule: "Never be the first to say 'I love you' to a man. Wait for him to chase you. It doesn't hurt if the man is more in love with you than you are with him, because marriage is built for women, not for men." I'm thinking, *Mom, you're talking about marriage too? What's the matter with us? I just met the guy!*

Mercifully, Andy saved me from breaking Lily's rule. He told me that twenty-one days after we met, he had tripped on a sidewalk on his way into work, and literally, as he was falling, he realized, "Oh my G-d, I'm falling in love with Tovah Feldshuh!" While Andy's realization was a little more high impact than mine, the result was the same. I decided that before we went too much further, I had better address the grease-painted elephant in the room. I waited until Andy's thirty-second birthday—March 20, 1976—and then over a very romantic dinner, I took a deep breath, and could feel Mother Lily gently pounding on my sternum with her fist: "Remember who you are." Was Mom giving me a signal that I was entitled to emotionally express myself much more fully than she was able to? *Courage, Tovah, courage*, I said to myself.

"Andrew Levy, I have known your family since I was thirteen years old. Every bourgeois cell in my body obligates me to tell you that you have absolutely no business dating an actress. You should be dating an Ivy League professor or a writer or an Advanced Placement teacher."

"An Advanced Placement teacher?" Andy said, suppressing a smile.

"Whatever," I said, getting flustered.

"But where did you come up with Advanced Placement teacher?" Andy started to laugh.

"I don't know, I think I might have played one on TV," now laughing heartily despite myself. "The point is, what do you want with an actress? I rehearse, and I tour frequently; when I'm in town, I do eight shows a week. There's press around all the time, and on top of that, I'm always looking for the next job. I take classes daily whether I'm working or not. And my dearest Andy, the truth is, I love it this way. I know I'll never leave my work. So I say again to you, what are you doing dating an actress? I think you could do better . . . *but* to tell you the truth . . . I am getting tired of protecting Clarice Levy's son. So now, on your thirty-second birthday, I'm warning you for the last time: *don't date me.* After this, if you persist, you're on your own."

I expected a lot of reactions from Andy in that moment, but I could never have imagined the one he gave me. From watching my mother, the idea of being a wife conjured up visions of spending my life waiting for a man, anticipating his every mood, every wish; picking him up at the train station with the Thermos full of iced Jack Daniels, a tray of Ritz crackers and evenly spread Velveeta, and an eternally patient smile. I would magically keep the dinner warm (yet never dry), until I lovingly walked with my man into the house. My mother Lily was Wonder Woman in all these areas, but I was not. I had based my path in life on my father's vision that you should follow your bliss in the choice of your life's work, and thus I had no intention of waiting on, or for, any man. How could I do that *and* have a profession?

"Don't you know yet, Tovah?" Andy said gently. "I don't need to be in the spotlight. I'm happy to stand next to you and simply feel its warmth. Your life is exciting to me. I don't want a woman who is totally dependent on me—I too need my space. I have other interests, and I'm just as passionate about mine as you are about yours."

"Really? What's your favorite hobby?" I asked.

He answered instantaneously: "You."

I chortled.

"Seriously," he said, "I don't need a woman hanging around my neck. I want time to read my books, to play my tennis, and to think up new business solutions for my clients. I enjoy my pursuits as well. I work hard, you work hard. I'm dedicated to excellence, you're dedicated to excellence. I love travel, you love travel. We both like space in a relationship. We're the perfect match."

"Seriously?" I echoed.

"Seriously," he emphasized.

"Well, OK then, kiddo," I said, "I feel that I've given you fair warning, so let it be on your head. From this point forward, if you want to continue this relationship, I'm here. Please apologize to your mother for my falling in love with her son." I can hear Lily reiterating: "Remember who you are. He should be so lucky to have your love. He should be so lucky to share the same *air* you breathe!"

Four short months later, Andy invited me to Washington to see the D'Oyly Carte production of *The Mikado* at The Kennedy Center. Parasols were twirling and fringe was flying. We were seated in prime orchestra seats. Sixteen weeks into our relationship, Andy, bless him, clearly knew how much I valued a good location to ensure a great experience of a show. To this day, I may skip buying a dress or a lobster, but I will never sacrifice buying myself the best seat in the house.

It was summertime. I was wearing a sleeveless tank. During the show, I felt Andrew tracing letters on my left arm very softly and quickly. I finally picked up that he was tracing the letters: M-A-R-R-Y-M-E. I almost dislocated my neck during the chorus of "Myasama myasama orinaya myani." Then the first act ended and the house lights went up. I didn't say a word, but my heart was knocking against my chest. We were on a double date that night with close friends, so Andy and I couldn't just cut and run. Earlier in the day, Andy had invited them back to have a drink with us after the performance. What was he thinking? Was this arm-trace marriage proposal a whim?

Once Gilbert and Sullivan had finally rhymed themselves out, we walked back to Andy's apartment. Still, I didn't say a word. Andy could not contain his ear-to-ear smile. We had a quick drink with our sweet friends and bid them goodnight.

Alone at last, Andrew suddenly left the living room. He re-entered a moment later with washable red finger paint, and began Act 2 of the proposal. Just as carefully as he'd traced "marry me" on my left arm at The Kennedy Center, he now wrote "W-I-F-E-?" in red finger paint across my clavicle. What was he going to do for a third act? Skywrite?

If this was going to be a moment to remember for the rest of our lives, I needed the classic proposal as much as Mother needed classical piano. I was hoping to see Andrew gazing up into my eyes while down on one knee, not standing in front of me with bloodred fingers.

"If this is actually happening," I said to him gently, "will you please go wash your hands, come back, and really ask me the question?" Andrew went, washed his hands, took a fine, red cotton pillowcase with white stars, and placed it carefully on the ground. Then he got down on one knee, looked up at me, and said, "Tovah Feldshuh, will you marry me?" There was a pregnant pause. Out of the silence, I finally replied, not "yes," but, "of course!"

Andy, ecstatic, immediately questioned, *"When?"*

"Let's not get ahead of ourselves," I quipped.

I very much wanted to marry Andrew Harris Levy, but I needed to feel sure that I was capable of marriage. Thus, we began what would be a secret summer engagement. This was nothing compared to my parents' two-and-a-half-year secret marriage. Truth to tell, when it came down to it, marriage scared the hell out of me. Being a wife, even during this second wave of women's liberation, still looked to me like being a waitress, a call girl, a chief cook, an event planner, a chauffeur, a gofer, a cleaner, an organizer, a wardrobe mistress, and a nanny. With all of that going on, where the hell do you fit anything for yourself, let alone a career? What I was also looking for was whether Andy was up to the task. I wanted to give him time to come to his senses and call the whole thing off if necessary. Could we both manage marriage?

What a ten-week test it was for Andy!

When he proposed on June 28, I was in the middle of the summer season at the American Shakespeare Festival in Stratford, Connecticut, playing the lead ingenues under the baton of the elegant and polished Michael Kahn. I played Abigail Williams in *The Crucible* and Celia opposite Eileen Atkins in *As You Like It*. The great Walter Cronkite came to see us, and I had the honor of meeting him for the first time. A few years later, I met President Ford with Walter, and the President asked if I was Walter's daughter. Walter answered, "I wish!" That was a thrilling moment. Walter Cronkite was right up there with Davy Crockett and Abraham Lincoln, as far as I was concerned.

That season at Stratford, Christopher Plummer was also directing an evening of scenes and sonnets. It was wonderful to see him and his beautiful wife Elaine again. Stratford was as intellectually inspiring as it was beautiful. What a place to be secretly engaged! I had rented the barn that Katharine Hepburn lived in when she did her *As You Like It*. The entire setup was Yankee romantic.

That summer, I also filmed my first soap opera in New York, *Ryan's Hope*, playing journalist Martha McKee of the *Village Banner*. It was impossible to forget my name or that fictional newspaper because of my character's terribly creative, incessantly repetitive catchphrase: "Hi, I'm Martha McKee of the *Village Banner*."

Between the Stratford Shakespeare Festival and the soap, it was a busy and exciting time with a crazy commute fueled on love. Andy would fly up to Stratford on the weekends, and sometimes I would fly down to Washington with him at the crack of dawn on Monday, my day off. If all this commuting didn't scare him off or exhaust him, I didn't know what would.

Andy didn't budge.

As we entered our tenth week, I took a deep breath and said we could announce. On the Saturday night of Labor Day, we found ourselves sitting on the couch in my parents' living room waiting to break the happy news at last. I knew Sidney and Lily were both going to be over the moon about Andy. He was charming, intelligent, articulate, successful, and how many times have I mentioned that he had an undergraduate *and* law degree from Harvard? He had even gone to prep school at Andover, spoke French, played the trumpet, and read the classics for G-d's sake! My mother could not have dreamed up a more ideal husband for me if she had tried.

It had become increasingly difficult to tell either of them anything over the phone because they were both hard of hearing. I felt it was important, therefore, to do this in person. I wanted my mom to get the joyous message loud and clear.

"Lily, Sidney—Tovah and I have something we'd like to tell you," said Andrew so endearingly and eloquently and politely. I expected my mother to stop everything on a dime and turn around at last to hear the words she had been waiting my whole life to hear from a Harvard lawyer! It was either that, or pull me into the utility room. Instead she said, "Can it wait a minute, Andrew? We're in the middle of *Rosemary's Baby*." So Andy and I sat with them and waited another hour and seventeen minutes while they watched Ruth Gordon's Oscar-winning performance one more time. Then, as soon as the credits rolled, we stood and turned off the TV. Dad and Mom followed us into the living room. My mother looked at Andrew.

"Now, what was it you were saying again, Andrew?" Lily asked loudly.

"Lily and Sidney," Andy began again very formally, since it was the most auspicious of auspicious occasions. "I would like to toast my bride-to-be."

"Wait, *what?*" said Lily fortissimo. I sat there wishing she had gotten the better hearing aids like I'd asked her to because she was really murdering the moment.

"I'd like to toast my bride-to-be," said Andrew again, a little more loudly, but with as much enthusiasm, joy, and pride as the first time.

"*What . . . you're married???!!!*" my mother screeched, horrified.

This wasn't going at all the way my husband-to-be expected. The look on Andy's face was priceless.

Welcome to Lilyville, Andrew!

"Lily," my father mercifully intervened and with a litigator's diction: "He means they're *engaged.*"

Recognition dawning at last, my mother screamed, "Engaged! Sidney, they're engaged!" and then to us, "Congratulations!" My father beamed and kissed both of my cheeks, then shook Andrew's hand vigorously over and over again. Andrew broke out the bottle of champagne he had secretly tucked into the fridge for just this moment, and we all toasted to our future. It was a wonderful, memorable day, even if it had to be organized around the network premiere of *Rosemary's Baby* and shouted directly into my mother's ears.

Our engagement was a hectic, electrifying period, scattered between two coasts. I had been commuting back and forth from Los Angeles for work and I had beginner's luck. In six weeks, I had landed six different guest-starring shots on six different television shows—666? Well, it was devilishly exciting work!

I was so busy professionally that I felt like a one-woman repertory company. Each week was a different character. I played everything from sexy psychologist Victoria Kidd on *The Bob Newhart Show*, to Katharine Hepburn opposite Tommy Lee Jones in *The Amazing Howard Hughes*.

I loved commuting to Los Angeles for work. I had a ball. I would arrive at LAX and be in front of the cameras within twenty-four hours. I adored Broadway, but the pay scale and the exposure was far greater on television. Hollywood gave me a living wage at last! Even my cautious, "don't trust anyone" mother was starting to find all of this activity quite exciting. Once I was on television, she could tell her friends, "My daughter is on TV, and the world is watching," instead of, "My daughter is playing a little Orthodox Jewish boy and has to kiss a girl eight times a week."

This was a first: watching my mother, Lily, be pleased with me. It was an eye-opening experience. I realized how much I missed out on my mother's approval for the first twenty-five years of my life.

With my engagement and the increased quality time I spent with my mother planning the wedding, something started to shift. She was allowing me to take the lead for the first time. I couldn't tell what inspired her to do this, but I assumed it was her great satisfaction that I was going to marry Andrew Harris Levy, for whom she was building a pedestal with a throne on top! This much I did know: something as big as a tectonic plate under Lilyville was already in motion, and I liked the rumbling.

Lilyism on Marriage

"Tovah, you wanna know how to have a good marriage? I'll show you how to have a good marriage. Just shut one eye," as Mother slammed her cupped right hand over her right eye. "And selective hearing doesn't hurt."

Marry Like a Jew,
Divorce Like a Catholic

MARCH 20, 1977 STANDS AS THE BIGGEST TURNING POINT of my life. On that day, I walked down the aisle to marry Andrew Harris Levy in The Plaza's landmarked Terrace Room, dressed in an antique, Belgian lace wedding gown from Henri Bendel's, rose-petal white Delman pumps from Bergdorf Goodman, and a twenty-foot veil of fine imported French silk tulle with Parisian wax flowers at its crown. The veil and the pumps were a bridge too far for the budget my parents had generously given me. The dress alone had reached that limit!

My mom chimed in, right in the bridal salon at Bergdorf's, "If you want a fancy veil and shoes, you will have to pay for them. You're a famous actress now, you can afford it!"

She was right—I could afford it, so I paid for it. Fair was fair.

I think in that moment, my mom was reminded of her sister Rose, the oldest of the four Kaplan girls. For her wedding, Rose had her heart set on a pair of white satin wedding pumps. They cost an outrageous fifteen dollars, a fortune in 1924. Never mind—the whole family went into action. They all contributed to the wedding-shoe cause. My mother was barely thirteen years old at the time and remembers contributing the pennies that she would have otherwise used at the nickelodeon. It gave the family pleasure to procure Rose's wedding pumps. It gave the family pleasure to deliver dreams, and Rose had made a great match.

Rose's little sister, my mother, also married well. Lily's father-in-law was a wealthy silk-mill owner named David Feldshuh, after whom my brother would be named. The Feldshuhs also owned a Pierce Arrow driven by a chauffeur and lived in a lovely house on the more posh side of Paterson, New Jersey, near East Side Park. My father was the youngest of the four Feldshuh children and the only boy. Like my mother, he was placed in Rapid Advance at Paterson Elementary School and graduated from Paterson High at sixteen, university-bound—I'm sure, hoping for the Ivy League.

But on November 27, 1926, catastrophe struck father's life. Fresh from a tour abroad to buy silks in France and visit family in Austria, Germany, and Poland, while on the ocean voyage home, Grandpa David must have caught a cold, which ultimately turned into pneumonia. In 1926, penicillin had not yet been discovered. Four days later, David Feldshuh was dead. I remember my father telling me how he prayed for his father's life by his bedside all Friday night November 26 into the wee hours of Shabbat morning, November 27. Grandpa David kept patting his young son's hand, saying, "Sonny, sonny, it will be alright. It will be alright."

Unfortunately, it was not alright. David Feldshuh did not win his battle against the Angel of Death, and Sidney's prayers were not answered. The Feldshuh world imploded. Dad had to enter a "local school" to stay close to his family. The obvious choice was New York University, where his sister Sylvia was a junior. Grandma Marion, now a widow, would need the frequent visits of her son as well as the then-affordable tuition at NYU.

Grandpa David's funeral took all day, as he was honored by all the organizations he headed: from the Paterson-Passaic YM-YWHA to the Friendly Building and Loan Association to the Humboldt Lodge of the Freemasons—and that's not even half of the institutions that honored his leadership and guidance, now gone in a breath.

Sidney commuted to campus until he joined the Square Club, which consisted of a brownstone on Washington Square that he and his chums rented so they could sleep right in the lap of the university—and maybe sleep right in the laps of some of the coeds. New York University College of Arts and Sciences brought Sidney more than an education, it brought him the love of his life: my mother. She was seventeen, he was eighteen. Thus began a sixty-eight-year alliance. At twenty, Dad graduated NYU and was accepted to Harvard Law School—on scholarship!

Now here I was, engaged to a Harvard lawyer of my very own, and my parents could not have been happier. My mother was ecstatic. For once, she could relate to where I was coming from. For once, I had lived up to her hopes without having to be coaxed in the direction of her no-nonsense, pragmatic vision. Mom and I worked joyfully on the wedding. We saw eye to eye on practically everything, which was a brand-new experience for me.

My mother was a quintessential party planner with a Rolodex of practical pointers: go for quality, be generous, take care of your guests first, make the celebration early enough so people are alert but not so early that they don't have something to look forward to as the main event of the day. Don't be rushed. Overprepare by rechecking the details well beforehand, so you can go with the flow at the celebration. Sleep well the night before, and if there's something special you want at your party, seize the opportunity, and make it happen. Andy's modest request at our wedding was to have white hearts of palm in the salad course, and you can bet they were there in abundance. Leave it to Andy to make it easy for everyone.

As a team, Lily and I accomplished a magnificent event, and we did it in *six weeks*. (I know what you're thinking. No, I was not pregnant, mind you—but more will be revealed!) With celebrations, my mother and I played an effortless duet. In so many elements of our relationship, we were in contrapuntal harmony. Sure, it was music, but we were singing two very different songs. For my wedding, however, we were in pure harmony—heck, we were in unison!

"Where would you like to get married?" my mother asked me. After a search of various beautiful synagogues including Temple Emanu-El on Fifth Avenue (too Reform), the Spanish Portuguese Synagogue on Central Park West (too Orthodox), and Temple Israel Center in White Plains, New York (too far away), I asked carefully, "Mom, do you think the ceremony and reception could be held at The Plaza Hotel?"

My mother's face lit up. "Yes!" she exclaimed.

This was when The Plaza was still The Plaza, years before the Donald got his hands on it and turned it into gold-painted, overpriced condominiums sitting atop a shopping mall. All of the quiet elegance and sophistication of a piece of Gilded Age New York left the place on the day The Plaza became a Trump property, and I still deeply mourn its passing.

In 1977, to walk in through those grand front doors was to know that every detail would be expertly executed and authentically beautiful. As Mom would say, "You don't have to worry about a thing when you are at The Plaza."

My mother and I were met in the Palm Court by the head of catering, a dapper Austrian gentleman wearing an Italian-cut suit with a crisp pink pocket square. His name was Werner, pronounced "Verna," and his precise, irresistible accent bespoke his fastidious attention to detail. He led us upstairs to the catering office, which was lodged in a tulip-yellow parlor with satin white wainscoting, dainty Baccarat sconces, and portraits of Plaza brides adorning the walls.

Tea was served out of a heavy silver pot alongside a three-tiered silver stand filled with delicate decadent pastries and crustless cucumber sandwiches. Wedding brochures were fanned out in an eye-catching display to deflect from the heart-stopping price lists folded within.

We told Werner that we definitely wanted the Terrace Room. He replied, "Excellent choice. A New York landmark, with chandeliers made by Charles Winston, Harry's brother, and built as a replica of the Terrace Room in the Petit Trianon at Versailles." *Versailles at last!* Lily and I smiled at each other knowing this was it.

Handing us the sample menus, Werner pointed out the highlights: Beef Wellington with tiny pearl onions, Gravlax curled into heavenly pink roses, and blinis that looked as light as clouds.

He continued, "How about a vat of delicious fresh shrimp? Zer veddy populah." We replied, "Oh no, Werner, we have to have a kosher-style wedding out of respect for the more observant members of the Feldshuh family. Shrimp is considered high *treif* (incredibly *un*-kosher). Definitely not."

However, to the "performance dessert," a flaming Baked Alaska served by seamlessly synchronized waiters descending from every staircase in the Terrace Room, we said, "Definitely yes!" Werner personally guaranteed that they could deliver two hundred plates of fire and ice before a single flame went out.

Our mother-daughter duet continued as we searched for my wedding gown. The dress I fell in love with was from the rare and beautiful Bendel's Antique Gown Collection. It was handmade completely out of Belgian lace and dated from the turn of the century, when it was worn by a Belgian noblewoman—or so they told me at Bendel's. It had a Victorian collar so high it had to be boned, and a fitted bodice with long lace sleeves that came to a gentle point at my wrists, drawing the line of the dress all the way down toward my fingertips. The dress itself had just the slightest hint of a train, but it was all about the veil. That Parisian masterpiece was like an ivory waterfall, dramatic but demure, cascading from the crown of my head. I adored that veil.

Ruth Gordon—who not only won the Oscar for *Rosemary's Baby*, but played Maude in the treasured classic feature *Harold and Maude* and

Dolly Levi in the original Broadway production of Thornton Wilder's *The Matchmaker*—was my matron of honor. It's essential that you stop right now and find a moment of her on film so that you can appreciate this extraordinary being, whose voice and delivery alone is the quintessential Quincy, Massachusetts, busybody feast. The sight and sound of her by my side as my matron of honor was as much a delicious delight as anything Werner could've put on the menu. When I asked Ruth to join the wedding party and for her husband, Garson Kanin, to be a legal witness at the private ceremony where we signed our *ketubah* (marriage contract), Ruth said, "Mahvelous!" Garson said, "Anything you need, *shaynaleh* (little beauty in Yiddish)."

Off we went to Saks Fifth Avenue with Ruth, where Mom and I selected with her a lovely floor-length petal-pink chiffon gown with a relaxed bow at the neck and a floating white capelet. Broadway designer Barbara Matera, who designed clothes not only for Ruth, but for Bette Davis, Lauren Bacall, and Hillary Clinton (for Bill's inauguration), created a matching pink-and-white chiffon confection, topped with orange blossoms, to be nestled in Ruth's signature chignon. This floating vision, Mom and I thought, would be gorgeous. With her perennially kittenish grin, Ruth asked for the full-length skirt to be cut to above the knee. "I want something short and sexy. Always use your sex, Tovah." She was eighty-one. I said, "Ruthie, if you upstage me at this wedding, I'm going to throw you through the windows of the Terrace Room right into the Palm Court." Ruth leaned in conspiratorially and whispered, "Gotcha!" giving birth again to her signature Cheshire Cat smile.

In the middle of this express train of planning, someone from Merrill Lynch called my agent at ICM, Milton Goldman, and said that the company was making a television commercial and would love to film my wedding at The Plaza as footage for selling Merrill Lynch as an investment wealth management firm to the public. In exchange, they would foot the bill for the entire wedding. My first reaction was, "Wow!" My second reaction was, "What's the downside?"

Milton explained: "Well, they'll need klieg lights overlooking the room, and of course there would be a camera crew there to film."

We were planning to have a candlelit ceremony in a room that was a New York historical landmark. I was so afraid that my wedding would turn into a circus (and this was years before *Pippin* when I craved a circus). I consulted with my parents, and they simply said, "Whatever you want is fine with us."

I didn't want to chance it. This was to be the only wedding day of my life. So I said no. Dad didn't say a word. Bless him.

In hindsight, it might not have been such a bad idea because we would have archival footage of broadcast quality . . . and residuals!

Garson Kanin, in his best Pierre Cardin tux, looked like a wizened gentleman of stately perfection in a 1940s drawing room comedy. The rest of the groom's party was in formal morning suits with high hats, gray spats, and gloves. For the flower girls, I chose delicate blush organza dresses that were floor-length and fully supported by pale-pink crinolines. Their sashes were also organza and ended in a gorgeous starch bow in the back. They carried baskets of pale-pink rose petals and wore wreaths made of fresh antique pink roses in their hair. The outfit would not be complete without lace anklets and white gloves, just like the ones my mother dressed me in for every important occasion since day one. I sometimes wondered if I hadn't been born in a pair of lace anklets.

All too quickly, the day was upon us. There was my wonderful Broadway dresser, Howard Rodney, who had been with me since *Yentl*, fussing over every stitch of that Belgian lace wedding gown and every puff of tulle. Howard, Mom, and I took that antique masterpiece, having been steamed and stuffed with tissue by Bendel's bridal staff, out of its gigantic box. Because of the age of the fabric, I was told never to hang my dress, only to lay it flat, like a human figure taking a nap. To this day, that dress reclines atop our new cedar closet in our country home, waiting to go vertical for the next celebration. That dress was as anxious as I was to get married, and it looked like it was going to start dancing on its own at any moment.

Jeffrey Bruce, my incredible makeup artist, was brushing the magic on my face and dramatizing my eyes, while Patrick Moreton, my exacting hairdresser, created the perfect Gibson Girl coiffure. As the champagne and hors d'oeuvres arrived in the bridal suite, we could barely indulge ourselves, we were so excited. This day was better than an opening night. This day was the opening night of *my life.*

My brother flew in from the Twin Cities, and he and my father looked proud as peacocks in their morning suits, high hats purposely tipped askew, gray gloves, and spats.

And then there was my mother, looking like a queen in blushing pink chiffon with two strands of long, shimmering pearls that my father had given her for one of their anniversaries. My mother delighted in the Old World elegance of this wedding.

My parents were married on the roof of the St. Moritz Hotel on Central Park South, Flag Day, 1935. It was the height of the Depression, so for money they substituted thoughtfulness. Ada and Gershan threw their daughter a 3:00 p.m. ceremony followed by a high tea with dainty tea sandwiches, cake, and champagne, all of which was "just like high society," Mom quipped. Now look where she was today.

Suddenly, the clock struck five, and it was time for the wedding to begin. *Places!*

My mother, by my side in the bridal suite, squeezed my hand and leaned in close to me and said, "You can do anything you want now, Tovah. Anything you want."

I said, "Yes, Momma!" thinking that she was referring to my upwardly spiraling career.

Instead she said, "Because you're marrying a Harvard lawyer!"

Forget the fact that I had just won five major awards on Broadway, all in the same season. Never mind that I had spent ten months starring in the surprise hit *Yentl* that garnered me my very first marquee billing. My name was literally up in lights, but in my mother's eyes, success wasn't marquee value, success was marrying the Harvard lawyer. She could relax now. After all, she came from a generation where a woman was defined by the man she married.

As I descended the stairs alone into the Terrace Room (because the three of us could not fit together on that staircase) my parents, who had preceded me, waited at the foot of those elegant steps. My knees wouldn't stop shaking. I channeled the teaching of famed choreographer Donald Sadler, who had taught me how to descend a staircase without ever looking down. This was during my time in the 1974 Broadway show *Rodgers and Hart*. As you bend your right knee, you touch your left ankle to the back of the next step coming up. That way, you don't ever have to drop your eyes. He had learned this technique in Vegas, and on March 20, 1977, Vegas visited The Plaza. Though I was trembling, I never looked down. I gazed at my destiny in front of me and floated down that long aisle as if I were being carried on the river of my first twenty-seven years of life. As I grew nearer and nearer to my *beshert*, my destined one, with my mother on my left and my father on my right, I realized my entire existence was about to transform. Like a mantra, I kept repeating: *step touch, step touch, step touch, no rush.* I was thrilled to have both my parents with me. I was grateful. Traditional Jewish weddings always honor the father *and* the mother of the bride and groom—a brief but treasured moment of gender equality that has existed for millennia.

Despite my penchant for Handel, it had been my mother's ardent request that I should walk down the aisle to—wait for it—"Here Comes the Bride" (officially "Bridal Chorus") by Wagner, Hitler's favorite composer and an arch anti-Semite. Despite Wagner's history, I should tell you, there is a reason that melody from Lohengrin is a cliché—it's a cliché because it works brilliantly. The orchestra repeated the first phrase of the F-natural octaves in 2/4 time at least twice so I could get down those stairs that cascaded into the Terrace Room. As I stepped onto the starched white runner with my parents, Wagner's "Bridal Chorus" conjured up visions of my parents' wedding, with my gorgeous mother Lily step-touching to the same melodic line, just as she had done in 1935.

All two hundred guests stood, and my mother—who had fussed over me, and dressed me in crinoline skirts and lace anklets, and tamed my curls, and reminded me to practice piano, and constantly corrected me, and loved me in the best way she knew how—experienced a shining moment as her only daughter, her baby, was fulfilling her deepest hoped-for dreams. Beaming, she held my arm proudly.

Then my father—for whom I symbolized the continuity of life after the ashes of war, for whom I was his only child he knew from infancy, who felt that my every breath was a miracle, who taught me to "reach for the stars so you can land on the roof, reach for the roof, you'll never get off the ground," who was my greatest cheerleader, my closest ally, my protector, my first great unconflicted love, that *Pater Heroico*—took my right arm, and the three of us together walked down the resplendent candlelit aisle, gratefully devoid of klieg lights.

Under the George Winston chandeliers, we walked toward the ivory satin *chuppah*—the marriage canopy—embroidered with lilies, roses, and the Hebrew saying *"Ani L'dodi V'dodi Li." I am my beloved's, and my beloved is mine.* Our names would soon be embroidered inside that chuppah.

Andy stepped off the wedding platform to meet me, and after hugging my mother and father, he extended his hand to take me with him up to the marriage canopy. I hugged my parents and kissed them from the depths of my soul. It was an embrace that said, "Thank you for my life. Thank you for a universe of depth and meaning." I took Andrew's hand, and with that touch began our journey to create our own family, the next generation of Feldshuh-Levys.

Under the chuppah, I started with the *hakafot*, the custom of circling the groom to create a protective, loving wall around him. Ruth Gordon held my flowers as she handed me the train of my long veil. Nowadays, the groom also circles the bride. Fair is fair. Then the wedding ceremony continued with the betrothal, which consists of the reading of the ketubah and the exchange of vows—which was sanctified by the singing of seven blessings, called the *Sheva Brachos*. Andrew and I placed our wedding rings on each other's right index fingers and pledged our love to one another forever and always "according to the laws of Moses and Israel."

Finally, Andrew crushed the glass underfoot. A broken glass cannot be mended, and this tradition symbolizes the idea that marriage is irrevocable. It is a publicly declared miracle where two previously unrelated people declare hereafter, "We are now one," and having a child is the embodiment of that oneness. The minute the glass was crushed, even our assimilated crowd screamed, "Mazel tov!" and the orchestra sailed fortissimo into Mendelssohn's ebullient "Wedding March."

In 1977, despite having done *Yentl* on Broadway, I did not observe the marvelous Orthodox Jewish tradition of *yichud*—repairing to a private room with Andrew for an hour to take in our new bond of marriage. Normally, the parents escort the young couple to that room, and then the newlyweds lock the door, since now, for the first time, they can be alone . . . and intimate. In Talmudic days, this is when the marriage was consummated.

Instead, like good Americans, we formed a reception line. Little did Andy realize that passing up the tradition of *yichud* would foreshadow a lifetime of sacrificing intimacy in the grand reception line of my career. After each guest congratulated us, they went on to a fabulous cocktail hour in the large marble foyer. There, to my mother's and my horror, a huge vat of shrimp arrived, which we had specifically instructed Werner was *verboten*. As for the shrimp's fate at our kosher-style wedding? It was devoured in seconds. Somewhere else in The Plaza, some unlucky bride was getting our vat of matzah balls!

The entire night was sublime, my parents and the Levys were ecstatic, and the world seemed our oyster.

Ah yes, I left out one little detail: the *reason* this masterpiece was crafted in the record time of six weeks. I received a call from my father in January 1977. Uncharacteristically, he said, "Sweetheart, I'm having a little business problem, and I have to ask a favor. Could you possibly get married sooner rather than later? As a matter of fact, as soon as you and Andrew can manage? I fear that if you wait until July 7, 1977, I won't be present at the wedding." My good luck numbers, 7/7/77, faded from view.

"What?" I said, my heart pounding, "Are you sick, Daddy? What's the matter?"

And my father repeated, "I'm having a little business problem. My ex–law partner is serving a two-year sentence for tax fraud and has turned state's witness to accuse me and members of his own family of tax violations to lessen his sentence. Despite my plea of innocence, and a first trial, where there was a hung jury, the US attorney wants a second trial."

I thought to myself, *First trial, second trial? Where have I been?*

Dad went on, "There could be adverse publicity for me, and to be honest, to walk down the aisle with this in the newspapers would be very hard on our family."

I was glad this was a phone call so that he couldn't see my tears, which probably would have broken his heart on top of an already painful admission. I held my breath as he continued.

"Tovah, to avoid the risks inherent in any trial, I've come to the tough decision to enter into a plea bargain. Please remember, Angel Cake, I have not been convicted of anything. I've decided to come forward and plead guilty to one misdemeanor to lessen the legal consequences for me and to protect our family. At least, I hope so."

I knew intuitively my father was again operating as an unbridled optimist. *My* whole world was reeling. My first and only thought was to rewind the tape of this conversation. I wanted to deny its existence. Dad's news felt like a torpedo in our family ship. All I could think about was how to save my father, how to be his life jacket. I gently replied, "Of course, Dad, whatever you need."

It was unthinkable that my father would not be at our wedding. I knew I was going to walk down the aisle with both my parents by my side. It was also unthinkable that my father could possibly be indicted for income tax violations. After all, wasn't he a lawyer and a man of impeccable integrity? Here was the man who made me walk back to the local drugstore at Heathcote Five Corners to return a stolen Three Musketeers bar when I was three years old. Here was the man who made me apologize to the pharmacist for pinching his candy. That walk of shame and confession was an agonizing experience for me, but valuable—I never stole again.

Where was that man?

I called my mother. Bless her, she had known for some time about this problem and never exhibited one moment of upset in my presence, and per usual, kept her lips tightly shut. She remained silent, stoic, and strong.

When Mom and I hung up, I faced the difficult task of calling Andy. I assumed my future hung in the balance. I told him my father's law partner was already in jail for dreaming up a tax scheme and had sought to implicate my father to curry favor with the authorities and to lessen the jail time he was already serving.

"Andrew, do you still want to marry me?" I said, then started to weep because I was so afraid his answer would be "no."

He replied without hesitation, "Of course I still want to marry you. This is about your father, not you. We will all get through this."

I called my mother back. Ecstatically, I said, "Momma, I don't just have a Harvard Lawyer, I have a *ganza mensch* (Yiddish for a great being). We have a wedding to plan!" And in six weeks, instead of seven months, my remarkably poised mother and I put together the most elegant wedding at The Plaza Hotel, down to the last detail. When the bullets are flying, you want to be in the trenches with Lillian Feldshuh.

One week after our wedding, on Monday, March 28, 1977, my father, who hung the world for me, volunteered to cop a plea to one count of attempted tax evasion. Andy comforted me and said, "Remember, Tovah, Sidney was not convicted. He chose to plea bargain."

As my father had stood by me all of my life, so I would stand by him through this ordeal. I went down to the Federal Courthouse for the sentencing the day after Lily's sixty-sixth birthday. Against an April spring sky, and as a bride of less than a month, I wore all black, in mourning, I suppose, hiding behind large Jackie O sunglasses.

I heard the judge sentence Sidney Feldshuh to two years in minimum-security federal prison. My heart stopped. Then came the saving six words: "to be commuted to ninety days." My father asked the judge if he could go home to finish arranging his affairs. The judge denied him that privilege, and I saw my father taken away in handcuffs from the courtroom.

The young lawyers at his firm whom he had generously mentored were also in the court that day. We were all distraught. Soon after, the *New York Post* printed an article stating that my father had plea bargained to one count of "the attempt to evade taxes." The last phrase read, "He is the father of Broadway actress Tovah Feldshuh." To which my mother said, "Remember, the day after you read a newspaper, it's wrapping fish."

And that was the last time we spoke of the matter.

In Lily's silence was her strength. I had grown up with it, under it, beside it, and begging to get inside it. Hers was a silence that had simultaneously protected and tormented me, born out of a shyness no infant could comprehend. Her silence felt to me like the great "no," a black hole, infinitely dense and with a gravitational pull that could have sucked up the furniture. I realize now that Mother loved me deeply, and probably relentlessly, but silently. Somewhere, somehow, she was given the message that silence meant she was a lady, and a lady doesn't bother anyone. A lady is discreet. A lady doesn't intrude. And a lady doesn't, G-d forbid, overshadow her husband.

My father served his ninety-day term in minimum security at the base of Manhattan Island right across from the *Sesame Street* studios. During his stay at Manhattan Correctional Center, he became the head of the prison law library, forever checking the stacks for the tomes of federal and state law in order to advise inmates who didn't have the benefit of being able to afford a lawyer. "There is dignity in work," my parents always said. That was a fundamental motto of my family, and my father lived by it.

We could speak only when he could call me from one of the few pay phones. There was never enough time because there was always a queue and a limit to how long you could stay on the line. And even if we could have chatted for an hour, it wouldn't have been enough. How I longed to hear his voice. When we did connect, it was chin up all the way.

"Dad! How are ya today?" I would ask.

"Great," he would answer. "I'm getting some exercise, sleeping a good deal, and working in the law library. I'm looking forward to seeing you soon, my Angel Cake."

Despite the huge adjustment in his life, my father fared quite well in his new surroundings. His survival skills were honed from the war, and this minimum-security facility across from Big Bird and Elmo was a honeymoon compared to the dangers and battles of World War II. His characteristic eternal optimism helped him adapt to his new circumstances quickly. He could talk to anybody, and chose always to turn a sow's ear into a silk purse. I heard from my brother that once an inmate had threatened my father. The Italian mafia guys in prison accosted that inmate and said, "Don't touch Feldshuh or there will be consequences."

He called me on the phone one afternoon and I said, "Dad! How are ya today?"

"Great, Angel Cake," he replied. "You know how I love the color red? Well, our jumpsuits have been changed from yellow to red this week, and I feel marvelous!"

My mother spent the summer of 1977 alone. She continued to go to Mamaroneck Beach and Yacht Club every day, and when people asked where Sidney was, she simply said, "He's away on business." She told me she imagined Dad was at camp, just like he was during the first summers of their romance, when he was a camp counselor in Upstate

New York. "He's at camp," she thought, "He'll be home soon." That was her mantra.

When I look back on this experience, I can see myself standing in that gown, a New York tintype of American elegance in a moment of true joy, textured by tradition and informed by family challenges. I was joined to a great man who made the commitment to weather any pathway for better or for worse, sacrificing so much of the fundamental normalcy he so richly deserved. He was there, standing by my side, with the belief that together, we would find the unexpected shrimp when life was ready to deal us matzah balls. This boy was the answer to my dreams *and* my mother's. Now there were three of us steadfastly longing for caviar all the way.

My Crazy Ex-TV Show

S o I GET A CALL FROM MY WONDERFUL AGENT, ARTHUR Toretsky, and he says, "Tovah, there's a new series on the CW (CBS/Warner Brothers Cable) called *Crazy Ex-Girlfriend* and they'd love you to play the mother of the crazy ex-girlfriend. They need someone who can sing and dance, and the part is on a platter for you. No audition. Firm offer."

My heart starts racing. Every phone call should be like this.

"In episode one, you'd only be a voiceover, but they'd pay you for the week, and then they'll start to write for your character. At the moment, this is only a three-episode arc, but you never know!"

I'm thinking, *Just get me in the room.*

"Look up the girl who wrote the series, Tovah. Her name is Rachel Bloom. She's a graduate of Tisch, and she's teamed up with a show-runner, a graduate of Harvard, Aline Brosh McKenna, who wrote *Devil Wears Prada!*"

"Harvard? Prada? Singing? Dancing?" By now I'm salivating. "Send me the script."

He says, "Let me send you the rough cut of the first episode instead."

Arthur sends me the link, and I watch episode one. It's astonishingly great; completely unbridled and wacky, and oh, so skilled. I'm thrilled to play Rachel Bloom's mother and hope they will send me some scripts equally as brilliant.

The mother's name is Naomi Bunch, and she's the most judgmental, difficult, "let me improve you by fixing you" Jewish mother ever. I'm thinking, *Hmmm, what could I possibly draw on for inspiration?* Thank you, Lily!

I accept the deal, and the next thing I know, I get a five-page solo entitled "Where's the Bathroom?" Here's just a taste of the lyrics:

Where's the bathroom?
Where's the bathroom?
I need to use the bathroom
Tell me that you have a bathroom
In this hovel you call home
I don't know which was bumpier
The plane ride or the taxi
All these freeways are a nightmare
Where's my purse? I need my comb!
By the way, you're looking healthy
And by healthy, I mean chunky
I don't mean that as an insult
I'm just stating it as fact—
I see your eczema is back

——BY PERMISSION OF SONY

Thank you, composer and lyricists, Adam Schlesinger (of blessed memory), Jack Dolgen, and Rachel Bloom!

I'm told, in typical Hollywood fashion, "Don't worry about anything. We can shoot your song in small takes. You don't have to memorize the whole thing."

I'm thinking to myself, *Yeah, right.* And I remember what Lily ingrained in me: "You only have one chance to make a first impression."

I practiced that song in New York until it was Bird's Eye—Ethel Merman's term for "frozen." I knew it cold.

I was scheduled to record at Columbia Recording Studios, 6121 Sunset Boulevard, Studio A. Studio A was where Garland and Sinatra recorded!

The network sends a big, black SUV and flies me business class to Hollywood. Yes, I'm in my sixties. *Yes*, it still excites me. *YES*, I'll have the free champagne!

The next day, on the *Crazy Ex* set in North Hollywood, we whip off the staging and the song in two takes. At the end of it, Rachel says to the director, "I told you to believe in Broadway. *This* is why we need Broadway actors."

I loved *Crazy Ex-Girlfriend.* Women conceived the show, ran the show, and starred in the show. I was hired for three episodes, and stayed for all four seasons.

Naomi Bunch, in true Lily "Why must you do such wacky things!" fashion, thinks, *Rebecca . . . how could such a person come out of* my body?

Unlike Golda Meir, Naomi is not the Jewish "Bubbe mother." Naomi Bunch is a satirical take on the Jewish Princess mother, plagued with a daughter who does not meet her standards. In trying to save her, I have to change her. Sound familiar, Terri Sue?

———

PATTI LUPONE JOINS THE SHOW for one episode in season three. Patti is a Broadway giant, one of those names above the title that on its own can sell out a run. We went up on the marquee around the same time; I through *Yentl*, and she through *Evita*, and have been pals ever since.

And now we get to sing together! To have a duet with Patti LuPone to show my grandchildren puts a smile across my face. Patti is brass-tacks brilliant, and if she respects your work, you can fly with her through any scene.

She is brought in to play the rabbi at a Bunch family Bar Mitzvah. Together we sing a number called "Remember That We Suffered." Picture Patti and me surrounded by a hall of celebrants doing the Hora, an absolutely jubilant celebration—except for the diatribe of Jewish atrocities that make up the lyrics of our song. Not since Mel Brooks's showstopper "Springtime for Hitler" has a song so irreverently satirized the Third Reich.

Later that season, I'm reading an upcoming episode, and it says "the mother opens the door in bra and panties." I'm thinking to myself, *I wonder whom they're getting as my body double?* So I call the producer and they say, "The body double is *you*. Don't be alarmed."

Don't be alarmed?! I say to myself. *I'm a senior citizen. Even if I had a great figure, it's down to the ground. Facelift? I need a body lift!*

My Victoria's Secret underwear debut on television created a week of endless push-ups, sit-ups, laps in the pool, and lettuce. In the scene, my doorbell rings. I'm expecting my daughter. I open the front door in the aforementioned bra and panties, and instead of just Rebecca, I see she's with her Asian boyfriend, Josh Chan. One look at me, and all the color drains out of my daughter's face.

She screams, "Mom what are you doing?"

Naomi replies, "I didn't know you were bringing the Oriental."

In the very next scene, I say, "Excuse me, I need to go upstairs to change for the evening," and as I exit, with my back to them, I unhook my brassiere and take it off and twirl it like a stripper, walking upstairs naked to the waist. It was an award-winning moment for AARP. I realize as I get older, I get bolder. Thank you Father Time.

How I wish all of my Hollywood experiences had been this sweet . . .

ACT II

What's a Nice Kid Like Me Doing in a Picture Like This?

"MOMMA, I'M DYING OUT HERE. I HAVEN'T WORKED IN months. I feel like the *Three Sisters* in Chekhov's play, wailing, 'Moscow, Moscow, Moscow,' but for me it's 'New York, New York, New York.' Momma, what am I gonna do?"

Her best ammunition was, "Remember who you are."

I'm suddenly thinking, "Who *am* I?"

I could visualize her three thousand miles away thumping her fist on her own sternum the way she used to thump on mine whenever I felt defeated. All I could think of were the nuns banging their chests saying, "*Mea culpa, mea culpa, mea maxima culpa.*" My fault indeed. Why did I move here?

"Mom, in New York, I'm Tovah Feldshuh. In Los Angeles, I'm 'Tovah *WHO?*' I feel like I have moved from Greece, home of ideas, art, philosophy, to Rome, home of freeways, power, and plastic surgery.

Hollywood has been one big bait and switch. It wasn't like this when I was commuting in the fall of '76, when Andy and I were engaged and I went back and forth to the West Coast to work. I got those six jobs in six weeks on six different shows. I played Katharine Hepburn for G-d's sake! And now my phone sits here like a dead pet. Surely I booked those jobs because of my talent. That hasn't gone anywhere . . . has it?"

Silence

"Hello? Hello, Mom?"

"Tovah, what pet died?!"

Who would've thought that with New York three thousand miles away, Hollywood would end up being just on the outskirts of Lilyville? My relationship with my mother had become a series of transcontinental calls—that is, after 8:00 p.m. Pacific time when the telephone rates went down for Lily back on the East Coast. Now I was tethered umbilically to the wall by a coiled, beige phone cord, hoping for some kind of encouragement.

I could hardly expect her to be a cheerleader. Both Mom and Hollywood had always been complicated for me. In 1973, when I first came out to the West Coast, Monique James and Eleanor Kilgallen offered me a contract with Universal Studios for five hundred dollars a week. I was called into their office, which was decked out with Sidney Sheinberg's fantasy of being an equestrian. Sheinberg was the head of Universal along with his partner, the legendary Lew Wasserman, who headed MCA. There were pictures of horses on the hunt everywhere. Jews playing polo. Ralph Lauren, born Ralph Lifshitz, could've ponied right up. And there I was with my unbridled *chutzpah* (Yiddish for balls), "Ms. James, five hundred dollars a week sounds fine, but would you mind giving me a stipend to pay for my singing, ballet, and tap lessons? I did them every day in New York."

Ms. James replied, "You paid for them there, you can pay for them here," probably thinking, *Who is this kid?*

"I bet you didn't say that to Judy Garland or Mickey Rooney," I said, tongue in cheek, only making the situation worse.

"You're *not* Judy *or* Mickey," Monique said flatly, moving a little closer so I could hear her very well. So close that I could see the creases in her lipstick and the eyes that told me in no uncertain terms that I was the colt she was about to tame. "When we gave you that small part in the Bette Davis film, we thought that you were marvelous—you hear me? Marvelous—even though you died before the opening credits. . . . And do you know *why* we thought you were marvelous?"

"No," I replied innocently.

"Your skin," she said. "Your skin looks like Elizabeth Taylor's. Now, would you like to work for us at five hundred dollars a week and see where that takes us?"

"Well . . . ," I said, politely pushing against her lead, "May I . . . may I please think about it?"

"*Think* about it?!" As if to say, "Does this girl know how to spell small fry?"

"Tovah, some of the greats started as contract players right here at Universal: Suzanne Pleshette on *Bob Newhart*, James Brolin on *Marcus Welby MD*, Sharon Gless in *Cagney & Lacey*. Even Henry Winkler— sure, he graduated from Yale, and maybe he *wasn't* a contract player, but it was Hollywood that made him famous. People still remember The Fonz," she brayed.

I feared that if I did only television I'd become an actress with an emotional range from A to B. I wanted A to Z!

Worse than telling my agent was telling my mother:

"You're turning down a contract from Universal? You can afford to be so choosey? Tovah, let me talk *tachlis* (Yiddish for truth). Are you *mishug?*" (Yiddish abbreviation for crazy.)

"Momma, listen: television's like a straitjacket. The networks—and there are only three of them—don't let you change a word of these scripts—and they're pablum. If I want to make a suggestion and want to change a line, they begrudgingly say, "Stop everything! We have to call the network and ask permission." Then you've held up production. Directors expect us good little girls to show up on time, hit our mark, know our lines, do what we're supposed to do, and then get the hell out of the way. I know how to do that, Mom, and I do it well. But is it art? I don't know. To me, it feels like factory work."

And this was only the first time I turned down factory work from one of the fame factories of Hollywood.

The second time I had the naïve courage to say "no" was in 1976. *Yentl* was completing its run, and the incredible Alan Shayne, the debonair head of Warner Brothers Television, flew to New York and took me to The Plaza's Palm Court. He then begged me to take *Three's Company*. I said, "Mr. Shayne, I can't accept your offer. I don't know how to act yet."

With his shock of silver gray hair and his piercing blue eyes, he took my face in his hands and said, "Are you insane? You just won five awards on Broadway! Come to LA, you'll be in a brand-new series with John Ritter and this newcomer, Suzanne Somers."

I replied, "I know this sounds foolish, but I think *Yentl* was a lucky break in a role I was born to play. I've gotta do the classics. If I don't train my instrument now, I'll never be able to enter the Olympics of acting. I'm hungry for the high jump, Mr. Shayne." And I stopped speaking because I didn't want to insult him. And thus, the gifted Joyce DeWitt took that role and flew with it.

I can't say that I don't feel the slight pull of regret for not taking the offers that were given me and galloping down the television path. I'm sure my fate would've been different, maybe better with far reaching fame. But at the end of the day, I would've given myself to causes in which I didn't fully believe. And that's what I would've been left with. I had an irresistible drive to follow my bliss. Perhaps because my mother had tried to tame me when I was young, I had a primal need to run free.

Well, guess what turning down *Three's Company* made room for? The miniseries *Holocaust*.

"Mom? I just landed an eight-hour miniseries. Four nights of television! I have a principal role playing Helena the Czech freedom fighter, and they're flying me to Vienna for the shoot! *Vienna!*"

"Sidney, pick up the other line! Tovah's going to Vienna! Exciting! What's the name of the series?"

"*Holocaust.*"

"What?"

I repeated, "*Holocaust.*"

"Excuse me? I thought you said *Holocaust.*"

"I did."

"*Oy vey*, Tovah! You need a Holocaust like I need *luchen kop.*"

"Momma, we start shooting July 18—18! Chai for life—in the Vienna woods."

"The Vienna woods?! That's where the Feldshuhs fled the Nazis! And they got shot in the head! They got a literal *luchen kop*! You're going from a honeymoon to a Holocaust? Not a smart idea. You're gonna spend the first weeks of your married life thousands of miles from your husband? Oy, *gevalt*!" (A multipurpose Yiddish exclamation of wonder . . . or anything disastrous.)

Indeed, after two extraordinary weeks at Villa D'Este on Lake Como, then Calle di Volpe in Sardinia, Andrew and I flew from our honeymoon to a Holocaust. I arrived at the first rehearsal and Marvin Chomsky, the director, calmly said, "We would like a Czech accent," as if he were saying "Please pass the butter." I looked at him like he was insane. This is the kind of news I would have preferred to hear *six weeks before production.*

Thank goodness before the honeymoon I spent ten days in Czechoslovakia researching my part. I happened to tape-record my guide as she explained the sad history of her country. So between the Czech guide and the dialect coach, we made it. Barely. Then they asked me to speak Russian!

The night before filming, there was a cast dinner, and I met Joseph Bottoms, who would play my sweetheart, Rudi Weiss. Joseph was desperately handsome and wonderful to work with—until I wore electric hair rollers in rehearsal for our love scene. He kept accusing me of pricking his chest with the prongs of my rollers, which the hair department had insisted be kept in until cameras were about to roll. Mr. Bottoms bristled but begrudgingly behaved. Subconsciously, I must have been wearing them to remind him that flattered as I was, I wasn't interested in any of his overtures, on set or off. What a fuss made over a little prick.

Despite the roller incident, the first three days of shooting went beautifully. Then we were informed that the Vienna lab developing the footage had ruined every frame of our work. By accident? We braved an entire reshoot, and from then on, the film had to be sent where it was safe to be processed.

When *Holocaust* was released in the spring of 1978, it was a groundbreaking work revealing stories about World War II that had never been uttered on such a grand scale. The textbooks throughout Germany and Austria were rewritten, and German and Austrian children began to study this blight in their history. Holocaust monuments sprouted up all over Europe. In Berlin, the Museum to the Jewish People is right next to the Brandenburg Gates and the Reichstag. That would be like placing a memorial to the Native American the size of Madison Square Garden in the middle of Times Square.

Holocaust turned out to be a defining moment in television history. It was the second miniseries in the world after *Roots* (which was also groundbreaking in bringing the cruelty of slavery into the mainstream's consciousness). *Holocaust* was also a defining moment in my career. I received my first Emmy nomination and was awarded the Israel Friendship Medal in Washington, DC, by the Vice President of the United States, Walter Mondale, and the Israeli ambassador, Simcha Dinitz.

It was on the crest of this success that I had the courage to move to Los Angeles. Who wouldn't think that this was a town ready to embrace me? Plus, it was time to build our home together. Mindful of the conflicted relationship I had with my mother, Andy thought it might actually be helpful to live three thousand miles away. He had lived in LA before and loved the ease of life the city afforded. He also understood it.

Washington is a one-horse town: politics. Los Angeles is a one-horse town: entertainment. (Again, Jews on horses.) Both run on three essentials: power, a sliding social pole, and sex. (Wait, isn't sex a sliding social pole?)

As a transplanted New Yorker, after a very short time, I had no idea what to do with all the sunshine, the sorbet-colored houses, and the stretches of freeway. LA felt like another planet, and I felt very isolated in this sprawl of a town. I had come from a vertical environment, with each of us packed shoulder to shoulder. Los Angeles was a horizontal environment, with each of us contained in our own cars. Except for the music on our radio or a call on the newfangled car phones, there was a silence about the city. It reminded me of those isolated early days in my corner bedroom in Scarsdale.

Andy arrived in LA before me to rent a house. He picked me up at LAX in his gunmetal Porsche, then drove me to Brentwood, and said, "Shut your eyes." He pulled into a driveway, led me, eyes closed, to the front door, picked me up in his arms, then carried me over the threshold, exclaiming, "Welcome to paradise!"

I opened my eyes, and so it was. In an era of shoulder pads and foam-rubber epaulettes under my silk blouses, all the furniture was oversized and puffy. A huge taupe sectional graced the living room, sitting on planks of old oak, stained a burnt umber. The kitchen was paved in gorgeous Spanish tile that looked hand-painted. The size of each room with its vaulted ceilings and Spanish flair would've embarrassed any New York apartment.

Andy said, "You like the interior? You ain't seen nothin' yet." He led me to the backyard. We were on three acres of land, with a plum and a lemon tree ripe with fruit, a huge oval pool with a graceful dolphin spewing water at one end and a diving board at the other—and the house came with a housekeeper! It was right out of the movies. What an introduction to living on the left coast.

"Hello, Mom?"

"*Tovah?*" She screamed, "Is that you?" Mom's hearing was seriously going south. We were now *shouting* from coast to coast, as if there were no phones.

Overenunciating, I said, "Mom, Andy found us the most beautiful place to live. Our master bedroom is as big as your living room, and the bathroom is as big as the dining room!"

"What? You're taking a bath in the dining room?!"

"No, Mom, the bathroom is as *big as your dining room,*" struggling to clearly pronounce every single word.

"Got it. Go on!"

"We wake up in the morning, and we sit outside on fancy white wrought-iron furniture, just like Aunt Rose owned at Willow Downs! The housekeeper serves us fresh Arabian coffee, and I go down this little hill to pick plums and lemons, ripe from the tree. And after breakfast, I jump in our pool to swim laps. It's *so* glamorous!"

"You're living the dream!" Then, ever practical, "What's the layout?"

"Living room, dining room, kitchen, breakfast room, den, office."

"Is there a guest bathroom on the main floor?" Ever the party planner, she advised, "If you don't have a guest bathroom, you won't be able to entertain."

We entertained plenty. Mom would be delighted to know that despite having a guest bathroom on the main floor, the Hollywood crowd sometimes peed on the bushes outside. Too much wine, too little responsibility.

Unexpectedly, the owners came home in mid-August and we were banished from the master suite to the attic. I felt a little like Anne Frank—I waited for them to put a bookcase over the door. Soon after, we were asked to leave, two weeks before our original agreement was up. We scrambled and landed in Venice. Not Italy; we were in Venice Beach at the elegantly titled *Oakwood Garden Apartments.* Who was I to know they were being ironic?

Old mustard carpets, pale-green walls, dark-brown furniture. Details Lily would never know. Then, to add insult to injury, came a terror out of the sky. No, literally, *Terror Out of the Sky.*

"It's a sequel to *The Savage Bees*!" pitched my ICM agent Ina Bernstein, electrified with excitement.

"A sequel?!" I asked incredulously. Like *one* wasn't enough?

One week later, I found myself in the Mojave Desert starring opposite Efrem Zimbalist Jr. and a supporting cast of African killer bees. Who knew a bee wrangler could be a girl's best friend? Note to self: avoid projects that require bee wranglers. I could wax on. (Forgive me.)

I was embarrassed to be filming such a project. To cope, I found myself awake at 4:00 a.m. to swim sixty lengths in the darkness of the Oakwood Garden pool to brace myself for the scorching hot, dust-filled days of soul-swallowing work.

Trained to do Shakespeare, I was now working opposite trained bees. Working for "money and momentum" left me with "money and misery." With little artistic satisfaction to be found in this experience, this was a film credit I would never put down on my résumé. It may not have mattered to the world, but it mattered to me.

Andy was my rock. "You're meeting people. You're making connections. You're getting your name out there," he said. He was *right*, of course. That's exactly how I reframed it. That's exactly how I endured it. But how exactly would I explain this job to my mother?

And then came the dreaded call, long distance to Lilyville. The news did not land well: "Tovah, this is one picture I will *not* be seeing you in. All we can do is hope our friends are all *out* the night it airs. How could you take such *drek*?" (Shit in Yiddish.)

She was *right*, of course. There would be no Hollywood spin on *drek* in Lilyville.

And then came the *sequel* to the sequel—and a phone call to remember: "Hey Tovah, we need a pick up shot for the bee attack with you in the Volkswagen at the top of the film." It was the producer.

"Absolutely," I said, ever the pro.

"Yeah, I've got the Volkswagen here in my backyard. We'll pop you in it and get my daughter to shake it from behind. You'll do the screaming thing. Easy."

I said, "Your backyard?!"

"We're out of money. The budget's gone."

Talk about a "B" picture! (I can't help myself.)

After that, no jobs for two months.

During the shoot, Andy and I bought a home perched high in the West Hollywood hills, at 1619 Queens Road. In 1886, railroad tycoon Moses Hazeltine Sherman designated an area to house his railroad workers as he built two electric railways, the Pacific and the Pasadena lines, which connected Los Angeles to the small, beachfront town of Santa Monica. Pity those trolleys didn't survive. The tour guides tell us that by 1925, movie stars were flocking to live in Sherman to be near the studios in Hollywood. Soon the citizens voted to change Sherman's name to West Hollywood to emphasize its relationship to the movie industry. Douglas Fairbanks, Mary Pickford, and Charlie Chaplin all had homes in West Hollywood, and it was there that they founded United Artists. If it was good enough for them, it was good enough for me!

"Mom, we found a beautiful three-bedroom Spanish house, and before you ask—*yes* it has a guest bathroom on the main floor. It's one block east of La Cienega Boulevard in West Hollywood."

"Great on the bathroom, but where are you?"

"Up in the hills. Mom, it has a spectacular view. At night we see the twinkling lights of Los Angeles, and by day we see the Pacific Ocean. . . . Well, when there's not smog. We're only on a half-acre of land, but our *visual* real estate is twenty-five miles."

No sooner had Andrew and I nested in West Hollywood than I flew the coop. My East Coast agent, Milton Goldman, called with fairy dust to my heart.

"Tovah, you've been offered *Peter Pan* at the Municipal Opera House in St. Louis!"

Lillian Kaplan at thirteen months. 1534 Charlotte St., the Bronx. *Sol. Young Studios, 474 Tremont Ave., Bronx, New York.*

The Kaplan girls: Lily victorious over May, according to their referee and older sister, Nancy.

"Hortense," Lily's glamorous alter ego, with Nat. As she wrote to her girlfriend Charlotte Caesar on June 7, 1929: "Nat, he's alright, but I want my boyfriend."

Lily with her "boyfriend," Sid, at his graduation from NYU, June 1930.

"Hortense," 1928 Vice President
of the NYU sophomore class.

Lily with her secret husband,
Sidney Feldshuh, June 1933.

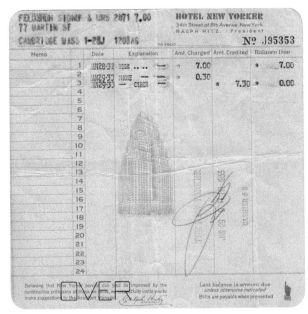

First night at the New Yorker Hotel as Mr. and Mrs. Sidney Feldshuh
after their secret elopement on January 28, 1933. (*$7.30!*)

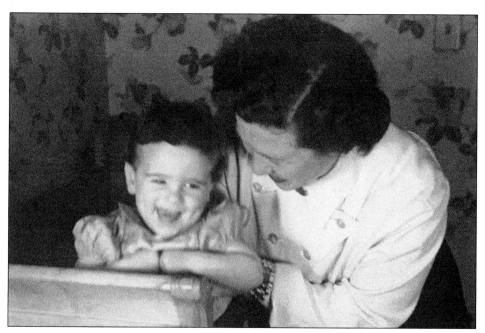

Terri Sue in the Bronx, 1950 . . .

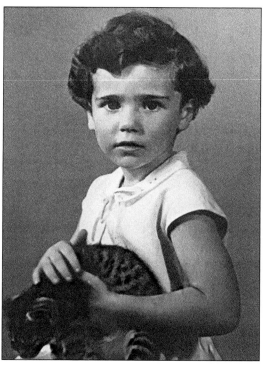

. . . Terri Sue in Scarsdale, 1952.
(*Need I say more?*)

Terri Sue, tomboy party girl, in brother David's
hand-me-down play clothes with Mary Janes and anklets, 1953.

Sarah Lawrence College graduation, 1970.
Holding my diploma, the last legal
document as Terri Sue Feldshuh.

As Peaseblossom in *A Midsummer
Night's Dream* at the Tyrone Guthrie
Theater, in 1972. Or: "So you want
to be an actress? I suggest you ACT!
Otherwise become an accountant!" . . .

. . . Eighteen months later: *Yentl*, my first starring role
on Broadway and my first marquee, 1974–1976.

1978: Starring in *Saravá* on Broadway and in the miniseries *Holocaust* (NBC).

"You can do anything you want now,
you're marrying a Harvard lawyer."
—Lily, just before the wedding

Mr. and Mrs. Andrew Harris Levy,
a "New York tintype of American
elegance." March 20, 1977.

I remember the seat for
the piano was just a single
chair, not a bench (1961).
David, Dad, and Lily look on.

Lily and I never played together. I made sure not
to repeat that pattern with Amanda (1997).

"There is no understudy
for a mother."

The Broadway Baseball
League with Amanda
and Brandon, 1990.

"Amanda, that dress . . . you look like
you're open for business!" quipped Lily.

Amanda's Bat Mitzvah, February 24, 2001.
Pre-party pose with Andrew and Brandon.

Lily's quip: "Tovah, I rate your parts by how you look.
Dolly Levi (and Naomi Bunch): a TEN. Golda Meir? a *ZERO!!*"

Golda's Balcony by William Gibson became the longest-running
one-woman play in Broadway history, 2003–2005.

AGING IS OPTIONAL
('cause G-d I hope it is!)

Tovah's tip: "A trapeze act eight times a week and push-ups before every take makes for guns of steel."

Sidney's quip: "If you pee and you poop and you cut a sweat every day, where can disease land?"

On the trapeze in *Pippin* with my "catcher," Yannick Thomas, and between shots with Steven Yeun, "Glenn" in *The Walking Dead*.

Andrew Lincoln and Norman Reedus, what a feast!
I loved *The Walking Dead* . . . till I was the feast.

I'm even an action doll, but look what I had to do for it!

 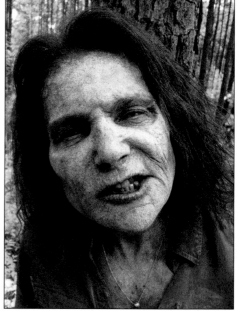

Look Ma, I made it to WALMART!

Selfies on the set of *Crazy Ex-Girlfriend* with my "daughter,"
Rachel Bloom, and my "rabbi," Patti LuPone, 2017.

In chambers with Supreme Court Justice
Ruth Bader Ginsburg, as I was studying to play
her in *Sisters in Law* by Jonathan Shapiro, 2020.

With Helen Hayes, First Lady of
the American Theater (1979) . . .

. . . and with Barbra Streisand,
First Lady of American Song
(Barclays Center, 2012) . . .

. . . and talk about the sound of music!
With legends Christopher Plummer (2014) and Leonard Bernstein (1979).

Lily at ninety, celebrating the one hundredth birthday of Walt Disney
(with Goofy and Chip) at Disney World, December 2001.

Joyce was our beloved caretaker. She would stay
with our family for more than twenty-five years.

Lily's ninety-ninth birthday with David, me,
and three of the "Four Musketeers" who saved her life:
Drs. Matt Williams, Martin Leon, and Susheel Kodali.

The last Vaudeville act at 103 . . .

. . . and the audience who saw it.

I'll Be Loving You Always

"The Muny Opera? The biggest house in America?"

"You got it, kid! You'll be singing 'Neverland' to eleven thousand people a night and flying across a 110-foot stage." I was over the moon and the second star to the right! I threw some fairy dust over my beloved husband hoping he would "Meet me in St. Louis." It was only a three-week engagement, after all. At the massive St. Louis Municipal Opera House, I was flown by Foy—the same people who flew Mary Martin. The more details I learned, the more thrilled I was to tell Mother. I was convinced this would wow her.

"Mom! I'm playing the Muny! One hundred and sixty thousand people will see me in these two weeks. I'm sharing my dressing room with Rudolf Nureyev!"

"How's that gonna work?" Lily asked dubiously.

"He dances by night; I rehearse *Peter Pan* by day." Now, making a joke: "Between his jockstraps and my flying harnesses, our dressing room looks like a brothel specializing in S&M."

"Is that a clothing store or a chocolate?" she joked back.

"Good one, Ma."

"I know what S&M means, young lady, so watch it!"

"Tuesday night, I went to see him perform, then went backstage to tell him how great he was. He smiled, Momma, but then was so sad. He said, 'No one comes backstage to see me.' I said, 'Mr. Nureyev, they're frightened, that's all. You are a legend—the first to defect from Russia at the height of the Cold War! It was incredibly courageous. The dance world owes you everything. To watch you is to watch a dancer for all time.' Then, Ma, he bowed as if he were taking a private curtain call and kissed my hand, saying, '*Spasibo.*' Thank you."

"A Russian thanking a Jew? We've come a long way since the Cossacks! *Momzers!*" (Bastards in Yiddish.)

"Momma, keep your voice down. It's a new world."

Maybe I'd never dance like Nureyev, but if this part of my life were a dream ballet like Laurie's in *Oklahoma!*, my career would be the music propelling me in a peripatetic allegro of the disparate artistic opportunities swirling around me. On stage right would be Andy repeating, "The way I love you is by never standing in your way"; on stage left would be my mother saying, "The heart of the marriage is in that marriage bed." Dancing between career and home, some of my choreography would be grand *jetés*, leaping through the air, and some of it would be crushing *retombés*, falling once again to the ground.

The great choreographer Agnes de Mille famously said, "The creative urge is the demon that will not accept anything second-rate." Carve that on my headstone! If she choreographed my dream ballet, I'm certain she would have evoked the tension of this tumultuous period in my life, with its feast in the East and famine in the West, by choreographing me frenetically bounding across the stage like an excellence machine, grasping for stature both at home and at work.

As you may remember, many of Agnes de Mille's ballets end badly, with the heroine's worst nightmare being realized. However, the dream ballet of my California years ended with a big Broadway break. OK, it was a flop, but it will live on in my heart, and in the historic TV commercial, forever: *Saravá*!

When I told Mom she said, "Sara *Vaughan?*"

"No, Mom. It's a Brazilian show, a musical based on *Doña Flor and Her Two Husbands,* by Jorge Amado."

"Oh, Tovah, the shows you do. They're as unpronounceable as your name. What about *Gypsy,* or *Mame,* something I can tell people without having to shout the spelling or use a dictionary!"

"Mom, I'm starring in a big Broadway musical. Who cares how you say it? Professionally, it's phenomenal."

Unfortunately, the production was riddled with problems. Mitch Leigh, a boy from Brooklyn, who learned early how to buy low and sell high, made a fortune as a jingle writer. Then he wrote *Man of La Mancha,* which made him another fortune. He was both producer *and* composer of *Saravá.* By 1978, he was married to his second wife, Abby Leigh, a renowned painter who was as beautiful as she was kind. They lived on Central Park South in a spectacular apartment that had an

A+ Lily view, and then moved to a mansion on East Sixty-Eighth. All this sounds like a fairy tale, except people had notorious trouble getting along with Mitch, especially the book writer and lyricist N. Richard Nash (American for Nathan Richard Nusbaum).

They stopped talking in Boston when *Saravá* was playing the Colonial Theatre. Nash left the production and from then on we were not allowed to change a word of it. No script adjustments could come into New York. This was effectively an artistic jail cell to which the cast could not find the key. *Saravá* was caught inside an unfinished draft and was Writers Guild bound to stay there. Every night at intermission I would say to myself *Tonight, Act Two is going to work. It's going to work. IT'S GOING TO WORK.* It didn't work. It would never work.

The pioneer producer Mitch Leigh told Santo Loquasto, the Tony Award–winning set and costume designer, that he could not have the second half of his scenic design. Santo, speechless, soldiered on, and had to make do with one half of a butterfly staircase in a half-baked set. We hobbled along the entire season. The reason we were able to hobble at all is that Mitch Leigh decided to never open the show.

We previewed for four months until the critics stormed the Broadway Theatre in March of 1979 saying, "If you're going to charge Broadway prices, you're going to be reviewed." And though they found the show flawed, the *New York Times* singled out my performance as "incandescent."

It wasn't enough.

We closed in three months.

Generously, Mitch Leigh gave Andy and me round-trip tickets from New York to LA every two weeks. At least that gave me some opportunity to "preserve and protect my man." My mother was always shouting, "Take care of Andrew!"

We bravely crisscrossed the country for a grueling nine months. It was too much. Mom was right. When I finally returned to California, Andy actually cried.

"Please don't ever separate us like this again. It's too hard."

Stunned, I replied, "I won't darling, I won't." And I never have.

That commute from Broadway to Hollywood was an enormous strain on our young marriage, particularly on my wonderful groom. Though *Saravá* had given me my second Tony nomination for Best Actress, it was time to settle in permanently with my patient and understanding husband.

I loved our West Hollywood house; I just had no idea how many hours a day I'd be spending in it without work. I was still represented by Ina Bernstein and Joel Dean at ICM and I proceeded to do two feature films, both of which made no money. Then, I proceeded to do nothing. And when I say nothing, I mean *black hole of the universe* nothing. The silence of unemployment in Hollywood is only paralleled by the stillness of a dead body.

Excellence has always been my game. My Daddy taught me that if I were excellent, all the rest would follow. It didn't follow. I would have to teach myself that relationship was easily of equal importance, especially in Hollywood. It seemed to me that in LA, you got cast at parties and seduced at auditions. In New York, you auditioned at auditions, and if there was a seduction, it happened at a party. In New York, at least for me, I found that there is a clear difference between what is social and what is professional behavior.

There was, however, one megastar who actually hit on me at a Hollywood party. I had just completed *The Idolmaker* with Taylor Hackford directing and Howard Koch (now Hawk Koch) producing. I was invited to Peter Bogdanovich's house for a party. He was living with the beautiful Cybill Shepherd. They'd had a scandalous love affair during the shoot of *The Last Picture Show*, which gave Peter multiple Oscar nominations (in addition to multiple orgasms) and made him the thirty-one-year-old "boy wonder" of Hollywood. During this shoot, he decided to leave his wife, Polly Platt, who was the set designer of the picture and with whom he had two children, for the irresistible nineteen-year-old Cybill Shepherd. That evening at Bogdanovich's was one of my first A-list parties.

The house was an enormous Spanish villa; apparently it was owned by Clark Gable's widow, Kay Williams Gable. I was in the kitchen, which I remember was in deep mahogany tones. The obligatory Spanish tiles were on the walls, and they were beautiful. It was a hot night, but the air conditioning inside the house was on full blast. I was cold. Cybill immediately said, "Here, please wear my shawl." She handed me a large black mohair shawl with a beautiful black diamond-knit pattern.

I said, "I haven't even met you and you're offering me your shawl?"

She said, "Don't be silly. Take it. In fact, keep it."

"My name is Tovah," I blurted.

"I'm Cybill," she said.

"I know that," I replied. "Who doesn't?"

"Enjoy the shawl, enjoy the party," and with that, she waltzed off to her next admirer. That shawl has kept me company for the last thirty years. In my one-woman shows, I wrap it around my crowning character, Grandma Ada, a girl who dreamed of being an actress, but instead lived a life of limited horizons as a wife and mother. That shawl holds a distinct memory for me. I touch it, and I touch the kindness of Cybill Shepherd.

There were many stars at Peter Bogdanovich's that night, but the only one that keeps coming to mind was the astonishingly handsome Warren Beatty. I don't recall exactly how our conversation started, but he asked me who I was and why I was there. I told him about *The Idolmaker*. He kept gazing at me with a tilt of his head, and those beautiful, sensual lips. Before I knew it, he asked me to sleep with him. Where I come from, that's right off the bat. I have to confess, I was incredibly flattered. He was well-known as a ladies' man who scored very high with any woman he wanted. As Lily's daughter, all I could think of was, *I wonder if he's healthy? STD? HPV? Ee i ee i oh?* He had a slew of famous exes: Joan Collins, Natalie Wood, and I thought he was currently with Diane Keaton. There he was, in a black T-shirt with his sparkling blue eyes riveted on my hazels. He was like a cool drink of water. Also in a town that is famous for being famous, he was much beloved. He had made *Shampoo, Heaven Can Wait*, and had just finished *Reds*. As much as I was in awe of the whole package, Lily remained on my shoulder.

So I told the handsome movie star, "Sleep with you? I can't. I'm married."

He replied, "So what?"

I said, "So what, to you! I have to wake up tomorrow morning and go back to my life."

He replied coyly, "You're making a big mistake. We'd have a hell of a time."

I said, "You mean a hell of a night. The answer is no."

I confided this story to my pal Patti LuPone when we were shooting *Crazy Ex-Girlfriend*. Her response?

"Tov . . . you missed a good one!"

It always amazed me how casual Hollywood was about liaisons. Maybe because we live one on top of another in New York, there's the strong possibility of people knowing your business. My apartment building is like a dorm. If you want to be promiscuous, just remember, everybody's gonna know. The elevator is quite telltale. In Los Angeles, the sprawl feels like the missionary position—horizontal! The relentless sunshine is the perfect backdrop for sunbathing, nude bathing, spiritual ecstasy in ashrams, and Topanga experimentation with drugs. All these body enliveners would naturally encourage sexual freedom. And we haven't even gone inside the Jewish Men's Club, those powerful, buttoned-up executives who run the studios. I'm sure those expensive Rodeo Drive suits come off often for a willing new actress or actor in town. As for me, I never played the casting-couch game. Ever.

It was my bourgeois values, I'm sure perceived as boring and predictable, that ushered me past those moral pitfalls. My values may have labeled me "Old World," but they also labeled me not an easy target. They also kept me safe. I wanted to be visible through my talent and intelligence, not my sexual appeal.

Gender equality was part and parcel of being a Broadway star. I believe the women were paid equally to the men, and you were judged on your gift first, not on your beauty. This entertainment was *live*—you couldn't cheat it. You either hacked it or you didn't. In Hollywood, so many other factors came into play. The editor can save your performance. A person brought in to dub your voice could save your performance. And of course, the director could save your performance. None of that held true on the stage. Once the curtain went up, you were on your own.

The other movie I made at that time was *Cheaper to Keep Her* with Mac Davis, also a financial flop. That star was the perfect gentleman and never once came onto me. His wife had just been stolen from him by his best friend, Glen Campbell, and Mac was so shattered by the experience that he said he would never make a move on another man's wife. Filming with him was smooth and without stress. I admired his integrity, and it made me feel safe. Pity the movie was a flop! The flop I had been in in New York still delivered me a Tony nomination. Back East, even if the plays weren't good, if you were good in them, it was noticed and it mattered.

———◆———

THE VACANT AFTERNOONS IN LA turned torturous. While New York had been electric in its towering energy, I found Hollywood to be an enervating, flat pancake, where even my best efforts seemed to vanish like vapor in the relentless sunshine. Even something as simple as spontaneously popping into a cultural event, one of my great joys in Manhattan life, was impossible in LA without a preplanned, often bumper-to-bumper forty-five-minute drive.

So I became a jogger.

"That's *ridiculous!*" Mother said, "What are you running *from*, Tovah?"

I wanted to say, "I'm running from Ray Katz." He was a well-known manager who took me under his wing. I met him through Mac Davis.

He said, "Tovah, my girl, you're too intellectual. This is Hollywood. You need to promote a more sexual side at these meetings. I have an idea. Why don't you *not* wear underwear to your next audition? Not wearing underwear might inspire you to be more sensual in the audition room."

Slamming calm across my face, I replied, "Ray, what is most disturbing about this request is that you are on my team. You only want what's best for me, and *this* is what you think is best for me?"

Let the record show, Ray, that in honor of your memory, I am writing this chapter without a stitch of underwear.

Back then, I was thinking, *I better pack up my Elizabeth Taylor skin and head back to New York.* But I couldn't. I was married, and I had commuted enough to disgust both my mother and my husband. Years later, everyone was in on that joke on the set of *Crazy Ex-Girlfriend.* Alexis Colwell, assistant director, pasted a big picture of Elizabeth Taylor outside my trailer as if it were my headshot with the caption underneath, "Tovah Feldshuh and her Famous Skin!"

———•—•———

ONCE AGAIN, ON THE PHONE with my mother, metaphorically grasping to suckle at her breast, instead of milk, I was met with castor oil.

"Tovah, what is wrong with you? Moving to Hollywood was what you and Andy wanted. Andy uprooted himself to cater to your career. Stop being selfish. Happiness is a choice and so is being miserable, young lady. And I did not raise you to be miserable."

"Mom, let me spell it out for you." Turning to the wall and pounding it with my fist, I said, "My managers keep 'advising' me to bring out my sexuality, not my brain, not my talent. *'Glamour and fuckability'* is the credo out here. That's what sells. Why, Mom? Because I suppose their eye is on the commission, not the career, and certainly not the art. They may hope for art, but that is not their priority. Their priority is 'making the deal and making money.' And Mom, these are the people who are my allies! There's no way you or Daddy or Andy could understand the value system here. *Glamour and fuckability*, Mom!"

There was a seemingly interminable silence on the other end of the line. I wondered if I crossed some unspoken threshold by sharing these truths with her.

Then she spoke.

"If G-d passes over Hollywood, he owes Sodom and Gomorrah a big apology."

Lily's Jewish Haikus

Is one Nobel Prize
So much to ask from a child
After all I've done?

A lovely nose ring,
Excuse me while I put my
Head in the oven.

—The Jewish Standard

There's No Understudy
for a Mother

HERE IS MY FAVORITE CALL THAT I PLACED FROM HOLLYWOOD to my parents:

"Mom, Dad? The rabbit said yes!"

"What?! What is she talking about, Sid?"

"I think she's telling us she's pregnant, Lily."

Indeed, I was. I was already in my second trimester.

"Second trimester? And I'm just hearing about this *now?* I'm glad we didn't have to read it in the newspapers. Are you healthy? Are you big? Send a picture."

"I'm not showing yet, Mom. First baby."

And indeed I wasn't—and wouldn't until the end of my fifth month. At that time in Hollywood, if you were pregnant, you would not be offered work. Unlike today, many actresses hid their bellies until the baby bump popped and it could no longer be camouflaged.

"Mom, Dad? The reason I didn't tell you any sooner is that the day I found out I was pregnant was the day we were leaving for our 'round-the-world trip, so the only people who have known are Andy, our travel agent, and me."

"The travel agent knew before we did?! Sidney, are you hearing this?" she blared. "*Oy, abbruch.*" (Yiddish for what a rupture.)

"He had to know, Mom. He changed our itinerary and got us out of the tropics and into the cold, from Thailand to China."

"Did it ever occur to you *not* to take the trip?"

"What occurred to us, was not to tell you till *after* the trip."

I had been filming *Daniel*, a movie about the Rosenberg trials, which I knew something about having been cross-examined my-self by Roy Cohn. Cohn was one of the prosecuting attorneys on the case who convinced Judge Irving Kaufman to give the Rosenbergs the death sentence. Ironically, this job was my ray of sunshine in the spiritual winter of relentlessly sunny California. Timothy Hutton was starring, Sidney Lumet was directing, and I was late. Not on set. *Never.*

I took the Daisy Home Pregnancy Test and bingo! I held my news close to my heart for twenty-four long hours. I knew that the next day Andrew was flying in from the coast to meet me at Eero Saarinen's sleek new TWA terminal at Kennedy Airport to begin our journey around the world. It was November 27, 1982. Twenty-seven—always my lucky number. He took one look at me and he said, "Oh my G-d, you're pregnant. We're canceling the trip."

I said, "We're getting on the plane." I was determined that Andy and I would take this trip. And we did. After all, traveling with a baby in utero is a very economical way to travel. You don't need a third seat. So we boarded, a reluctant Andy and an overjoyed me with my precious carry-on stowed securely inside.

Somewhere between New York and Paris, ever-practical Andy asked, "How did this happen?"

"Honey, you always ask me if I have protection. But when I flew out to California on October 28 to be with you, it was the one night you didn't say a word."

"Because I thought you were a responsible adult," said Andy.

"Well . . . I saw it as a sign."

"A sign of what?"

"To take matters into my own vagina!" He couldn't help but laugh. Then he started to plan. "The only way we're continuing this trip is to reroute it so that you're safe. The minute we land, we're calling Chaim Curlander." Chaim was our travel agent, a Jewish boy from Baghdad brought up in Calcutta. Another Hollywood story.

Mercifully, Chaim awoke to our middle-of-the-night trans-Atlantic SOS. From our end of the line, standing in the already bustling early-morning activity of Charles de Gaulle Airport, and listening together on a payphone with an inconveniently short black cord, we heard Chaim's ever-soothing, carefully modulated instructions. "For starters, you've got to go someplace where you don't have to take Malaria pills." Then he whispered, "It can cause deafness in the fetus. But no worries, it's easy. I'm pulling you out of Thailand and my hometown, Calcutta, and sending you to Beijing." *Beijing in December,* I thought. *Oh boy.* By some twentieth-century miracle of ingenuity, without Orbitz or email, Chaim Curlander rerouted and rebooked our 'round-the-world adventure all while we were waiting in the Paris airport.

When we landed in Israel on our way to Jerusalem, I cheered, "Let's go to the Old City!"

Andy replied, "Let's go to Hadassah Hospital."

We took the cab ride to Hadassah's Ein Karem campus. It was immense and beautiful—so clean you could eat off the floor. This is the hospital that received the Nobel Peace Prize in 2005 in acknowledgment of its equal treatment of all patients regardless of ethnic and religious differences. We were quickly directed to the OB-GYN floor and met with Dr. Shulamit Levine. She took a second test.

"Mazel tov! You're pregnant!" the doctor said.

"The rabbit said yes?"

"What rabbit, *motek?*" (Sweetie in Hebrew.)

Apparently the science was different in Israel.

Then we went to the Old City! It was a mystical experience to visit ancient, sacred markers of the Jewish people that were proof of our existence and our ancient history that went back thousands of years. Now with child, I was part of carrying that history forward into the next generation, or as the Hebrew saying goes, *"L'Dor V'Dor."*

When we returned to Los Angeles from our trip, thirty-three planes, eight languages, and twenty-six time zones later, with a strong pregnancy in its second trimester, I picked up the phone and called my parents.

While Daddy was demonstratively marveling at the surprise—"Oh, Tovah, Andy, we're thrilled with this news!"—I began to steel myself for the inevitable rain shower Mother was going to bring to this picnic of joy. Was she really going to begrudge me that this baby's prenatal passport had seen more of the world than she?

Instead came an unexpected rupture of excitement. "Then I need to hang up! I have phone calls to make! Sidney, don't talk long. I've gotta call Doris, Shirley, Rose, Nancy, May—" Her clarion trumpet riff ending abruptly, she hung up.

Hearing my mother's singular version of delight was all the caffeine I needed to conquer my jet lag and bounce back to California with renewed zeal.

For the next six months, I had a higher purpose in Hollywood. It just wasn't in movies, television, or theater. I was about to become a mother, and my pregnancy and the birth of Garson Brandon Levy were the happiest months of my life on the West Coast. My parents flew out on my due date, July 25. The baby took three more days to make his entrance.

The birth was *interesting.* That baby boy had the Feldshuh jaw: wide. Or maybe he just didn't want to leave me. At 11:05 p.m. on Thursday,

July 28 (four sevens!) our son was finally yanked out of my womb with an instrument that looked like firewood tongs. As a result, he came out looking like a Conehead from *Saturday Night Live*. Never mind, *"For unto us, a child is born."* Brandon is on the very short list of great unconflicted loves of my life.

At Cedar-Sinai Hospital, in the recovery room soon after Brandon was born, I turned to my husband and said, "Andy, we need to go home. I can't bring a child up in this place. For me, the values are from Krypton. And even if *we* don't share these values, they are everywhere, and I don't know that I will have the strength to protect our son from the Hollywood elements that pervade this town."

I felt a pull, now a mother myself, to return to my mother. Was this thought really happening? Why would this be my first instinct? From deep within me, like some sort of primordial lightning flash, came the realization that this woman had raised me with exactly the wisdom and discipline I found so absent in Hollywood. *These* were the values I wanted imprinted on my son, as they had been imprinted on me. Along with that thought came an inner reassurance to myself, *Tovah, if you are there by Brandon's side,* you *can be the one to give this child the missing maternal nurturing that you had so dearly craved.* With some sort of divine irony, I had the sudden and clear revelation that together, my mother and I could be a force of nature in the rearing of this child.

"Andy," I said, breathless with this new discovery, "I believe, with my overflowing unconditional love, Mom's vast wealth of experience, Dad's unbridled optimism, and you as my rock, with your parents right behind you, this child will have a perfect constellation of support."

Andy looked at me incredulously, shaking his head with an expression that seemed to say, "You're willing to walk back to the scene of the crime?" Then he paused, and a beatific smile came over his face. It was that same adorable expression that radiated in my dressing room on February 16, 1976. After a pause, he said, "If you want to do this, I want to do this. New York lies much closer to your essence, which is family and artistic freedom. New York is not just your preferred home, it's your *essential* home." If I could have gotten out of the hospital bed, I would have given him a standing ovation.

Meanwhile, the happy in-laws and my parents were all in town busily planning the bris. It was a new city to both sets, yet Lily Feldshuh along with Andy's mother, Clarice Levy, were able to source the best caterer in town. The bris took place on August 5, a day so blistering it felt like we were in *Cat on a Hot Tin Roof* by Tennessee Williams.

After the ceremony in our sunny, Spanish living room at 1619 Queens Road, I said, "Mom, Dad, I've never been happier. I loved being pregnant. I was never alone with this baby in my belly, and I'm never alone now. And breastfeeding? It's highly underrated. One beer and your tits pop out like Sophia Loren. The baby gets such beneficial nourishment from your milk, and it feels so good."

"So Mom, Dad, here's the good news. We're coming back to New York! Andy just got a great job at a prestigious law firm in Manhattan. But for the time being, we don't have a place to live. So here's the big ask: can we move in with you?"

Expecting a typical Jewish parent's rapturous affirmative, instead I heard, "How long?"

"Mom!"

"Aren't those movies paying you enough? That you should have to move in with your parents again, at this age?"

"Until we find an apartment!" I said defensively.

Sidney intervened, "Nothing would make us happier. We'll do whatever you need: buy the crib, paint the house, build a wing. Stay as long as you want."

"Sid!" she yelled.

"Mom, Andrew agrees with me that we need to raise this child back east. With grandparents nearby."

"Nearby? We'll be just down the hall!" Lily said.

Sidney whooped, "Won't that be wonderful!"

"Wait a minute," Mom objected, "Won't Andrew be hurting his career?"

Looking back, I realize it was a wild thing to ask of him, but he did it. Thanks to my extraordinarily adaptive husband, we were able to move three thousand miles back east by the spring of 1984. Three law firms by age forty, and he made partner at each—amazing!

Back in Scarsdale, I had my infant son to preoccupy me and the pleasure of giving my parents the endless joy of becoming first-time grandparents. Mom and Dad had me when they were almost forty. Now in the September of their lives, they were reexperiencing their own beginnings through the eyes of the greatest explorer: Brandon.

I knew the first tangible rapprochement with my mother was when I married Andy. Now there was an even bigger step toward our mutual understanding and connection: motherhood. The mortar smoothing the gaps between us was my overwhelming inner peace, the paradigm shift that came with knowing that life, miraculously, was good again. The metaphorical California smog of my soul had lifted and my lungs were being healed with the vibrant oxygen of nearby Manhattan and the neighboring environs of Lilyville.

Moving back to 47 Penn Boulevard, in what could have been a minefield of emotional challenges, was surprisingly seamless. I was thrilled to be in the sanctuary of my parents' dream house. Cautiously at first, I began to bond with my mother in a new, intimate way.

"Mom," I said over morning coffee, marveling as she made her entrance, bedecked in her fitted shirtwaist and daytime pearls. I was reminded that, as ever and always, she had already been to "hair and makeup" by 7:00 a.m., while I sat in a worn Scarsdale High sweatshirt, grateful *not* to be camera-ready at dawn. "We have something new in common, Mom. We both know what it's like to have a baby conceived, formed, and born from our bodies."

"Yes," she said with a touch of warmth, "and now you can appreciate that while you were in me you never sat still. You were a *vants* (Yiddish for running insect). You used to create waves in my belly. I would watch them at night. They were so fascinating, I couldn't sleep. They were also uncomfortable."

"Mom, I apologize if I was a hardship," I batted back. Her having missed my point completely, I made it plainer. "Mom, our lives have intersected!"

"Pardon me while I intersect my coffee with some sugar," she said, deflecting what was intended as a compliment. She got the sugar and pulled up the chair beside me. It was white wrought iron, perfectly painted, and it matched the white wrought-iron glass-top table where my family ate breakfast all my life. My mother always loved light because she loved to look out: big windows that opened out on nature, furniture graced with glass so you could see through and around it, soft translucent colors—pinks and greens and pale blues on ivory polished cotton curtains to bring to mind the flowers, the lawn, and the sky that flourished outside. My mother was a bird peering out upon the world, perhaps "A Bird in a Gilded Cage," as my grandmother Ada used to sing so many years before.

Moving even closer, I could smell her Arpège. "So tell me, Tovahleh, it's just the two of us here. What was *really* so terrible about Hollywood?"

What was really so terrible, Mom, was the pervasive silence. Hollywood was like you, is what I wanted to say. Instead I said, "There were days I couldn't get out of bed, Mom. Even swimming laps didn't help."

"Tovah, I'm gonna admit something to you, and we're about to 'intersect' again. Do you remember when my mother died, February 20, 1959? It was like a veil fell over my spirit."

"I remember, Momma. I was scared. I was only ten."

"You used to come to the bedroom and try to get me up. I'd say, 'Terri Sue, Mommy is doing the best she can.' There were days I couldn't move till afternoon."

Incredulous at her empathy, I said gently, "Yes, Mom, yes. That was the feeling for me too. I'm so sorry. I couldn't have understood how depressed you were."

"Tovah, you were a little girl. That wasn't your job. It was mine to fix. And do you know how I did it?"

"How, Mom?"

"I made up my mind *not* to be in that bed one minute longer. I willed myself to get back into action. Move a muscle, change a thought. Of course, the antidepressant Elavil didn't hurt. I had children to raise and a house to run and a husband who relied on me. It was *nonsense* to stay in that bed. My mother Ada would've spanked me. The sadness didn't go away, but the activity helped bring me back to life. Family, Tovah, family. Family first. And *that's* why you're feeling better right now. *There's* your intersection, Miss Fancy."

It was surreal to be back in my mother's orbit. It was as if she were filling me with helium that said, "Welcome home," even if a minute later she would puncture that balloon with her criticism. Nevertheless, there I was, deliciously beginning to defy the gravity that had held me earthbound and distraught out west. If I had to choose between Hollywood and Lily's criticisms, I chose Lily.

From April to September, we passed a smooth summer at 47 Penn—well, with a few bumps in the road. I called it a POA, period of adjustment, but it sure didn't feel like that when it happened.

One July afternoon, Mom had offered to watch Brandon so that I could take a walk past Quaker Ridge and retrace some footsteps from my own childhood. Sad that my English racer was no longer in the garage, I carefully walked along the Weaver Street gutter I had so skillfully biked every day in the sixth grade to get to school. Then I noticed the town had built a beautiful asphalt walking path so no child had to be afraid of being hit by a car on that two-lane highway anymore. I ran around the green manicured fields upon which I once played soccer and baseball. I remembered how I hated baseball. My position was shortstop, and once, in sixth grade, the ball banged me smack in the chin. I wailed. The ball was too hard, and the game was too slow. Baseball made me nervous—let David have dreams of Mickey Mantle, not me!

After a three-mile run around the sports fields, I cooled down on the huge circular driveway of Quaker Ridge where we once took our bicycle tests. Bicycle Day was our favorite day. The obstacle course was set up by the police department and the faculty to make sure we could master our bikes, and ice cream was served afterward—Good Humor ice cream, thanks to the generosity of my pal Lulu's father. Then I walked back home, absolutely invigorated by the memories I visited leaping back in time.

Now on the asphalt path, I thought, *It's 1984. I'm married, have a son, have starred on Broadway and struggled in Hollywood, and here I am coming home, returning to the source of the hidden nipple, the breast my mother tucked away six weeks after I was born.* Even at thirty-five years old, I couldn't wait to walk in the utility room door of 47 Penn and wipe my feet first on the horsehair mat that never said, "Welcome," but got the dirt off my sneakers (which was a requirement), to see my mother. I knew she'd be cooing over Brandon. I knew we were both members of the Mutual Adoration Society of G. Brandon Levy.

I walked in the door and there was my mother, spoon-feeding butter-pecan ice cream to Brandon, not an hour before his dinner time.

"Mom, what are you doing?!" snapped out of my mouth before I could temper my tone, my anger flaring. "Ice cream? Really?!" I said, swooping in to remove the spoon from her hand and snatch the bowl that sat between them.

Brandon immediately burst into tears, and my mother stood up defiantly. "Tovah, what is wrong with you? Look what you've done! We were having an absolutely wonderful time until you walked in the door."

"Mother," I said as I efficiently wet a kitchen towel and returned to Brandon to wipe his mouth, "Andy and I have purposely not introduced this boy to sugar the first year of his life. It was our decision. We did it for a reason."

"Well then, you should've made that clear."

"I thought I did."

"You know I'm hard of hearing."

"Hard of hearing, or *selective* of hearing?"

Now exasperated by the scene unfolding, and my son crying from my terse directives, Mother stood up and took us from the frying pan to the fire.

"Listen here, young lady. I know a thing or two about raising children. You and David ain't so bad, though how I ever raised a daughter to speak to her mother like this I'll never know. Remember, I gave you your life, and what's more, I was doing you a favor watching Brandon. Secondly, need I remind you that you are a guest in this house, and most importantly, it's *just ice cream*. And he loves it. Everybody loves it. Children are supposed to love ice cream. Your father lives on butter pecan."

I bit back. "Mom, not only is the sugar terrible for him, but he can choke on the pecans! He only has four teeth! I'm grateful he's breathing! And it's not just the ice cream, Mom," I continued, the heat rushing to my face and my solar plexus fluttering like an electric current. "It's the respect. You've been sneaking this boy chocolate chip cookies and even Daddy's hidden stash of Mallomars every time you think we're not looking. You will addict him to sugar. He's going to have the same terrible mood swings as Aunt Rose—or *you* when you're not taking your antidepressants. We want to spare him that."

She marched to the sink, the sound of her Cuban heels underscoring her rising temper. "I'm going to wash my hands of this," she said, literally washing her hands. "You and Andy can make up your rules and try to tamp this child into some Nobel Laureate of perfection, but children are meant to be children. It's the only time in their life when they're not worried. Please don't tell me how to do something that I already do quite well on my own, thank you, and considering our forty-year difference in age, Miss Broadway actress, perhaps I know more about mothering than you. On top of which, Daddy and I opened our hearts and our home to you without a peep."

"Mom, you peeped."

"That wasn't a peep. It was a chirp. You think you can just swoop in here with your rules, and that makes you the all-knowing mother?"

"Mother, the science is different today. Just like the path on Weaver Street that used to be a gutter and is now a perfect asphalt walkway. There are safety considerations you are not aware of—"

"Don't end a sentence with a preposition."

"Fine!" I yelled, exasperated. "There are safety considerations *of which you are not aware*! Satisfied? And parents today can make more informed choices on bringing up our kids."

"More informed choices?" she said, busying herself with her recipe cards at the yellow Formica kitchen desk, as if to minimize the assault she was about to launch. "Galavanting around the world while you're pregnant? Not having your own home in New York and landing at 47 Penn with an eight-month-old? Making rules up about one of our greatest pleasures, sugar? What's next? No playing outside? G-d forbid he should climb a tree. Have you forgotten who you are? How you would hang upside down on Dr. Clark's apple tree? Climb the street poles of the neighborhood? Speed down Franklin Hill, no hands? Go flying off your swing set? Then obsessively hang upside down on that trapeze bar?" Snapping the gray recipe box closed with a metal bang, she turned to me for her final assail. "You're ridiculous. Mothers have been raising their children perfectly without science for generations."

She repeated dismissively under her breath, "Ridiculous."

Steeling myself, I said as calmly as possible, "Mother, Andy and I are grateful to be *guests* in your home,"—how that word pierced me—"but how we raise our child is our business. Please respect our choices."

Undeterred, Mom continued, "Let me tell you something I can predict as plain as the nose on my face: you are going to get a job, maybe a movie in Hollywood or a Broadway play, and then watch what happens. You're going to leave him behind. You've got your nanny, right? And you've got your blessed husband, who like me, is there, dependably, every night. You with your women's-lib values, with your gender-equality rights, think you have it all. But you don't have it all, Tovah. You're just lucky you've got two substitutes for you the next time your career comes knocking. Remember, my daughter, *there's no understudy for a mother.* You leave this child for your famous employment, and mark my words, he will be scarred. This to me is selfish. But then again, your whole generation seems selfish."

And here comes the caboose of the guilt train: "Your grandmother gave up her dream of being an actress when she became a wife and a mother. Her theatrical dream turned to ashes on Seventeenth and Second Avenue. I gave up my dream of getting my master's degree because it never occurred to me that I would be entitled to be a teacher as well as a wife."

I inserted, "I gave up getting my master's degree because David told me I didn't need one to be an actress."

She responded, "That's not the same, and it was a stupid choice. You didn't have to listen. And you never discussed it with Daddy or me. I would've never advised you not to complete your degree. The point is: I was there. Look, I may not say 'I love you' ten times a day, but I was *there.* I gave you a home you could depend on, rain or shine."

"Well, remember the bunny incident?"

"Please! Once! I was late for you *once!* Stability, Tovah. Dependability. That's not science, that's common sense. Your child either comes first or he does not." Her tone and her words lacerated me.

I erupted. "Then why didn't you make me feel that I came first? The only thing that came first in my childhood were the rules. Now with Brandon you're breaking all of them!"

Silently pulling the freezer door open, then firmly putting the butter pecan back in its place, she added, "Ice cream is the *least* of this child's worries."

Brandon, clearly responding to the heated electricity sparking between Mother and me, was inconsolable.

I said, "Mom, where did you put his Boppie?" (His blankie.)

She responded, "On the counter. He doesn't need his Boppie when he's with me."

Ouch.

I grabbed the Boppie, went to his high chair, gently stroked his hair, leaned into him, and quietly cooed, "Sha, sha, my *laben* (my life in Yiddish). Sha, sha." I picked him up, putting my hand on his little *keppie* (head in Yiddish), and resting his head on my shoulder, I glared at Mother and said, "Mother, look what we've done to Brandon."

"*We've* done? Ridiculous! Who's the one who made this baby cry? Not me." And with that she sternly marched out of the kitchen and down the long hall to the master bedroom.

I turned to my boy and apologized, "Sweetheart, forgive me. I didn't mean to upset you. I was angry with Gramee, not with you. You did nothing wrong." I softly dabbed his tears and sat him on the kitchen counter.

Holding his little waist, I said, "OK Brandon, even though you're not talking much just yet, I know you're probably understanding all of this. Bwan, you're my lucky charm, you're my life changer, and holding you in my arms is going to give me the strength to do something that's a little tough for Mommy. So can you help me, my beautiful baby boy?" A smile began to form on his face. Then in my best singsong silliness—I could never stop singing around my children—I began "The Brandon Song" (my nickname for him was Bougie, which means candlelight in French, and is pronounced "Boujee"):

> *You are my little bougie*
> *My bougie, bougie, boy*
> *You are your mommy's dream child,*
> *You are your mommy's joy!*
> *You are my bougie*
> *My bougie baby*
> *You are my bougie, bougie, bougie . . .*

Get the audiobook.

By this time he was beaming. Holding him in my arms, I began to follow my mother's path from the kitchen down that long corridor I knew so well to her master bedroom. All the while I whispered to him, "I've got to make this right with Gramee, Bwan. We love her and she was only doing what Gramees do because she loves you." Taking a deep breath, "I'm also going to teach you how we apologize. These may be the five hardest words to say: 'I was wrong. I'm sorry.'" Tentatively, I tapped on Mother's bedroom door.

"Mom, may I have a word with you, please?"

"Come in, Terri Sue," came her reply, both infantilizing and chastising me for changing my name from the beautiful one she had given me.

I slowly opened her door, which was painted heroic blue, and, with babe in arms, hoping the sight of Brandon would be an olive branch, I saw Mother reclined on her chaise lounge, looking deflated.

I said, "Mommy, I was wrong to speak to you that way. Very wrong. Please forgive me. We are so . . . *I* am so grateful for all you do for us. Yes, it's our preference that Brandon not have sugar. And I know this is just your way of loving him. Could you possibly find *another* way?"

Did she even realize how painful it was for me to see her far more demonstrative with my baby than she had ever been with me? How she delighted in holding him, singing to him, and telling him how "*gawgeous*" he was? While with me, my mother had been stingy with compliments—"selfish and foolish" seemed to be her choice words in my childhood.

I held my tongue, I held my son, and I continued. "I know you just want what's best for him. Just please don't make me the bad cop and you the good cop. OK?"

Now sitting up erect, as if the last twenty minutes hadn't happened, Mother piped, "Oh, forget about it. Grandmas dole out the treats. Parents dole out the discipline. We're good. Now bring that baby back to his Gramee. Come here, sweetheart!"

I SET ABOUT TO PROVE to my mother that though the umbilical cord may have been physically severed at birth, this boy and I were inseparable. More than that, I was an excellent, vigilant mother.

On one memorable afternoon, as I was helicoptering dutifully, I hovered over Brandon, who was playing peacefully on the living room floor with the afternoon sun framing his body in a serene rectangle of warmth. "Peekaboo," I called from above. No response. "Bwannnnndon, peekaboo," I cajoled, slightly louder. Again, no response. He must be concentrating. "Brandon!" I barked. Again he continued with his toys, without budging. I thought to myself, "That's it, he's deaf." I ran to Mother's Formica kitchen desk and grabbed the Manhattan Yellow Pages, the larger of the two phone books neatly tucked in her filing cabinet. Quickly returning to my baby boy, I repeated in alarm, "Brandon! Brandon! BRANDON!" I held the cumbersome book up high and released it, letting it thump to the ground, careful to miss his beautiful little head.

He didn't budge. Panic mode. Leave it to my Jewish DNA to jump from serenity to calamity in a nanosecond. Fingers shaking as I navigated my mother's rotary phone, I called our family doctor, Robert Newburger, immediately. He said, "First of all, Terri, calm down. Breathe! Let me get you the name of the audiologist at White Plains Hospital." I scribbled the details down, scooped my boy up, put him in his car seat, and off we went, as close to the speed limit as I could possibly restrain myself. An interminable half hour later, Brandon finally got his hearing test.

In the medical office, I explained, "Dr. Wondro, I took malaria pills in the first month of pregnancy for a trip around the world before I knew that the chloroquine phosphate in it can cause deafness in a fetus." Then I confessed, "Today I dropped a phone book near his head and he was unresponsive."

Dr. Wondro shook his head quizzically. "Did it ever occur to you that you might have a calm baby, Mrs. Levy? Brandon's hearing is perfect, but *you* should go see a psychiatrist."

At dinner that night, I proudly told the family, "Brandon's hearing is perfect!" I left out the part about the psychiatrist.

My mother was wrong about one thing. For those first eighteen months of Brandon's life, the bright lights of Broadway that once called to me like a siren's song from just over Lily's shoulder began to lose their allure. It was like losing a taste for my favorite food. Indeed, I chose not to go back to what was once my salvation: the New York stage. Once I had a baby, I wanted nothing more than to be by Brandon's side. It was primal. He was the dazzling *son* around which our constellation revolved. With Andrew, my mother, my father, and me day in, day out, Brandon flourished, and I floated in the cloud nine of motherhood for eighteen months.

Mom and I both believed that children came first. The only differentiating factor that lurked in the shadows was: I was a mother who loved her kids, but also loved her art. Lily was a *balabusta* (Yiddish for house executive) turned *bubbe* (Yiddish for grandmother).

And then it came. The test that Lily so caustically predicted. In the fall of 1984, I was offered the lead role of Kate Hardcastle in *She Stoops to Conquer*, opposite Nathan Lane for the Roundabout Theatre Company.

"Would you turn down a show opposite Nathan Lane?" I asked my toddler. Now sure that he could hear, his silence said everything.

"Did you know, my son, when you were in Mommy's belly, I had a dream that your name was 'Broadway Levy,' not Brandon? And when I told my friends this dream, all our baby showers in Los Angeles were festooned with 'Welcome Broadway Levy' printed on the napkins, the balloons, the cakes, and even on gifts. I knew from that moment, you were destined to bring me 'back to the boards.' You were my good-luck charm. Without you, we might have never moved back East."

As for telling my mother about the Roundabout offer, I didn't discuss it with her. People have asked me if Lily was a typical stage mother. I have to laugh. If anything, she was an *off*-stage mother—she wanted me *off* the stage!

With timing from the heavens, Andy and I found our first New York apartment right before the beginning of rehearsals. I was to be given a reprieve from the acrid scent of disapproval that I knew would emanate from Mother if I began commuting from Scarsdale to Broadway, leaving Brandon behind.

"It's a glassed-in bird's nest," Mom said, stepping into 110 Riverside Drive for the first time. "I love it! Look at that view of the Hudson River. South *and* west! Have you tested the water pressure?" she began as she counted the electric outlets and tested the closet doors. "Put on all the spigots! Flush all the toilets! Where's the kitchen? What kind of stove?" She entered the kitchen. "Oy, this place is perfect. Buy it."

I added, "Mom, you won't believe it, but Babe Ruth lived in this building."

"It's a sign! One of my most thrilling memories was on my twelfth birthday, April 18, 1923." I chimed in in unison to finish the familiar sentence, "Yankee Stadium opened its doors."

She laughed, then frowned and said, "Riverside Drive. Impossible to get a taxi."

Still forever reaching for the Lily seal of approval, what better way to demonstrate to Lily that I was a good mother than by having a second child? Andy and I were at gorgeous Canyon Ranch in Arizona. It was the very end of May 1987. I had already had, not suffered but *had*, two miscarriages: one during the run of *A Shayna Maidl* ("A Beautiful Maiden") and one while skiing in Aspen. They were both very early in the pregnancies. Lily always said, "Don't worry about miscarriages. G-d throws out the bad ones to keep the good." That one sentence saved me hours of guilt and grief. I was just grateful that every time Andy looked at me, I got pregnant.

This pregnancy stuck, and in 1988, we were blessed with a beautiful little daughter, who was supposed to come out of her mother's womb around February 9. It was a Tuesday. It came and went. So did Wednesday, Thursday, Friday, Saturday, Sunday. . . . *Where is this little girl?* I thought. She was going to be named Amanda Claire after her great-grandmother, Ada Kaplan. It is Jewish tradition to name our children after the honored dead, connecting our forebears to immortality. Amanda Claire and Ada Kaplan would share the same Hebrew name—Adah, or "nobility."

Ada, as I mentioned before, died February 20, 1959—she was on her way to a poker game after a doctor's appointment. Wouldn't you know it, Amanda Claire waited eleven days until February 20, 1988, to be born on Ada's *yahrzeit*, the anniversary of her death. Perhaps there are no coincidences.

On the twentieth of February, I was reclining on a family heirloom, a swooning couch (can't get more dramatic than that!), and I was dictating to my beloved assistant, Wendy Radford: "Please take a letter to Orsid Realty and tell them we need to renovate the kitchen with a new rubber floor because I have a toddler who needs to drop things, and I have a baby on the way." Then the worst menstrual cramp ripped through me. "Ow!"

Wendy exclaimed, "Tovah, it's beginning. You're already eleven days late."

"Let me just finish dictating this letter," I said. Between cramps, which I refused to see as contractions, I gave a call to my ob-gyn, Dr. Hutson. He said, "Ms. Feldshuh, this is your second child. Please get to the hospital ASAP." That was at 5:00 p.m. Andy said firmly, "We're going!"

I said, "Just let me finish my letter!" By 6:00 p.m., at his insistence, he drove us in the trusty old forest-green Mercedes to New York Hospital.

By the time we arrived, Dr. Hutson examined me, and he said, "You're already five centimeters dilated."

"That's nice," I replied. "Can I please have an epidural? This is no party."

Staying very calm, Dr. Hutson said, "Let me look for my favorite anesthesiologist." Ten interminable minutes later, he came back and said, "You know, I can't find him. Let me just double-check in the OR."

Stopping him as he turned to leave, I yelped, "Doctor! I'm in full-out labor! Listen to me," I pleaded, trying to reel him in with the laser focus

I usually reserved for the stage, "I've been a good girl. I have not smoked marijuana since 1977. Do *not* walk out that door unless you promise to bring me—" The last words were swallowed by the arrival of a wrenching contraction. I felt like I was on the wave of the wrong surfboard.

As he left, Andy, garbed in a hospital gown and cap, looking unsettlingly like Hutson, calmly intoned, "Tovah, inhale expand, exhale release. Inhale expand, exhale release."

"I know! Like a rose, like a rose!" I screamed. Now snarling, "Are they crazy? *This* is state of the art medical care? Oh, my G-d!" Trying to calm me down, Andy said, "Puff, puff!"

Puffing rapidly through my pursed lips, "Fooo foooo, fooo, foooo, this is fucking ridiculous!"

Finally the door of the birthing room opened, and in came the doctor, again alone, again empty-handed. Before he could utter a syllable, I wailed, "Oh, you've got to be kidding me. Really? Nothing? Nobody?"

Then came five words no person anywhere should ever have to hear, "It's too late for anesthesia."

"Can we get a second opinion!?" I wailed. He smiled and said, "no," as he began the preparations to deliver the baby right then, right there. *They lied to us about natural childbirth. Painful? This is like pulling my lips over my head. And don't give me this BS about "second child."* And then it hit me: "You *lied* to me! This was all a ruse to trick me into delivering this child without an epi-*dural!*"

Hutson wasn't listening, he was calmly pressing an intercom to summon a nurse.

"I'm sorry, Mrs. Levy, but we knew immediately you were too far along for an epidural. Now push, please. Deep breath in, and push. *Push!*"

Push? I wanted to smack him. Instead I pushed. I pushed, thinking, *This is for lying to me.* I pushed, thinking, *This is for every birthing coach who lied to me about this pain.* I pushed, thinking, *THIS, Tovah, is for you and that fucking dictation*, knowing full well my own obstinance was the real culprit in this scenario.

I pushed two more times, and out the baby popped like a greased football.

Out went the pain like a tidal wave of relief, and in came a tidal wave of exhilaration and wonder. "Look at her! Look at her! What time is it? What's the exact minute?"

"It's 8:25 p.m., Mrs. Levy," came the nurse's reply, as she wiped, weighed, and swaddled Amanda Claire.

"Andy! Just like Mom before me, both of us at age thirty-nine and both of us on the Upper East Side gave birth to our daughters in just two hours."

"Look at this baby, Tov," Andy marveled.

She was pale blonde and blue eyed and her skin was made of alabaster. You could see all her veins and arteries. No question, Amanda Claire, like her Hebrew name denoted, was a real blue blood.

Calling to the doctor, now suddenly my new best friend, I said, "She looks just like my mother, so beautiful," as if he had some role in that part of the delivery. "Dr. Hutson," I said, "You've delivered a baby who will always remind me of my mother. Whenever I miss her, all I have to do is look at the face of Amanda Claire. It's a miracle."

If I ever needed proof of the power of genetics, it came to me the moment I gave birth to our children. Each came out with a distinct personality, different from the other, that rings true to who they are to this very day. Brandon didn't want to leave me and had to be pulled from my body with salad servers (which the doctor insisted on calling forceps). When he emerged, he was completely calm and never cried. I actually said, "Check his breathing." In an emergency, you want Brandon Levy on your team.

Amanda was eager to get out, and was born inside of two hours. When she emerged, she cried like a fire alarm. She was as emotionally sensitive as her delicate appearance foretold. When you want to gauge a room, flank Amanda Levy.

I can only describe the intense period of motherhood that followed in theater terms. When a show is in technical rehearsal—the grueling preparatory stage of mounting it that involves focusing every light for every scene, setting every sound cue and set change, wrestling with wardrobe that suddenly is too constricting or too intricate for the necessary quick costume changes—this nightmare is called "ten out of twelve," meaning the work days are twelve hours long, and the actors are hostage for ten of those hours until the job gets done and the show is locked. It's an endless problem-solving process, which becomes understandably exhausting because it is rigorous, sometimes thrilling, and sometimes disheartening. But the job gets done.

Motherhood is all of that, only the schedule isn't ten out of twelve . . . it's 24-7 . . . and the job is never done.

My baby boy Brandon was four years, five months old when we brought his little sister Amanda home in our arms from New York Hospital on February 22, 1988.

A few months later, I was diapering her on the changing table when her big brother pointed to Amanda's privates and said, "Mommy, Mommy, what dis, what dis?" I said, "Brandon, that's Amanda's magic button. Now you listen to Mommy. When you get older, women love three things: poetry, roses, and always take care of the magic button."

Skip forward to a phone call from Brandon, now all grown up and in love with his first sweetheart.

"Mom, we're in love and we're together."

"What do you mean together, son? Do you mean for coffee, for classes, or . . . biblically?"

"The last one, Mom," he said with understandable hesitance. I smiled, knowing not many sons share such news with their mothers. "And Mom, no worries," he said proudly, "I took care of the magic button."

Ahhh, thought I, *Mother's little dividend. Some lucky girl is getting a genuine mensch in the bedroom. Well done, Tovah.* But I only said, "Well done, Brandon. Thank you for letting me know."

Then, before I could help myself, I asked, "And is she Jewish?"

Looking back on these days, they are a swirl of gazing lovingly into my children's eyes, except for one afternoon. We were walking in Riverside Park at Eighty-Third Street, where Brandon's favorite playground was. I had Amanda in the stroller and Brandon had just pulled away from my hand to race ahead to the jungle gym. Interrupting this bliss came one of my well-intentioned neighbors, sporting a shock of red hair, a color nature never knew, with neon eye makeup much too busy for day wear, and her face wrenched in exaggerated concern. "Tovah Feldshuh!" she said in a voice loud enough to be sure that all the mothers took notice. "What's happened to you? We used to love your work. Have you retired?"

"This is what motherhood looks like," I answered, smiling, while thinking *fuck you*. "These children? You're looking at my best work!"

And as I pushed past her with my stroller to meet Pirate Brandon, now on the bow of his jungle-gym ship, I flipped my hair back and called over my shoulder so all the mothers could hear, "Go ahead, keep watching. This is the greatest role of my career." And off I went with my cubs.

INDEED, I HAD NOT RETIRED. A few seasons later, I went back to Broadway just in time to potty train my irresistible Amanda backstage. One of the happiest, wildest experiences of my career was playing Maria Merelli in Ken Ludwig's *Lend Me a Tenor*. Everything was first-class, including the cast. Victor Garber, Philip Bosco—who won the Tony for Best Actor—Ron Holgate, J. Smith-Cameron, Caroline Lagerfelt, and Jane Connell. And as the butler, Jeff Brooks stole the show every time he was onstage. We rehearsed at the opulent 42nd Street Studios, home to rehearsals for the American Ballet Theatre and big-budget Broadway musicals. It felt like the A-Team right from the start.

William Ivey Long had our wardrobe made at Carelli Costumes and our shoes handmade in Cleveland, where the play takes place. I had a large, blue fox collar on my passionate purple costume, and the director didn't think it was big enough, so Ivey Long went back to purchase the deluxe version. I had a hat with plumage that made me look six feet tall.

We had to convince PETA that no birds were harmed in the making of this millinery marvel. That hat-trick didn't fly.

I remember my fitting at Carelli's. William Ivey Long asked, "How would you like to look?" And I said, "Wide shoulders, small waist, an Italian derrière, and big breasts," as if I were ordering off a menu in a three-star Italian restaurant. He replied, "Done." And it was.

Our producer, Martin Starger, brought movie money to the show. Marty had enough financial cushion to bring the production from an A to an A-plush. I'd never been in the lap of such a pleasant success. At our opening-night party, I sat with the likes of Placido Domingo and Prince Edward of England. I'm so grateful that the vehicle was running so smoothly because, underneath me, the road was bumpy.

We were out of town in our ten-out-of-twelve technical rehearsals preparing to open in seventy-two hours at the Mechanic Theatre in Baltimore. I was offstage left, waiting to enter, when my cell phone vibrated on the prop table. The stage manager looked at me askance, but what mother doesn't keep a phone near her? My heart jumped when I saw the Caller ID. I picked up my brick of a cell phone, cupped my hand over the receiver, and in my best stage whisper, said, "Dr. Kahn?"

"Tovah, Brandon's come down with scarlet fever. It's going to be fine, but I thought you should know."

I said, "*Know?* I'm on my way."

I then turned to the stage manager and said, "May I please speak to Jerry? It's about one of my children."

I went out into the house. Surprised, my major mensch director Jerry Zaks said, "Everything OK?"

I said, "Brandon's sick." And before I could even get out the words "scarlet fever," he said, "Go." You can say a lot of things about theater people, but in that moment, Jerry was responding to an unwritten code of ethics that transcends the dictates of show business. It's as if we spoke a secret language: instead of "the show must go on," it was "family comes first."

"Go get the train immediately, *dahlink*," as only Jerry could say it. And I ran from the Mechanic Theatre to Baltimore's Penn Station and took the next Metroliner up. As I burst into 110 Riverside, Andy met me with, "No worries. I got him to the pediatrician, he's taking antibiotics. He'll be fine." Not stopping my pace, I continued directly to the nursery. "My G-d, Andy, Brandon's as red as a beet." I touched his burning face. "What's his temperature?" I kneeled down so I could put my face near his and grabbed the cold compress next to the bed. I leaned in and sang quietly in his ear, "You are my Bougie Brandon, my Brandon, Brandon boy . . . ," my voice dissolving into tears from guilt as much as from concern.

Andy came over to me, giving me the thermometer, and stroking my hair said, "It's going to be fine."

"We don't know it's going to be fine," I said, placing the thermometer in Brandon's mouth and leaning in and whispering, "Mommy loves you just because you breathe. Mommy loves you just because you breathe." *So just keep breathing, Brandon.*

After checking on our little Amanda to make sure at least one of my children was OK, I sat vigil by Brandon's bed, still in my travel clothes. Soon, Andy brought the phone in along with a cup of Throat Coat tea, mouthing to me, "It's your mother."

"Scarlet fever?" exclaimed Lily. "Your Aunt Nancy almost died from that. Put the phone by Brandon's ear. I want to talk to him."

"Brandon *dahlink*," now sounding as warm as Jerry Zaks, "It's Gramee. I love you sweetheart. Just remember who you are. We're a strong bunch. You're gonna get well, and you're gonna stay well. You're Brandon Levy. Now, put your mother on."

There wasn't a "please" or a "thank you" within a ten-mile radius of my mother's mouth. As Brandon handed me the phone, I motioned for Andy to stay and went into the hallway.

"Tovah, wake up! What's the matter with you? You have no business being in Baltimore with two young children in New York."

"I come home every Monday."

"Not enough."

"You're not helping right now. All of our energy should be focused on Brandon."

"Exactly. In this family, if you can't raise your children, you're a flea."

And I could see my mother flicking her hand on top of her left shoulder as if she were flicking off a speck of dirt.

"And where's your eighteen-month-old daughter? Is she happy seeing you only on Mondays?"

I clenched my jaw. There was no way I was going to be considered a flea in Mother's eyes. "Mother, Andy and I are excellent parents. Brandon's getting better now. We have the antibiotics. And Amanda was with me all last weekend."

"Weekend? Humph," my mother muttered. "Are you still going back to Baltimore?"

Tail between my legs, I answered, "Yes."

Silence

Guilty as Jewish hell, I went back to Baltimore. Brandon did get better, and the episode lives as one more black mark in Mother's invisible scorecard of my shortcomings as a parent.

She could've kept that scoreboard out for the entire run of *Lend Me a Tenor* because there were two more black marks on the way.

"You're toilet training your daughter *where?*"

"In the dressing room, Ma."

"That's ridiculous."

"No it's not, it's eccentric." It was also memorable—an event the cast members would never forget, nor would my mother. Nonetheless, I adored having my baby girl with me whenever possible.

The third black mark and the blind curve on the bumpy road was Brandon's reading. He was six-and-a-half now.

"What do you mean he can't read?" my mother hollered.

"It has come to our attention that his reading is not where it should be for his age, and we are addressing it."

"Ridiculous. What's going on in that house? Does this child even *have* a mother?"

And when I said we were addressing it, that was a euphemism for the afternoon that I officially became "one of those mothers" at Collegiate School. I marched myself into the office of the head of the lower school at the appointed hour, steeling myself with a page from Bette Davis's playbook and wearing my best casual yet crisp pantsuit. I greeted Ms. Tashlich as if it were a job interview and she were the applicant.

"Ms. Tashlich," I began. "Has no one in your school realized that Brandon is not reading yet? That he does not recognize vowels or consonants and that he is not decoding language? And that we are almost at the end of first grade?"

"We're trying a new reading program, Mrs. Levy, called the Whole Reading Program."

"Really?" I responded. "Would that be hole, as in H-O-L-E, to indicate 'there is a *hole* in his education'?"

She reasoned, "Twenty out of the forty boys haven't figured out this Whole Reading Program."

"And that's not the first clue you have a problem?" I bored in on the interrogation.

"Don't worry, he'll learn to read in second grade."

I replied, "He'll learn to read in the next six weeks because I'm getting him a tutor. I was counting on Collegiate to deliver a classical education on which we could depend."

Then, calling upon my best Katharine Hepburn reserves, and so as not to lose the intensity of my purpose, I shook Ms. Tashlich's hand only once quite firmly and said succinctly, "I appreciate your making this time in your busy schedule." And then, not being able to resist, I added, "Remember, I'm only a phone call away." Finally, conjuring my Guthrie training, I willed my presence up to "the height of skyscraper," all five foot two of me turned, crossed the room, closed the door behind me without looking back, and stood on the other side, imagining the exit applause for this private matinee.

Sitting down for tea with Mother at 47 Penn, I proudly told her of my prowess wrangling Ms. Tashlich. I said to Mother, "How ironic that Beth Tashlich's last name is the same word for the High Holiday tradition, *Tashlich.*" This is where we cast small crumbs of bread into a body of water as we name our many sins from the past year.

Shaking her head, Mom interrupted, "Brandon hasn't learned to read yet? Forget the breadcrumbs! Send Tashlich a *loaf*!"

The following day, I hired a highly recommended reading tutor for Brandon who taught our son to read in just six weeks.

Why did I go to the extra expense to make sure our son could read immediately? Because Jewish mothers do not settle for ignorant children. Intellectual intelligence is not an amusement for us; it is a survival skill. A Jewish mind is to be sharpened to a fine point like a beautifully honed pencil. A Jewish mind has to be trained to consider all factors in a society, both national and international, in order to gauge whether or not he or she is safe. Jewish children have to be taught to use their wits, should the stain of anti-Semitism return to mar a nation. Does this burden the Jewish psyche? You bet it does—so we need an early start.

In the *cheiders* (small Jewish elementary schools in Eastern Europe which usually met in the synagogue) on the first day of school, the teacher (or *malamud*) would take each child upon his lap and put honey on the Hebrew alphabet written on the child's slate. The *rebbe* would then invite the fledgling scholar to lick the honey off the *Aleph-Bais* (the ABCs). That way, the child would always remember that learning is sweet.

In his eleventh and twelfth grades, determined to be present in this boy's life at every possible opportunity, I volunteered to be the team mother for Collegiate soccer, basketball, and baseball, all of which Brandon captained his senior year. During the baseball season, after two weeks of bringing the preordained fresh strawberries to be served during the seventh-inning stretch, I thought to myself, "Well, this is deadly dull. What these boys need is a little *fress!*" (Yiddish for snack.) "Let me see . . . William's Barbecue should do it." The delight on the boys' faces the first day they swarmed around my folding card table, propped on the sidelines with a gingham tablecloth, and saw the designated strawberries *and* the platters of barbecued chicken was priceless.

By the third game, Coach Paul Mankowich pulled me aside and said, "Mrs. Levy, I know you mean well. But have you looked at how they're playing after all this food? The seventh inning is going down the tubes—they can hardly move. You're killing us, Mrs. Levy! Please, please," he pleaded, "If you have to shake it up, bring some carrots."

"Absolutely coach, duly noted, yessir!" I responded, duly shamed. "I'm on it. Never again," glancing over at Brandon who looked mortified to see his mother getting a dressing down from the coach.

On the way home he implored, "Really, Mom? Really? It had to be *my* mom getting a lecture from Coach Mankowich?" Glancing in the rearview mirror at Brandon but really seeing the specter of Lily, the omnipresent backseat driver of my life, I replied, "Brandon, always look for the ways you can meet and surpass an expectation. Underpromise; overdeliver!" With a triumphant Auntie Mame flourish, I said, "Those boys will forever remember the games they were given William's Barbecue chicken instead of just strawberries! People remember how you made them *feel* . . . and we made them feel *great!*"

Thereafter, in the spirit of compromise, I served the chicken *after* the game.

With Amanda, I had much the same approach, mindfully choosing activities for her that demanded the presence of the mother—not the babysitter—in the room. Somehow, while playing Tallulah Bankhead off-Broadway by night, I was able to be at her Suzuki piano lessons, I volunteered to coach her soccer team, and I watched Amanda get accepted at The School of American Ballet, no small feat (pun intended). All on her own, she was invited to join the children's corps of the New York City Ballet. While I was playing houses of two hundred, my brilliant daughter was playing houses of two thousand. Brava!

In film, we have the "crane shot"; the camera is perched atop a crane maneuvered from below to capture an aerial view of the action in a scene. That was how motherhood felt under the watchful gaze of Lily. She was my crane shot, whether she was in the room or not. Looming above, ever-observant of my choices and dialogue, Lily was present in every scene unfolding in my children's upbringing. I was going to prove to her, as her ever-critical gaze bore down on me, that I was an excellent mother, and arguably better than she. These children were going to remember not only what I did, but how I made them *feel*. They were going to fully know what it felt like to be loved unconditionally.

This was the intention I carried into my "scenes" with my cubs, as if to anticipate my mother's judgment. Silently directing myself, I'd call, *Action, Tovah! Get these scenes right. Get these lines spoken impeccably.* If there were a misstep or a line with an inflection that was tone-deaf, I'd call, *Cut! Let's do a retake! We're going to do this till I get it right.* My motivation? Simple. All the while I'm thinking, *Brandon, Amanda, you are loved. Unconditionally.*

So watch me, Mother. Watch how it's done. Watch how it can *be done.*

Did I get it right *every* time? No. Let's just say I'm perfectly imperfect.

After pulling her average up from a ninety-two to a ninety-six at the Spence School in Manhattan, after getting into MIT, Amanda came to me in her freshman year and said, "Mom, I'm majoring in physics," expecting an eruption of pride and a standing ovation. My reply? "Physics? How are you going to make a living?" *Oops! Was I channeling Lily?*

It should be noted nonetheless that all these years later, I have the gift of a daughter who says to me, "Our relationship in no way echoes your relationship with your mother. Mama, you were immediate, you were present, and I knew you loved me," and here came that magic word, "unconditionally." I did, and I still do, Amanda.

Mind you, these quiet artistic years from 1983 to 2003 were darker professionally than I would have liked, but what I am left with is not merely treasured memories, but more than that, intimate, unbreakable ties with my children, because I was there in a way they could understand and appreciate. I also picked a thoroughbred to marry. Never has there been a man so quietly sure of himself that he would not just tolerate, but *celebrate* my passion for my work. None of this would've been possible without Andrew.

In those early days, every evening before Andrew came home from the office, I'd gather my cubs; just as I called Brandon "Bougie," my candlelight, so I called Amanda "Nunz," which stood for the letter *nuhn* in the Hebrew alphabet, epitomizing femininity and infinity. The three of us would perch ourselves on the window seat of 110 Riverside Drive, and together we'd watch the sun set over the Hudson. Even Lily, the mother of the mother, applauded me for that.

Tovah on Justice Ginsburg

Justice Ruth Bader Ginsburg was one of my father's favorites. Ruth and he both believed in gender equality, long before the term even existed. Because of that, Daddy made sure I got a fair shot.

I recently played Justice Ginsburg—twice. Once quite reverently in a play called *Sisters in Law,* by Jonathan Shapiro, and once with the proverbial wink in my eye in my one-woman show, *Aging Is Optional.*

In *AIO*, I delivered RBG with a nod to BIG in the form of a rap:

> I'm always optimistic,
> I never get rattled;
> Each day's an opportunity
> To win another battle.
> Don't worry 'bout my health,
> I'm performin' at my peak.
> You'll find me on the bench
> Doin' push-ups next week!

—James Bassi, Composer and Musical Director

Reach for the Stars, You May Land on the Roof

"*T*ERRI *S*UE, *DOODLELUDOO DOO, I LOVE YOU DOODLELUDOO doo . . . Yes I do, doodleludoo doo.*"

On this night, like most nights, my father Sidney was putting me to sleep with songs and stories. "Once there was an old, old, old, old man," he stressed each elongated "oh," sounding like someone had just fallen off a cliff in slow motion, "Who lived in a tall, tall, tall, tall tree . . . ," He would chant, with each "al" sounding like a skydiver plummeting to the earth.

Anticipating this routine, I said, "Oh no Daddy, not *that* again!" Mercifully he stopped. I looked over in gratitude when I noticed that he had merely stopped because his own story had put him to sleep. It didn't matter; I loved having him there on top of my navy-blue bedspread, while I lay squished underneath my blankets. My bedroom was always cold; it was only my father's presence that transformed my room into a toasty oven.

"Sidney, get up, get up!" came the voice like a sharp challah knife, slicing through the tender moment of father-daughter bonding.

"You're supposed to be putting *Terri* to sleep!" she said, now successfully waking both of us. Then, pulling him off the bed, she complained, "He's so exhausted from his work. If he doesn't fall asleep on the train and miss his stop, he falls asleep during bedtime stories." It was true. But my father loved his work. His exhaustion was a badge of honor denoting the standard of excellence to which he held himself. It meant the world to me that at the finish of his heroic days, he could find the energy to make this time for me.

"Say goodnight to Terri," my mother said, pulling him out of the door, her voice trumpeting more like "Reveille" than "Rockabye."

"Goodnight Daddy, I love you," my voice reached.

"I love you too, Terri Sue, *doodleludoo doo*," came his groggy reply, just as the door snapped shut. As she led him to their bedroom, I could hear my mother's muffled muttering, "You two are ridiculous."

In the darkness of my room, it occurred to me that *not once had my mother ever come in to tell me a bedtime story.*

It's endlessly fascinating to me that I see my life as taking place in Lilyville. Why does Lilyville take up so much emotional real estate in the map of my mind? Why would my mother usurp the narrative when in actuality, right by her side was this benevolent man, in whose eyes I could do no wrong? The truth is I couldn't flee to Sidneyville. During those formative years, for long stretches of the day, Dad was away at work. There was no one to take the bullet for me in my mother's line of fire.

So let me take this overdue opportunity to welcome my Daddy back to the stage for a proper introduction and a list of some of his greatest credits during my childhood.

I'll never forget the Sunday afternoon when my father called me into the vast pale turquoise living room and sat me down in front of our high-fidelity phonograph. This was one of the many pieces of furniture I was not allowed to touch without parental supervision. I was pleased to be able to approach it under the *protectia* of my father. He pulled open the custom mahogany armoire that housed the hi-fi, and from the gold metallic LP rack where my parents' prized record collection was carefully filed, he picked up an album I'd seen him hold before. Then he sat down on the floor next to me and said, "Terri Sue, it's time for you to meet George Gershwin." He pointed to the picture of Gershwin on the album: "George, meet Terri Sue; Terri Sue, meet George."

Like a fairy tale, he began, "I'm going to tell you the story of how George and I first met. It was 1924, and I was fourteen years old when your Grandpa David took me to Aeolian Hall on West Forty-Second Street for a concert of a new work. It was called *Rhapsody in Blue*, and George Gershwin had composed it, and George Gershwin was at the piano playing it." I looked at George Gershwin's face on the album cover and marveled that my daddy had actually been in the same room as this famous man.

"And Terri Sue, I want to be here with you when you hear this music for the first time."

He pressed the lever that automatically raised the tone arm, which dropped the record down to the spinning turntable, and gently rested itself on the first outer grooves of the perfectly shined record. All of that was like a marvelous magic trick, the applause being the gentle scratching sound coming from the speakers just before the music began.

Rhapsody in Blue launches with a clarinet tremolo, and I suddenly began to imagine I was back on my bike, climbing up Franklin Hill to speed down, no hands, and continue on a journey pedaling as fast as I could around my neighborhood; past the brook where one day I would take my horse; past the Hutchinson River Parkway where the cars sped no more quickly than I believed my two-wheeler did; past my neighbors (I wondered if *they* listened to such music). The unstoppable energy

I had pedaling my Raleigh up or downhill made me feel like Wonder Woman. I was preparing for takeoff and wondering where George Gershwin would take me next.

When the music finished, my father—beaming in blissful reverie—lifted the needle, turned to me, and asked, "What did you hear?"

I said, "It's probably silly, but it made me think of biking no hands down Franklin Hill," wondering if I had missed the whole point.

"Wonderful!" my daddy said, setting off a sparkler in my heart. "What a wonderful image to have with this music. Now let me tell you what I hear, and see if you hear it too. It's not just the melody that is so beautiful, it's what's beyond the melody and between the notes. Inside Gershwin's melodies are the melodies of the Jewish people, of our history. Inside his melodies are also the history of jazz and the sounds of New York City. Do you hear them?"

I hadn't. I replied, "Not yet, Daddy, but I will! Play it again! I want to hear what you hear!"

Learning how to truly *listen* was life changing. In that moment, the world became more vivid through my ears. Somehow I grasped that not only is music there to delight us, it's also there to impart something much deeper, like a secret code underneath and in between the notes. With some sort of miraculous precocity, I intuited that it was, in fact, the task of the composer to have a special message to carry forward to us through his art. Just like my father, I don't think that I've ever heard music the same since that moment.

And my father made this discovery even richer by drawing the line to our Jewish heritage. George Gershwin had hit a special bull's-eye. He had told a universal story by letting us hear melodies that belong to the ages, in this case, the melodies of our Jewish ancestry, as well as our newer American heritage, embedded in his work.

"I understand, Daddy, I understand!" I said elatedly. "Play me more Gershwin. I want to see if I can hear what he is telling us!"

"How about 'Lady Be Good'?" Dad said.

"Terri Sue," my mother's voice interrupted from down the hall. "How long are you going to spend cooped up listening to records on this beautiful day? Sid, let her get outside and play. Go, young lady."

Dad slowly shrugged then said, "Don't worry Terri Sue, you can carry this music inside your heart anywhere you go. That's the real gift." And he called after me, "And the whole world will look different!"

Not only did my father introduce me to the portal of enchantment that music would forever hold for me, he taught me to always look beneath and between the notes. That's a lesson that has touched my entire career.

Then there was my father's ukulele. He had been playing it since his youth. How I loved any time Daddy appeared with it in hand. Its very presence seemed to announce, "Daddy's going to be silly!" Oh, to have someone else under that roof join me in being silly, a word Mother used so often as a pejorative about my behavior.

I remember one school night when my mother was sewing in the breakfast room, my father knocked on my bedroom door and said, "Come on. Let's surprise your mother with some music." Then he whispered, "I've got the ukulele." We tiptoed into the dinette where the light was best for my mother's stitching, and burst into our gleeful rendition of a very committed, "Oh sweet and lovely lady be good." I thought I hit the melody perfectly, but Daddy was singing way off-key. We were quite a combo.

Lily immediately implored, "Sid, you're killing me. I beg you, give me one note on pitch. I can't concentrate with this racket. You want your trouser cuff fixed or not?"

I pointed out enthusiastically, "Mommy, Dad's singing it for the ladies of the house. You and me!"

"Then tell him to sing in tune! I'm getting an earache."

I guess Daddy wasn't born with a voice either.

As a child, I was the keeper of a magical secret: my father preferred me to everyone else in the whole world. I never had any question that I was his sun and his moon. Looking back, perhaps *that's* why my mother went silent.

Was she thinking, "How dare he choose his kids over his wife?"

Oblivious to Mom's side of the story, I delighted in knowing that I was Dad's *zeisele* (his sweetness). Together, we created our own private universe of unstoppable optimism. I see now that Dad was revisiting his childhood through my eyes. Dad celebrated his life, his kids, and his wife—in that order. Lily must've felt it endlessly.

I remember one morning I was tagging along with Mom to her dressing room, as every four-year-old does, announcing, "Mom, I've decided to become a nurse. I'm gonna set up a nursing station on the front lawn with methylate, Band-Aids, ice water for the grownups, and lollipops for the children—"

She turned and said to me, "Are you sure you're not adopted? I think you must be adopted."

I couldn't breathe. At the age of four, you're still at the literal. I ran to my father in his upstairs study and I said, "Daddy, Daddy, Mommy says I'm adopted. Am I?"

And my father, first in disbelief and then with a gentle smile, said, "Of course not. You came out of Mommy's belly. I was there."

Still scared out of my mind, that night I wrote a letter in pigeon print to my father: "Dear Daddy, you are the only one who loves me. Mommy loves David. I am alone. Please don't ever leave me! Love forever, Terri Sue."

These feelings still haunted me until I finally had the courage to confront my mother about this memory decades later. Why did I wait so long? Was I afraid of confrontation? Was I afraid to hear the truth?

"Didn't you understand that I couldn't believe that a person like me could possibly give birth to such a capable, extroverted daughter like you?" my mother explained as if it were simple logic, and I should've known all along. "I just couldn't believe you were mine. When I said you must be adopted, you were setting up your nurse's stand, at four years old, using words like *methylate* and trying to cure the cuts and bruises of the entire neighborhood. Amazing. And for you to hear it any other way is ridiculous. "

"I was four, Mom."

"And you've been holding on to this all these years? You're so sensitive? Drop it, Tovah. It was a compliment."

"All I can say is thank G-d Daddy was upstairs to let me know that I was part of this family and belonged in this house. He was my hero that day."

She just gave me a look that said, "What a terrible thing to say to your mother."

My mother's love and my father's love seemed like polar opposites. His was unconditional. Hers was corrective.

When I wanted to ride my bike on Weaver Street, Daddy said, "Let her fly." Mommy said, "She's biking in a gutter on a two-lane highway."

When I went to New York City, Daddy said, "What an adventure. Everywhere you look will be like a picture postcard." My mother said, "Where you look is *straight ahead*. No strolling. No window shopping. Walk like a soldier. One false move and you're dead."

When we went to Rye Playland, Daddy was up for riding all the big thrill rides: Over the Top, the rollercoaster, even the bumper cars. My mother would say, "You're gonna knock your teeth out. Then what? Why risk it?"

Even when Mom was at her practical best, my father could take the practical and lift it to the extraordinary. I was eleven and a half years old, and was riding home "in the gutter" from Mrs. Clay's sixth-grade class on my trusty Raleigh English racer. The bike was red, the brick school building was red, and this memory is red.

I made it home in an easy ten minutes flat, yet I was sweating. *Well,* I thought, *we had just had a class party. We've been dancing, and I never sat down. The Lindy, The Philly, The Stroll!* Still ready for more, I thought, *I wonder if* American Bandstand *is on?*

My first stop after calling out, "I'm home," was the bathroom. To my astonishment, as I took my panties down, I saw they were stained bright red. I froze.

I could see my face reflected in the domed, shiny chrome hot water faucet. The image was clear but distorted—so was the moment. I didn't know what to do; I was in a state of shock. After much thought, I slowly cracked the bathroom door open and tentatively called my mother, hoping she was nearby.

"Mom? Can you come into my bathroom, please?"

"Coming," echoed the call from the kitchen.

Lily was wearing the colors of spring: a blue-and-yellow polished cotton shirtwaist, her double strand of choker pearls with a circular sapphire and diamond clasp adorning her neck, and matching cultured pearl earrings. She filled the soft yellow-tiled bathroom with the familiar fragrance of Lanvin's Arpège. I found this comforting in the rush of this overwhelming moment.

I mustered up the courage to point down to the object of concern.

Her eyes widened with surprise. They were sparkling. To my amazement, she said, "This is wonderful. You are developing just as you should."

With her perfectly applied red lipstick emphasizing her approval, a wide smile broke out across her face.

In a hushed tone, she clarified, "You're menstruating, Terri Sue. Congratulations, you're a woman."

I couldn't believe it: for once, my mother was not correcting me; she was not asking me to fix myself and hide this condition. She seemed delighted. It was clear, nothing about this moment was bad or sad to Lillian Feldshuh. What a shock! "You know, Terri, when I was your age, we were never even allowed to utter the word 'menstruation.' When I got my first period, I never told my mother. Everything was hidden as if we were supposed to be ashamed. And who wanted to get slapped?"

"Get slapped?" I asked.

"There was this Eastern European Jewish tradition that when daughters began menstruating, their mothers would slap them across the face to literally 'slap some sense into them' as a reminder not to get pregnant out of wedlock. Barbaric," Lily muttered, "I vowed I would never do that to my daughter. You were right to come and tell me."

I thought my mother was explaining that this was meant to be our special, marvelous secret, a covenant between women. However, when Dad flew *in* the door that night, that covenant flew *out* the window. In his dapper gray spring business suit with matching tie, crimson-silk pocket square, and stunning navy Italian loafers, he exclaimed, loud enough to stretch across a football field, "Congratulations on becoming a woman! This is a moment to remember!" And from behind his back with a flourish, he swept out a bouquet of eighteen long-stem red roses worthy of any Broadway star's opening night.

Was he happy? He was beaming! And Mom, ever sensible, added, "Terri Sue, sexual development is a normal part of life."

"It's a *cherished* part of life," Dad added, making the moment take flight. "This is not only a milestone for you, but for your mother and me as well."

Leave it to my father to turn this milestone that my mother had framed as a precious secret into a public family celebration. We were still in the fifties, but my Dad with his *chai* of roses was the one person I knew who could break down barriers of social custom with his enormous heart. This filled me with confidence and the ability to jump barriers in my life as well.

My mother, to her credit, didn't do so badly either. And her gift to me? Kotex mysteriously arrived that night.

ON AUGUST 15, 1995, MY eighty-four-year-old mother found my father lying on their bedroom floor at 4:00 a.m., naked, covering his genitals with her bathing suit that had been lying on an adjacent chair.

Mother told me later, "I will never forget his eyes. They were the eyes of a deer who had been hit. I thought Sidney had merely fallen. It was the middle of the night. I screamed for Joyce to help me put Daddy back in his bed so he could go to sleep." Joyce was their cherished caretaker. She would stay with our family for more than twenty-five years.

Mom continued, "My only thought was to make him safe and to protect his dignity. He was naked, but he could walk. It all looked normal. I put the covers over him, and it wasn't till morning that I realized he couldn't talk. That's when I told Joyce to dial 911."

I was at the Eugene O'Neill Center up in Waterford, Connecticut, when I got the call from Joyce. She said, "Tovah, your father's in White Plains Hospital. He doesn't seem to be talking. Please come quickly."

I drove like the wind from Waterford to White Plains. Usually, that parkway is a thing of natural beauty to me. On that sunny morning, all I saw was a road that was too narrow, too windy, and too crowded.

When I finally arrived at the hospital, Mother was with the doctors in the ER. A specialist had already examined my father. I joined them.

"Mrs. Feldshuh, your husband Sidney has had a stroke." Thank G-d my mother was sitting down. "With these situations there's a ninety-minute window of opportunity where we can intervene medically and try to trap and remove the clot. That's our only hope to regain a patient's full brain function."

Mother said, "Ninety minutes? I should've dialed 911 immediately. Please don't tell me this is my fault. Please. I'm not a doctor. I didn't know, *I didn't know*. What's going to happen to Sidney?"

The doctor answered, "He will survive, but I don't believe he will ever fully recover."

Mom was in agony. She felt responsible. She blamed herself.

The doctor continued gently. "Mrs. Feldshuh, the embolism affected the word retrieval center of Sidney's brain."

"May we see him?" I requested.

"Of course," and he pointed to the curtained area next to us.

I drew aside the curtain, and there was my father, pale and mysti-fied. He looked at me, I looked at him—my love was pouring out of my heart like a tsunami. I plastered a smile across my face.

I said, "Hi Dad, I love you. It's so good to see you. Can you lift your arms?" His arms shot straight up. Then I said, "How are you, Dad?" Si-lently, he pointed to his head and struggled to say one word, "Stroke."

I said, "Well, you're talking," and he shook his head "no." Mother was ashen.

This was the man I worshipped, the man who wrote his own bril-liant scripts to defend his clients in the courtroom because: "Every hu-man being is entitled to a fair trial and is innocent until proven guilty through due process of law." Now, my father could no longer find words in his clotted brain to speak coherently. How was *this* fair?

My dad struggled so to get well. The doctors at the hospital said Sidney was not going to come back, that the damage was too great. For months he refused to give up hope, and thus we never gave up hope. I remember one of Dad's best mottoes, "Every day is a new day." I have that quote glazed into the porcelain tiles on my kitchen wall in New York.

Lily protected him like a fierce guardian lion at the gate of the Chinese emperor. During the early days after the stroke, clients were clamoring to get into White Plains Hospital to speak to Sidney—one of them literally banged on his hospital room door. They were desper-ate to get his advice to finish up their matters with him. My mother wouldn't permit anyone whom he represented to see him. This great problem solver now could barely put together a sentence that made sense. He was thinking clearly, but the connection from his brain to the word, for the most part, was blocked. She was concerned with pre-serving his dignity.

We found a marvelous, optimistic gerontologist named Dr. Paul Pressman. The minute he walked into Dad's room, an ear-to-ear smile would come across his face. That smile was contagious; it lifted every-one's spirits, even Dad's.

"Mr. Feldshuh!" exclaimed Dr. Pressman. "Great news, you're going home! And you're on your way to getting well. We've got a speech therapist lined up for you, you're walking, your body is fully functioning, you're on your way!"

Once Dad was released from the hospital, I remember the speech therapist coming to 47 Penn and my father's agony and frustration during those sessions as he repeatedly experienced, in disbelief, what had happened to him. This rage against his setting sun was frequent. He knew what was going on, and he bravely weathered on, but privately, I knew he was shattered. It was heartbreaking to watch Dad realize he would never have dominion over his speech again.

Lily and Sidney stopped going out publicly, and family started visiting 47 Penn continually.

Dad could only sleep sitting up in the soft, French provincial chair in the living room, the very chair that our cat Rusty so relentlessly favored as his clawing post in my childhood. Mom used to scream when she caught Rusty attacking her precious chair, and now that chair was the setting of even more pain for her.

Every morning, Joyce and Mom would dress my father meticulously. He could walk around the house fairly well, though his left shoulder slumped on a diagonal as his right proudly held its own. But he never appeared disheveled. You are what you wear, and no one was going to allow Dad to descend into a hopeless, helpless, disintegrating old man. He could barely speak, and when he did, G-d knows what was going to come out. These were the saddest ten months of his life and of mine—and some of the funniest. This once great litigator now conversed as follows:

Tovah: Dad what do you do?
Dad: I'm a lawyer.
Tovah: What kind?
Dad: French toast with syrup.

Our eyes locked in bemusement at what he had just uttered. Trying to make light of his malaprop, I said, "Oh, you do stand-up too?"

As Dad was out of the hospital by early fall, I asked Mom, "Shouldn't we take Dad to synagogue for the High Holidays? It will do him good."

"Do him good?" she exclaimed, her face expressing, *you're an idiot.* "I would *never* do that to him. I don't want them to see my Sidney diminished. Look at the state he is in now."

I said, "Are you sure that *he* doesn't want to go to synagogue, that *he* doesn't need the spiritual and human connection? Is it *you* who is ashamed?"

Lily replied, "Your father has always been proud as a peacock. Every morning, he meticulously showered, shaved, put on his eau de cologne, and dressed for the day. He always took longer in the bathroom than I did to 'do his ablutions.' I wouldn't dream of pushing him to see people in his current state. I believe he would hate that."

During the Days of Awe, Dad did not go to synagogue, and I called home to check in. Mom picked up:

Tovah: Hello, Mom?

Lily: *(now terribly hard of hearing)* David?

Tovah: No, it's Tovah.

Lily: Oh, Tovah, what do you want?

Tovah: Can I come for dinner?

Lily: What?

Tovah: Can I come for dinner?

Lily: What?

Tovah: Can I come . . . .

Lily: *(yelling)* Sidney, get on the phone! It's Tovah.

Sidney: *(picking up the phone)* Hello, David?

Tovah: No, Dad, it's Tovah.

Sidney: *(in halting speech)* Hello, Tovah! What do you want?

Tovah: Can I come for dinner?
Lily: *(yelling)* What'd she say, Sid?
Sidney: She said, "Chrysanthemum!"

Dad may not have been able to talk properly, but that did not stop his nighttime activities. During the ten months of his grueling, frustrating illness, I often called my mother to make sure *she* was surviving the stress. Here's one memorable exchange:

Tovah: How are ya, Mom?
Lily: *(barking)* I'm exhausted.
Tovah: *(concerned)* What, you didn't sleep well?
Lily: *(bristling)* Are you kidding? He may not be able to talk,
    but he can't keep his hands off of me! *Oy!*

DAD WAS IN AND OUT of White Plains Hospital from August 1995 through May 11, 1996. He fought valiantly to get back some level of normalcy and functionality that echoed who he used to be.

By spring of 1996, I was doing my first one-woman show off-Broadway in New York City. It was called *Tovah: Out of Her Mind!*, one of my favorite pieces. The show inhabits a gallery of characters, ages eight to eighty, comic and dramatic, in monologue and song for a nonstop ninety minutes, eight shows a week (and is still available for bookings!). Like all of my favorite performing experiences, it demanded a precision and dexterity I found exhilarating . . . and exhausting.

Every night after the show, I'd drive up from Manhattan to White Plains Hospital, and the nurses would admit me through the emergency ward and let me go up to my father's room well after visiting hours, often between 11:00 p.m. and midnight. I would tiptoe in, watch him sleep for a while, then lay my head on his right shoulder. I learned to snuggle him on the right because his left shoulder was near his pacemaker, and his pacemaker was starting to protrude through his chest. It looked ominous and certainly not welcoming to a tired head. Sometimes he would wake up, stroke my face, and say, "I'm responsible." I never knew whether he meant "I'm responsible for my demise" or "I am still your father. I am a responsible adult. You can count on me." Sometimes I would fall asleep on his shoulder. If he was awake, I would sing Gershwin to him.

On May 9, 1996, I visited Dad during the day. He was so frail at that point that I could carry him. I decided to put his armpits on top of my shoulders, and I literally hoisted him out of his bed. "Let's dance, darling Daddy."

We danced as best we could as I sang to him "Lady Be Good." His body was so weak I was holding him as one would hold a hospital-gowned rag doll whose feet only moved in response to my moving his torso. But he sang with me, and the words came out in order—"Oh sweet and lovely lady be good, oh lady be good to me"—because the music center of the brain is separate from the word center where the clot lodged. When he wanted to speak, I would say, "Sing it to me, Dad," and strains of *Terri Sue doodleloodudoo* would emerge perfectly.

After a few measures of "Lady Be Good," my father raised his right fist in the air, and in a rainbow arc said, "That's enough." As his fist descended, I laid him back in his bed and kissed him on his forehead, and then his cheek, and then his shoulder, and finally on his hand. My last words to him were, "I'll see you on Saturday."

The next night, Friday May 10, as much as I had wanted to see my father, I had promised the Gay Men's Chorus I would be their entertainment on their annual fundraising cruise. Even though my father was not well, I felt that I needed to keep my promise. My father always said, "A promise is a promise!"

Indeed, I saw my father on Saturday, May 11. At 8:00 a.m., Gina, my father's nurse, who had just returned from vacation, called. She said in a hushed but urgent tone, "Your father's going. Come quickly."

I rushed to the garage and, once again, furiously drove up the winding Bronx River Parkway from NYC to his room at White Plains Hospital. I arrived by 8:45 a.m. Too late. My father was gone.

His body was still warm, just like Romeo's when Juliet discovers him in the tomb scene of Shakespeare's classic. I sat alone with Dad for some time. My brother was driving down from Cornell University, and my mother was just awakening.

By 11:00 a.m., there was a knock on the door. Looking up and expecting David or Mom, in came my new assistant, Jennifer Westfeldt, whom I had just hired fresh out of Yale. I said, "What are you doing here?"

She said, "I took the train up to White Plains because I didn't want you to be alone with the body of your father."

Stunned, and holding back tears, I said to this extraordinary young woman, "If you ever need a favor from me in the future, the answer is 'yes.'"

A few months later, she asked me to play her mother in her film *Kissing Jessica Stein.* Ever honoring Daddy's "A promise is a promise," I said "yes." Add to this that Jennifer named my husband in her movie "Sidney" and placed our home in Scarsdale. All I could think was, *Thank you Jennifer for this beautiful tribute.* We have remained lifelong friends.

My mother, dressed meticulously as always, arrived at White Plains Hospital before David. She was wearing her pearls and wedding rings she had cherished for sixty-three years. She went right to my father's bed, leaned down, and on top of the sheets that covered his still body, she kissed his genitals and said, "Thank you for my life. Thank you for my children," without shedding a tear. Remarkable.

I just sat there in a daze, holding Dad's hand till it was cold, then holding his arm till it was cold, finally putting my hands gently on his shoulders. When David arrived, brother and sister, we sobbed.

Mother said, "Enough," as she began to collect Dad's valuables. She opened the metallic drawer next to his bed and put Sidney's wedding ring and his watch into his turquoise Tiffany drawstring jewelry bag.

"Let's discuss the plans for the funeral. Tovah, alert the family. David, alert the synagogue. I'll call the caterer for the shiva. Oh, the casket. Tovah, that's you."

"Me, Mother? Really?"

"Of course. You're the New Yorker. Call your rabbi. Get some instruction." Then she called out into the hospital corridor, "Joyce, take me home!"

David and I remained in the room until sunset, end of day for the earth and my dad. The last thing I did before I left my father was to check his plastic identity bracelet to make sure it was on tight. I didn't want Plaza Memorial to grab the wrong body.

The day Dad died, Saturday, May 11, I was still in the middle of the run of my one-woman show, and I decided to go on that night. A promise is a promise. At the end of the show, I made a curtain speech telling the audience my father had left his body that morning. I said, "You being with me on this night means everything to me. You stand as my mighty *minyan* to say Kaddish for Sidney." (Minyan: a group of at least ten Jews needed to formally witness a prayer to G-d.) And then I recited the prayer for the dead, and those who knew it joined in. "*Yisgadal v'yisgadash sh'mei rabah . . .*"

When I went into the lobby to leave Playhouse 91, to my amazement, the entire audience stood waiting to extend their condolences. It struck me that while my father was in a morgue surrounded by cold strangers, here I was, in the warm embrace of these anonymous new friends. And people say New Yorkers are coldhearted.

On Sunday, May 12, I picked out Dad's casket. I had fallen into a deep sleep and even had a moment of blessed amnesia upon awakening. And then, like a bullet, I realized Dad was gone. My ground of being was forever changed, and I could barely pull myself out of bed. I wanted to keep hiding beneath my covers to avoid the task that awaited me, but I was determined to show up for my father in death as he had shown up for me in life. He had been gone less than twenty-four hours. I followed the instructions of our beloved Rabbi Roly Matalon at B'nai Jeshurun:

"Go to Plaza Memorial to buy the casket. It's right there on Ninety-Second Street. The funeral director is named Andy, just like your husband. Do this as a service to your mother, and of course, do this to honor your father. Remember, the highest mitzvah a Jew can do is to honor the dead because the deceased are not here to thank us."

The walk to Plaza Memorial was two of the longest blocks of my life. I trudged there like a Russian caught in a Siberian blizzard, even though it was the middle of May. My steps were leaden, though the trip was short. Too short, since at my destination my father's lifeless body awaited me.

"Welcome, Mrs. Levy," was the warm but measured greeting from Andy, the funeral director. I knew he had likely escorted hundreds of grieving families down to the Plaza Memorial basement to make this tender purchase. I listened to his voice, so professionally soothing, well-scripted with comforting words. As we descended the stairs, he said, "I must prepare you." He then stopped before the oaken door to the casket room, "the sight of so many coffins on display can be upsetting." I nodded. He slowly pulled back the door.

Here's the odd thing about grief: in that moment, the Plaza Memorial basement seemed to instantly transform into Bloomingdale's. The lighting was bright, and all the walls were painted white.

I stood up straight with a sudden *whoosh* of intention, and set off to shop! What was happening to me? I felt like a bargain shopper at a Memorial Day White Sale, skirting from casket to casket as if they were designer clothing racks. *A tisket, a tasket, I want an oak wood casket*, I quietly sang to myself.

At that surreal moment, I saw what Dad would love: a handsome blonde oak casket with the Star of David carefully carved in the top and a simple piece of thin white, sateen lining inside. It was restrained, but elegant. There was no need to look further.

I had been afraid to put Dad in a rough-hewn, pine box, as was Orthodox tradition. I wasn't Orthodox, and I was concerned he'd get a splinter in his *tuchus*. (Yiddish for derrière.) Well, that was simply not acceptable, particularly if you are what you wear. I was not about to let my father wear splintered wood for eternity.

A huge wash of peace came over me knowing I had indeed found something of which Daddy himself would approve. I knew that he was smiling that it was I, his Terri Sue, who had chosen exactly what would please him for this most significant of final gifts.

As Dad was swaddled when he came into this world, so he would be swaddled as he left. Two emblems would accompany him that signified his years on this earth as a Jew: a *yarmulke* and a *tallis* (a skullcap and a prayer shawl).

I placed my hand on the freshly sanded, blonde oak casket, signaling that this was the one. Andy nodded, then broke the silence and asked, "Would you like to see your father?"

I said, "Sure," not realizing that this was code for, "We want to show you that we are giving your father a kosher burial, that we have bathed him, cut his nails, cleaned under his cuticles, washed and combed his hair, and made sure his body is purified."

So we ascended the stairs, and I went into the main chapel. Empty and pin quiet, it was bathed in a golden glow reflecting off the golden carpet and the soft warm mahogany pews and matching double exit doors. Against this peaceful embrace, two men dressed in dark suits wheeled my father in on a well-used steel gurney.

Dad was a startling Michelangelo yellow-white. Unlike the way I had found him in his hospital room, he was stone cold. I kissed his freezing forehead, and all of a sudden from some unknown depth of my soul, I started to howl like a wolf. It was quite sudden, like a wounded animal who had been shot. It was so primal as to barely be human. My futile tears fell on a face that remained undisturbed. I yelled to my father as if to awaken him, the words of my childhood note, "Daddy, you are the only one who loves me! I am alone! Don't leave me!"

At that moment, the double doors of the funeral home blew open with a startling, unearthly energy. It was as if my father were with me. I glanced up to see the two attendants rushing to pull the doors closed against the force of wind that was emanating from the sanctuary. I looked at my father. Was he trying to signal me that he was a life force that could reach out to me even after death?

Walking back to my apartment, there was a lightness in my step because I was holding another precious secret: I knew my father had been with me.

We buried Dad on Monday the thirteenth. On that day, the theater was dark.

The funeral was held in Temple Israel Center's majestic main sanctuary. Fifty-foot ceilings and crimson velvet upholstered individual seats along the mahogany pews graced this holy refuge. The bimah was carpeted like the sanctuary, in deep cherry red, with the Holy Arc covered by maroon velvet and two Lions of Judah embroidered in gold thread, framing an even more richly embroidered Ten Commandments.

Friends and family arose; the mourners then entered slowly: my mother followed by her children and grandchildren. Everyone immediately came to their feet. Mother was standing pin straight, the way she always asked me to stand. In her best St. John black knit ensemble, with all her wedding rings and her favorite diamond and gold rose pin my father had given her, she walked slowly to the front row. She chose to wear only the little lace head covering that the synagogue gave out in baskets at the entry of the sanctuary, probably so it wouldn't ruin her hair. The only thing that told us she was eighty-five years old were her shoes—they were black comfort pumps from Eneslow on Park Avenue South, but they were new. Ever mindful, she realized she would be going from carpeted floors and hard, asphalt parking lots to the soft earth at the gravesite, and G-d knows she didn't want to lose her balance.

I followed in my black Chanel suit with a Bergdorf hat on my head, now graced by a black tulle veil that dear Faust, our family dressmaker, carefully basted on for the funeral. This was the final fashion parade for my father.

We walked with David and our spouses to the first row. I turned to Andrew and said, "Mom hasn't shed a tear. I think she's is in a state of shock because she lost her boyfriend." That's what she called Dad: her boyfriend.

One of the highlights of the eulogies was my brother David's tribute: "My father always said, 'Even a train stops,' but no one could believe that Sidney would ever stop."

Then it was my turn. I stood, collected myself, clasped my mother's hand as I left our pew, and walked slowly up to the bimah.

"To quote my father," I began, "'Every day is a new day . . . ' but this is a day I hoped would never come."

No sooner had I finished the sentence than all the doors of the synagogue violently blew open onto the parking lot. The congregation was agape. There were no words for what had just happened. I was caught off guard. Onstage, when something unexpected happens, we ad-lib. These were the unscripted words that came out of my mouth at this startling interruption:

"I think my father is here." Incredulous that this was happening again, I explained, "My darlings, yesterday, Sidney blew open the doors of Plaza Memorial as I howled for him in pain. Today, on this windless May 13, he is blowing open the doors again to signal to us that he's still right here, right now." We all stared to our right at the wall of double doors that were blown open onto the parking lot. Shouting in their direction I said, "We feel you, Dad. We hear you. We know you're here."

There was a hush that swept over the *shul* (temple) as my father's casket, with its star of David emblazoned on the top, was slowly wheeled down the long aisle of the synagogue, flanked by his children and his grandchildren, and out the doors he had just blown open into the waiting hearse.

Mother, David, David's wife Martha, Andrew, and I; our children, Amanda and Brandon; and David's children, Noah, Zach, and little Hannah, one by one gently slid into the limousine next to each other, as if one false touch might shatter the thin barrier holding back the tidal wave of grief, or so I thought.

Once the car door slammed shut and we were finally safe from the watchful gaze of those who joined us to mourn Sidney, the children, as children do, burst into merriment and seemed to pick up on conversations wherever they may have paused just before the service began, unable to resist the joy of simply being together. Mother wasn't bothered because she couldn't hear a thing.

Glancing over at Mother, sitting stoically and looking aimlessly out the window at the passing trees along the Garden State Parkway, I wondered what might possibly be going through her mind. I reflected on one of her Lilyisms: "If you love nature, you'll always be rich." I wondered how rich she felt today.

We pulled up to Riverside Memorial just over the George Washington Bridge in New Jersey and approached the Kaplan family plot, which was nestled in its own patch of greenery amidst the miniature city skyline of headstones crowded elsewhere in the expansive stretch of lawn, beyond which the forests of New Jersey circled protectively. The family plot is comprised of a single, large, gray granite, elegant stone marker, with the name "KAPLAN" proudly etched in bold capital letters. Emanating from it were ten attendant gravesites.

What was impossible to ignore at that moment were the two unclaimed spaces, seemingly waving over to the new generation of cousins, as if to say, "We're here for whoever in the family goes first." Mortality was inescapably gripping me by my shoulders.

To this somber setting, I had brought my boombox. I had caught my mother's sidelong glance as I loaded it into the trunk of the car earlier. "The least we can do is bury Dad to *Rhapsody in Blue*," I had explained.

The gravesite ceremony was beautifully presided over by Gordon Tucker, head rabbi at Temple Israel Center, and *El Male Rachamim* (Hebrew for G-d of Mercy, Prayer for the Soul of the Departed) was sung exquisitely by our cantor, Jack Mendelson. Then I solemnly pressed the play button. Out came the wail of the clarinet's ascending scale, beginning the *Rhapsody*. It was a clarion call to my father. As I looked across the cemetery at the assortment of markers within earshot, I felt some comfort thinking everyone at rest here might be loving Gershwin's masterpiece too.

"Mom," I started. "We need to bury Dad properly." We had all dropped roses on his grave and thrown a little bit of symbolic dirt on his simple, beautiful casket. "It's time to take a shovel and create the mound of earth that's supposed to be over Dad's body."

"What?" honked Mother, as if I had spontaneously invented this custom.

"Momma, Jewish practice dictates that we need to create a mound of at least three feet over the body. It's the mound that tells the world, 'There is a person here. There is a human being, who led a good and meaningful life, buried here. And to lose a human being is to lose a universe.'"

My mother said, "You're going to shovel in Chanel? And David, in Paul Stuart? This I've gotta see."

Understanding the symbolism of this gesture, the family, one by one, took turns with the shovel, to be part of building this final testimonial to Sidney. Mother merely watched. In fact, she lasted about sixty seconds before she grabbed Joyce by the hand and headed back to the limousine.

David and I took over again when everybody had a turn. We had barely reached ground level when my mother started to scream from the stretch limousine, "That's enough already! We need to go home!"

We kept shoveling until Mom yelled, "I'm getting dizzy!"

Then David and I obediently put down our shovels. The gravediggers waited politely until we got into the big, black car. "Mound-schmound," Mother bugled. "He's dead. Let him rest in peace. The gravediggers will complete the job. All of a sudden you're religious? Don't be so dramatic."

At a moment when I couldn't have been more vulnerable, Mother's words landed like a punch to the heart. I never saw my mother shed a tear. Not from May 11 right to the unveiling a year later. She was a rock.

Was she trying to set an example to the whole family of what dignity looked like when it was visited by personal tragedy? Was she trying to show us how not to burden others with our grief? Or was she masking her fear? What I saw was an unexpressed life making sure we didn't get to fully express our lives, either.

My father, Sidney Feldshuh, who was my home plate of unconditional love, had now left the field of play. Here I was, earthbound in Lilyville. My husband and my children would be by my side, on that I could depend. But now came a startling conundrum: going forward, whenever I would be at the epicenter of Lilyville, face-to-face with this maternal enigma, without Sidney as my protector and deflector, would I be defenseless? Then came the real question: who was going to be on *my* side?

Everyone Comes on *The Walking Dead* to Die

I WAS ON MY WAY TO THE GALAPAGOS WITH ANDREW, AND THE day before I was to board the plane for Ecuador, I got a call from my Hollywood managers to ask if I could audition for a series on cable called *The Walking Dead*. "Have you seen it, Tovah?" they asked.

"No," I replied. "I'm close enough to death that I don't have to watch it walk."

"They want you to audition tomorrow at Bernie Telsey's. I am sending you the scenes now. The scenes are not from the series, but you need to sign a non-disclosure agreement."

I said, "Disclose what? I know nothing. I'm happy to sign it, but I'm unable to audition tomorrow. I'm flying to Ecuador to board an expedition boat."

They firmly urged, "Do whatever you need to do to delay your flight. This is an important opportunity."

The next day, I went down to Bernie Telsey's with my luggage for my "important opportunity." I was literally escorted into a cinder block closet. There, a lovely twenty-two-year-old intern turned on a camera and I auditioned for the part of the head of the CIA from some series I did not recognize.

It was my first audition in my career where I wasn't given the material from the script. I looked at myself, I looked at the twenty-two-year-old, I looked at the little camera that was the size of an iPhone, I looked at the cinder block closet, and I said, "I think I'm at the end of my career. Forty-five years on the marquees of Broadway, and now *this*. This is leading *nowhere!*"

I auditioned, thanked the person who was young enough to be my grandchild, excused myself, and rushed to the airport. What I didn't know was that the Hollywood casting agent for the show, Sharon Bialy (named for the bagel), was watching the tape and immediately called the *Walking Dead* showrunner, Scott Gimple, and said, "I have found what you're looking for." Scott had to see the tape, the AMC executives had to see the tape—and I was on my way to Quito, Ecuador.

I boarded the Lindblad *Endeavor* and we were sailing to the Galapagos. We met marvelous people, saw Darwin's finches, the blue-footed boobies, the red-footed boobies, and the renowned giant tortoises. Three days into the trip, I got a call from my assistant Morgan Sills, who said in his North Carolina accent, "Hey Tov, I think you got a job. They're trying to reach you."

"Who?" I said.

"The people from *The Walking Dead.*"

"What's the part?" I said.

"They wouldn't tell me," he said.

"That's OK, they wouldn't tell me either," I replied.

"Can I give him this number for the boat?"

"Of course," I said.

A few minutes later, Scott Gimple called. He said, "Ms. Feldshuh, we would like you to join *The Walking Dead.*"

I said, "OK . . . may I ask what the part is, please?"

He replied, "It's the mayor of a town called Alexandria. She's an ex-senator from Ohio named Deanna Monroe, and she has been able to protect herself and her constituents behind the walls of this community for over two years. Can you be here this weekend?"

I said, "I'm here with the marine iguanas, and the Lindblad *Endeavor* doesn't dock in Cartagena till Sunday morning."

"You need to get on a flight to Atlanta Sunday night."

I said, "Mr. Gimple, the part sounds wonderful, but I have one request: my mother just died less than two months ago. I'm pleased that you're honoring my talent, but I would ask that you also honor my time. If this part, when it appears, doesn't have at least one scene in each episode that bats it out of the park, you should give it to another actress. I'm not going to be useful to you as a supernumerary. And I just don't have the time to waste."

Gimple replied, "Ms. Feldshuh, I promise you, I will never waste your time."

Scott kept his promise, and I stayed with *The Walking Dead* for two years and there wasn't one episode where I was peripheral. Deanna Monroe turned out to be a fantastic heroine, role model, and action doll!

The show takes place in a post-apocalyptic planet Earth ridden with zombies and follows a posse of protagonists who somehow are clever enough to duck the odds (or should I say the oddities?) and stay alive. These intrepid survivors come across Alexandria, a pristine sequestered community with Deanna Monroe as its leader. I offer them sanctuary, at least until—and here's where I encountered a non-disclosure agreement like none other. We were shackled from whispering even a breath of the impending plot twists to anyone. If you don't believe me, I invite you to the meeting we had before shooting began with the entire AMC legal team, who explained the gravity of breaking this agreement. They made it very clear that it would cost us our jobs.

"Not to *anyone*?" I asked Scott incredulously.

"It's an absolute, Tovah. Not even your husband. Here's the thing, the thrill of the series and why it's staying number one, is the element of surprise. These fans, The Walking Dead Heads, are ravenous for leaks. One shared detail to anyone will go viral and ruin the mystery."

"Fellas," I announced, "my lips are sealed . . . with Krazy Glue!" And they were. Andy understood implicitly because he has lived, and I have put up with, fiduciary client relationships for decades.

Having never been on *the number-one show worldwide*, I couldn't appreciate what this exposure would mean. But between seasons, when I was in an ice cream store across from the Duomo in Milan, Italy, to buy a gelato, the young man behind the counter said,

"Scusi signora, lei è in televisione?"

"Sì," I replied.

"Che ha fatto, per favore?"

"Ho fatto *Law & Order*."

"No, non è *Law & Order*."

"Ho fatto la mini-serie *Holocausto*."

"No, non è *Holocausto*."

"Forse è la serie *Il Walking Dead*?"

Screaming, he replied, "Sì sì, è *Il Walking Dead*!" Then the whole gelato store started screaming, "*IL WALKING DEAD*?! Posso fare una fotografia con lei, signora?!"

There was mayhem, the whipping out of dozens of iPhones, one on top of another, scraps of paper and requests for autographs a mile a minute. People followed me on the streets from Italy to New Guinea, Borneo, Mongolia, Siberia. . . . No place was remote enough. Even in New York City where I used to ride my bike anonymously, I was flagged, photographed, and—frankly—flattered. *TWD* gave me a whole new fan base: people with tattoos and nose rings. Come one, come all. I was thrilled.

Other than something going viral on the Internet, television is the most powerful media source I know. Fame, I realized, is just "agreement." Instead of one thousand people in a Broadway house thinking your work is good, there are over six million people across the world watching their screens and thinking your work is good—and then feeling somehow personally connected to you. Don't forget, you're appearing for free, on demand, and frequently binged!

Frankly, *The Walking Dead* was an artistic dream. The cast was fantastic, the directors the same, and nothing was taken for granted. I kept thinking of my soccer-coaching days. After the girls would make a goal, I would say, "Stay humble, stay vigilant!" Once *TWD* was number one, its entire community stayed humble and stayed vigilant, to make sure it *stayed* number one. It did.

The lead in the series, Andy Lincoln, couldn't do enough for me. He called my hotel the second I arrived.

"Whatever you need, I'm here for you."

I shyly requested, "Would you mind if we rehearse on the phone a bit? Run the scene for tomorrow a few times?"

"Of course," said Andy. "That would be great."

We spent over one hour going over the eight-page scene we had to do the next morning, which was my first day on the set. At 8:00 a.m., we whipped off that scene in three shots. The director was thrilled. It felt like theater by the seat of your pants. That night, I immediately hired a line tester.

If Mother were alive, she would've said, "The walking *what? The Walking Dead?*! All of a sudden, Golda Meir is starting to look good."

One of the most memorable scenes I filmed in the series was the last. And by that, I mean *my* very last. Spoiler alert: Deanna dies. It feels so refreshing to be freed from the NDA. But of course, given the premise of the show, Deanna was destined to rise from the dead, this time transformed into a . . . (don't tell anyone) zombie.

How did I find out I was going to die? I was talking to Scott Gimple about renting an apartment in Atlanta for my third season. Scott replied, "I wouldn't take a long lease."

"What?" I said, feeling like I had been gut punched.

He began, "Tovah darling, you will be dying at the end of this season. And you cannot mention it to anyone, including other cast members. I am telling you this to save you from getting stuck down the road."

I said to him, "You know my father said excellence was everything. If you're excellent, all the rest will follow."

He reassured me, "You're not just excellent, you're superb. We love you, you do a magnificent job," and whatever else you say to an actor whose time has come.

He explained, "The way this works is we get the audience to fall in love with you, and then we take you away. Everyone comes on *The Walking Dead* to die."

What Scott had to say wasn't personal, but it felt like shit . . . which happens to be the line I said when I was bitten, "Oh shit."

What I loved about this character is that Deanna, like my forebears, was incredibly courageous. As the army of raving zombies cornered me in the upper bedroom of my home, I had the wherewithal to grab a revolver, and rather than take the easier way out, shooting myself, I chose to shoot the enemy until my bullets ran out.

On my last day of shooting, the entire cast of *The Walking Dead* came to the set to watch me work. When the scene was over, everyone applauded, loudest of all the four leads, Norman Reedus, Danai Gurira, Melissa McBride, and (the sensational epicenter of this juggernaut) Andrew Lincoln.

The experience on *The Walking Dead* was simply perfect on all levels: artistic, intellectual, above all human, and, well . . . *inhuman*.

ACT III

Lily's Turn

E VEN THOUGH I WAS NEARING FIFTY WHEN MY FATHER DIED, there is no good time to lose a parent. I knew the curtain was reluctantly rising on what would be a sorrowful new act for the residents of Lilyville. From this point, all of us would be walking forward without our guiding beacon of optimism; without the benevolence of this man who could wrap the loving arms of solution around any problem that might dare to cross our borders or raise his fist in the air to communicate, "We will persevere."

For me, it was as if a spotlight without a forgiving filter was harshly singling out two of us, the two whom I knew were going to feel this loss perhaps most significantly: my mother, who had hitched her identity to my father and whose primary daily purpose orbited around her husband and children; and me, the daughter who drew some special sort of life sustenance from each beat of her father's oversized heart. My father hung the moon and the stars for me.

I can't forget my brother, David, who couldn't forgive himself for not making precisely the right medical decisions that might have helped Daddy live longer without a stroke, but hindsight is no sight at all. In fact, David—after he had a PhD in theater and was the associate artistic director of the Guthrie—put himself through medical school principally because he wanted to extend our parents' lives. Can you imagine, he paid his tuition by directing plays!? As Gershwin put it, "Who could ask for anything more?"

Lily and I were both starting out on this terrifying new frontier sans Sidney, ill-equipped to meet the challenges that lay ahead of us . . . and between us.

There we stood in stark relief: my mother and I. If ever I needed compassion and nurturing, it was now. Sadly, my life history to this point had told me, "You will not find what you need coming from your mother." Dad's death was a cataclysmic loss, and a terrifying new reality for me.

How did we handle it?

For myself, I dove into the work at hand, *Tovah: Out of Her Mind!*, a one-woman show whose very title seemed uncannily prescient. We had an extended ten-week sold-out run underway and—ever mindful of Daddy's credo, "a promise is a promise"—Sidney's daughter was determined to go on.

"Tovah, you must take time to mourn. For the sake of your mother and your immediate family, you must sit *shiva*. And I don't mean just today," Rabbi Tucker had instructed me, as we stood graveside.

"Of course," I replied and I did. Shiva is normally observed for an entire week. Shiva actually means "seven." Less religious Jews sit for three days (shiva-lite?), and had I not been in the middle of a run, I would've done what was right and proper in a Conservative Jewish household. I decided to sit shiva at 47 Penn Monday, Tuesday, and Wednesday until the evening performance, and have a memorial service for my Dad in our apartment on the following Monday off.

"Tovah, are you sure you can go on while you're grieving?" asked our producer Louise Westergaard as she walked me into her elegant apartment on Park Avenue. We were meeting to clarify our playing schedule. I outlined my intention to be back onstage as quickly as possible. "Don't do it for me," she replied. "We can manage. You just buried your father forty-eight hours ago. You don't have to go on tonight. You have my blessing to do whatever you need." I was incredulous at her generosity as I listened on. "We will reschedule the performances, we will rebook the audiences, we will accommodate this. I repeat, whatever you need. I'm afraid you might hurt yourself psychologically if you soldier on as though nothing has changed. Denial does not work when you've lost a parent."

The maid appeared from the kitchen with a silver tray of typical Westergaard hospitality, including the honey-vanilla chamomile tea that Louise knew I loved.

"Louise," I said, firmly resolved, "this is what my father would want. This is how I can honor him. He was the one who emblazoned on my heart: 'keep your commitments.' He was the one who taught me: 'there is dignity in work.'" The words caught in my throat as I valiantly continued. "Besides, nothing made him happier than seeing me onstage.

"I remember once we were in technical rehearsals for *Yentl* at the Walnut Street Theatre in Philly, and there was a man sitting in the back of the house for five hours. I thought it was my producer, Moe Septee. When we took our dinner break, I walked up the aisle, and there was my father! I said, 'Dad, what are you doing here?' He said, 'I had business in Philadelphia, and I thought I would stop by and watch you work. And once I sat down, I couldn't leave.'

"From then on, I put my father in every audience, and when I need him, in every seat." Holding back the tears, I said, "You see, Louise, I can be closest to my father when I am on the stage. He'll never miss a show, so neither can I."

"Tovah, we'll do as you wish. Go to the theater, and if you insist, go on tonight. But promise me you will send up a flare if it gets to be too much. There's no understudy in a one-woman show, kiddo. You're the only Tovah we've got."

Hugging her as I stood up to go, I said, "Louise, do you know how many shows I've missed on and off-Broadway in my entire career?"

"How many?" she said.

"None," I replied and left her beautiful apartment thinking to myself, *Wow, there really are angels when you need them.*

In the lobby, the multitude of elegantly uniformed doormen asked me if I needed a taxi. "Taxi? No thanks," I said. And in true Tovah-mode, after the funeral, the burial, an abbreviated shiva, and a meeting with my producer, I climbed on my bike and pedaled to Playhouse 91.

Signing in at the stage door, I spotted my director, Sara Louise Lazarus, waiting for me. With a warm hug, she said "Oh Tovah, I can't believe you're here . . . and early! I thought I would come in today in light of what's happened for whatever you need."

I thought to myself, *another angel.*

"Thanks," I said, but to my surprise, what came out was a squeak. *What was that?*

We both suddenly stood still. *I must be imagining things*, I thought, my heart beginning to speed up. Slowly, I tried to vocalize. The first sound to come out of my throat was a raspy squawk.

"Oh no," I whispered, looking instantly terrified. "Where's my voice?"

"Can you sing?" Sara calmly asked, not revealing an ounce of alarm.

Leaping into the character of Molly Kelly Kugelberg, and trying her lyrics in my head voice, "When your Mommy is a lapsed Catholic and your Daddy is a cultural Jew . . ." Dry air was coming out with very little pitch. "Sara, do you think I have time to run to Dr. Kessler?"

"Go," she implored. "Go!"

Off I sped on my bike, while Sara kindly called ahead for an emergency appointment with Scott Kessler, voice doctor to the stars.

Sitting in his waiting room, I was appropriately *Scared: Out of My Mind!* My eyes darted around the signed memorabilia. Michael Bolton's platinum record with the inscription, "Thank you Dr. Scott Kessler for your tremendous efforts and support. With love and gratitude, MB."

Next to it was Madonna's *Rolling Stone* cover where she wrote, "For my savior, Dr. Kessler," and signed it, "Living to sing." There was Rihanna, Tatiana Troyanos, Lady Gaga, and Justins Bieber *and* Timberlake! All of whom shared the same humbling terror: everything depends on the health of those two little cords. Misery loves famous company. The only sound in the office was the receptionist's voice saying, "Dr. Kessler, it's Nathan Lane. Can you see him?"

Sitting in his exam room, wallpapered with celebrity autographed CD covers, each one a valentine to the "miracle cure" this highly respected doctor had bestowed upon them at their dark hour of the arytenoids. *Oh, let this magic work for me,* I prayed quietly. I spotted my CD cover on the wall and was reminded, *Oh, yes, this has worked for me before. Please, oh please may it save me tonight.* Nothing is lonelier or longer than a performance of a solo concert with a compromised voice. You keep having to forgive yourself as you are drowning in catarrh, sinking into the mediocrity of your work like quicksand.

Dr. Kessler said, "We're going to give you a cortisone shot, a B-12 shot, and a prednisone pack to start tomorrow, but I need you to go into silence. Immediately. Not a whistle, not a whisper."

"But I'm performing tonight."

"This will get you through tonight, but you have to remain silent at every moment offstage."

"I'm never offstage."

Promising G-d that I would enter a vocal monastery and take a vow of vocal chastity if he delivered me from misery tonight, I flew back on my bike to Playhouse 91 and went on.

I would like to formally apologize now to any of you who may have been in the audience Wednesday, May 15, through Sunday, June 30, because clearly nothing helped.

Not being able to sing made a sad time even worse. There was no medical reason for the swelling, it was just my broken heart choking in my throat. Grief, sorrow, and stress were the culprits, and I couldn't seem to tame them. I was panicked.

In the midst of this, it was weighing on me that my mother must be suffering something equivalent, if not worse. I knew I needed to reach out to her. I decided to drive up Friday morning. Now *I* had the legal pad and pencil. She was deaf, I was mute. We were both in mourning. "Sounds perfect," I squeaked to myself as I made a large sign to hang across my chest that shouted, "I AM ON VOCAL REST!"

As tragic as I anticipated my mother's collapse to be in a Sidney-less existence, nothing prepared me for what I saw.

I raised the garage door with the clicker she had given me, and whether she had heard it or felt the vibrations, she was waiting for me when I entered the utility room.

I knew the house, I knew the furniture, but I didn't know the face. Walking toward me from the kitchen was a person I had never met before. It wasn't a change in clothing, it wasn't a change in hair, it was the light she brought into the room and the unmistakable joy she had in seeing me. Mind you, she was carrying a Hershey bar, so that may have given her pleasure as well.

But instead of the expected veil of sorrow over her spirit that she had experienced with her mother's death so many years before, my mother was unexpectedly radiant.

Scribbling quickly on a notepad, I wrote, "Mom, Hershey's?"

She said, "I've got a new motto: chocolate and laughter on a daily basis. They say chocolate is an aphrodisiac, so I live in hope."

I laughed and pointed to the sign around my neck and started to silently mouth my words.

Scrunching her eyes, even though she was wearing drugstore spectacles, she said, "Vocal rest? But you can still eat, can't you?" And then, thrusting her arm toward me, "Here, have some Hershey's."

"Dairy and caffeine," I wrote, as I started shaking my head "no."

"Dairy-schmairy," she laughed. "Take a square."

Leading me into the solarium, she said, "You can't talk? So I'll talk, you listen." And looking out at the back lawn, she mused, "Remember

Daddy literally cantering through the streets of Quaker Ridge like Paul Revere to come see me? Right up the front lawn he would gallop to give me a private horse show in the backyard on his beloved Wildwood King. He'd shout, 'Look Lily, Woody has five gaits.' And I'd shout, 'Look Sidney, Woody is ripping up the lawn.'"

Mom and I both laughed, and then she mused.

"He was such a show-off and he loved to shine for me. But the backyard? You should have seen the gardener's bills! Ridiculous!

"But I gotta tell you, Tovah," leaning forward conspiratorially, "I loved seeing him in his riding habit. He looked like an English country squire. So elegant. So sexy."

I grabbed my pad and scribbled, "SEXY?"

She nodded and continued, "And then he would lean down and whisper, 'Hey Lil, can I have a vodka and orange juice?' Do you know what that really meant?"

I drew in a breath, thinking, *Is my mother telling me something about her sex life?*

Reading the look on my face, she said, "Exactly," and then popped another square of chocolate into her mouth.

Was I with my mother, or was I with Hortense, that alter ego of her adolescence who was outgoing, joyful, and glamorous? The one who played tennis and rode horses and imagined going to parties with Noël Coward? Was she just having a good day or would this be the new normal? It had been barely a week since Dad had died, and she had nursed him for ten months before that, night and day, fighting against the dark angels who eventually claimed my father. Was this her version of grief . . . or relief? In theater we say, "If it works, use it." And so I broke off a piece of her chocolate bar and thought to myself, *I'll have what you're having.* Then I kissed her on her rosy, porcelain cheek and drove back to the city.

As the weeks wore on, Mother seemed to be navigating her new normal valiantly. She and I were sitting in my apartment at 110

Riverside Drive looking at the Hudson, and I said, "Mom, am I calling you enough, am I visiting enough? Everyone brings the chicken soup the first week of mourning, and then nothing. Are you OK?"

She replied, "Happiness is a choice. Sometimes we have to will it so."

"Is that what you're doing, Ma?" I asked.

"You bet your life."

—••—

IF EVER THERE WAS A moment I thought Mother might have an emotional setback, it was Dad's *yahrzeit*, the first anniversary of his death. As is the custom, the family had assembled for the drive to Riverside Memorial Cemetery for the unveiling of the gravestone. The tradition of waiting a year is designed to protect the loved ones from the shock of seeing the deceased's name etched in stone immediately after death, a sign of inescapable finality.

I, as is custom, was in black, the same Chanel suit that I wore to Dad's funeral. (I hoped no one would notice, but *you* might, dear reader, if you read page 210!)

Mother came separately from 47 Penn, with Dad's driver, Milton. Mother always accused Milton of driving well under the speed limit because he was paid by the hour. So I have no doubt on the way to Riverside Memorial, she was probably shouting, "Faster Milton, faster! Fifteen miles an hour, it's ridiculous!" As she stepped out of her shiny silver Chevrolet, I couldn't help but smile to see Mother wearing not black, but navy blue. "Mom," I exclaimed, "I love it. Shaking it up with navy blue!"

"Tovah, I'm not breaking any rules . . . just bending them."

As we walked toward the marker, still covered in its sacred white gauze, which was held in place by two strings, I continued my assessment of Mom's outfit. "Mom, you look like you're dressed more for a world cruise than an unveiling."

"Well, why not?" she said, leaning in closer. "Am I not setting sail on a whole new life?"

The rabbi greeted us and, once we were gathered, started the service.

Once again, we were gifted with a beautiful day. Once again, we each took turns to speak a few words about Dad. We each placed a small stone on Dad's marker and then on the large Kaplan gravestone to tell our forebears, "We have been here. We remember. We are grateful for our time with you."

Mom was the last to speak. She said, "I want you all to know what I had the masons carve on the headstone. It says, 'Sidney Feldshuh: Beloved husband, father, and grandfather.'" Now taking time to look at each of us: Tovah, David, Andrew, Martha, Brandon, Amanda, Noah, Zach, and baby Hannah—with Mom we were a minyan (well, a very un-Orthodox one)—she continued, "But I couldn't resist adding something I know Dad would've loved."

She then asked David to unfasten the strings. There, underneath that epitaph, in bold caps, were the words, "THE GREATEST."

We all began to chuckle silently at this unexpected flash of humor. She caught the family off guard, and she loved it. "Do you see that, Sidney?" she said, focusing on the marker. "I'd say 'How are you *schmeerkate?*' You'd say, 'I'm great.' I'd say, 'Only great?'"

And turning to us, "With fist in the air, Daddy would exclaim, 'I'm the greatest!'" and she imitated Dad's Rocky Balboa victory stance.

Now quietly, to him, "Yes, Sid, you're the greatest.

"Rabbi," she commanded, "Say Kaddish.

"Then lunch!" she whispered, cupping her hand in an aside to us.

We all stood quietly and said the prayer for the dead over my father. This marked the end of the formal mourning period. David and I, however, had still not recuperated. We went on to say Kaddish for our father for another year.

Breaking this sacred silence, came Lily's clarion call, "We're going to Gimelli's Ristorante. You all go ahead."

And then staring at Milton with a cold gaze, "I'll get there as fast as I can with *Milton* driving me." Shooing Milton toward the car, Lily yelled, "Go, Milton, go!"

My father's unveiling became my mother's *unexpected* unveiling. Lily was blossoming like the Rubrum Lilies she loved.

In the months following the unveiling, I received three voicemails that were priceless:

"Tovah, it's your mother." (As if I didn't know.) "I know it's your day off, let's go out to dinner. In Manhattan! I convinced Joyce to drive me in. Oh, and I fired Milton. How about Sardi's? Get us the corner table on the banquette. That way I'll have a full view of the room and a full view of your *fakakta* (Yiddish for fucked-up) caricature on the wall. See you at six. We're gonna have vodka gimlets and I'm gonna give you the skinny about eloping with Daddy. Whoo whoo!" *Click.*

"Tovah, it's your mother. Take me to the Frick. I love family mansions, and this is one of the best. Also, it's all one floor. The first ranch house. Aren't they clever?

"Then we can go to dinner. Your treat." *Click.*

"Tovah, it's your mother. Take me to the movies. It's gotta be foreign. . . .

"I need subtitles." *Click.*

She flirted shamelessly with waiters, chauffeurs, and the handsome leading men with whom I worked. "Don't tell Daddy," she whispered, looking over both shoulders, "but these are the *best years of my life!*"

I turned to Mom and said, "What's going on?"

She said, "If not now, when?"

This wasn't an aberration. Underneath my mother's quiet silence lurked a thousand desires that now had space to emerge. She rediscovered her rights to the full life movement and entitled herself once again and at long last to be vivid.

So when I thought no one would be by my side, there was my mother, right next to me, in a renovated Lilyville now in dazzling Technicolor.

Lily on Same-Sex Marriage

"Tovah, your cousin Jeff came to visit me with his husband, Christopher. They're having a baby, and whoever's sperm they're using for their first-born, they're gonna use the partner's sperm for their second-born. It's OK with me. They're such a nice couple, and they always keep in touch, but it's a *lebedik velt.*" (Yiddish for crazy world.)

Prying the World Open

L ILY ASCENDED TO THE ROLE OF FAMILY MATRIARCH, AND SHE met her new status with gusto and compassion, doling out hugs, marriage blessings, and words of wisdom to an ever-more ardent flock. And as for the two of us, we were "Together Wherever We Go," in growing harmony.

Once my father died, I fully realized *tempus fugit*, and I intensified my running around the world. Whenever I could, I would take Mom on trips. *Travels With My Mom* could be its very own Jerry Herman musical. Here's just one melody that lingers on.

I took her to Spain to visit our British cousins, Karen Shafron and her mother Beatrice. Karen owned a condo in Marbella. We stayed at the Puente Romano, had a fantastic reunion with them, ordered overpriced lobsters, and, of course, toured the environs. I couldn't resist taking Lily to Hemingway's Ronda, where the famous bullfight took place in *The Sun Also Rises*.

Returning from Ronda to Marbella should've been an easy drive, but being the adventurer I am, I decided to take the road less traveled. Obviously, I had not yet learned the credo of the mountain climber: "Always go down the way you came up." In our little blue rental car, as we tooled along, we noticed the country road turned into a rural dirt road which turned into a bridle path, complete with horse manure. We were in the middle of the woods, hoping our tires would not sink into the *mierda*, trapped on a path that was getting smaller and smaller.

Suddenly out of nowhere, a red pickup truck appeared behind us and started to follow. Through the rearview mirror, I could see the driver was a man with a shaved head, his heavily tattooed left arm dangling out the driver's window. Terrifying images from the movie *Deliverance* sprang to mind. Meanwhile, all Lily could focus on was the horrific bumpiness of the terrain. "Tovah, you're killing me!" she said. "I'm ninety years old, and my hip's gonna pop out!" I said, "Mom, we're being followed by a very angry-looking Yul Brynner, and the road maps are not clear on how to get out of here." She said, "We're not on a road. We're on a horse path! Stop the car and ask Mr. Brynner for directions."

Scared to death, I reluctantly, but obediently, stopped the car, but wisely kept the engine running. I got out and waved my hands politely in the air. The truck stopped immediately and much to my horror, the driver climbed down. Instantly assessing his outfit, I started chronicling these details in case a future forensic artist needed to create a composite sketch: He was wearing a ripped white T-shirt and black jeans that were worn through at the knees, tucked into dirty black boots. He had dark brown eyes set close together, a broad black brow, a flat nose, and his unshaven face had a scar on the left cheek. From whatever distance I could keep, I asked the driver, *"Por favor, direcciones?"* He responded in German. Oy! He didn't speak Spanish. He didn't speak French, he didn't speak Italian, and I certainly sensed he didn't speak Hebrew. Was he a stranger here too? He certainly looked strange. In my mind's eye, I kept seeing the statue of the huge bull in front of the Ronda Plaza de Toros, horns down, ready to charge. The situation felt ominous.

Wait a minute! My mother was a German major at NYU. Maybe she could help! "Momma, can you help me?" I asked, overpronouncing each word.

"Can I *hub* you?" she replied, quite deaf.

"No, can you help me?" I repeated, loudly. "Can you speak to this man in German and find directions out of this place?"

Lily replied, "German? We're in Spain, Tovah. *Spain.* Find directions? I can't even find my way out of this car! We're surrounded by horse shit. Tell him to get over here."

Asking the driver to come near our car was a terrible idea. The hairs on the back of my neck were starting to curl. How do I get out of this overgrown forest?

Then it hit me! Call "Ever-Ready Eddie!" That was my dependable Andrew, back in New York. Actually, the nickname had more to do with his aptitude in the bedroom, but over the course of our marriage, the moniker had expanded its scope as he had repeatedly proven himself ever-reliable in every pinch, a great virtue. So, in the middle of some woods somewhere in south central Spain, I hopped back in the car and called my husband's office, which was on the top floors of the Pan Am Building over Grand Central Station. The red truck did not budge.

Surprised to hear from me, he buoyantly asked, "Where are you?" as he took the call.

"I'm on a bridle path in Spain and we're lost. Andy darling, do you have MapQuest on your computer?" These were the early days of GPS, but it was my only hope. Meanwhile, Lily was loudly muttering, "Oy, my coccyx!"

"Please get me out of here," I said.

"Where's *here*, Tovah?" Andy asked.

"It's a rural, hilly area going toward Marbella from Ronda. And there's a German guy with tattoos following us in a red pickup truck."

"How long has he been following you?" Andy asked.

"It feels like an eternity. It also feels like *The Texas Chainsaw Massacre*."

"That movie didn't end well," he sang to me, trying to inject some levity, as he scanned his computer. "Hold on." And miraculously, my brilliant, resourceful husband somehow found a road where he thought we might be. He told me to make a U-turn.

"U-turn?" I said, "Andy I don't think you're quite visualizing the terrain." Then to myself I asked, *How many trees am I going to hit? How much horse shit is gonna fly?* thinking any fancy maneuvering would surely make this shitty scene only shittier.

I gently signaled the German truck driver to please back up. Mercifully, he did. Perhaps he was just a very nice man with a very bad barber.

With Andy's help, somehow we retraced our steps and went back to the road sign that eventually led us to Marbella. Only then did Andy sign off. We arrived just before nightfall and breathed a sigh of relief.

And for a Bar Mitzvah's worth of years, I had to hear Mother retell that tale, with the epigraph, "Here she is, 'Tovah the Tour Guide.' Good in a crisis she's *not!*"

The adventures with Lily not only had to do with adventure travel, it also expanded into *adventure technology*. Thanks to a successful cataract operation, Mother could read perfectly without glasses. Deaf as a post, she remained sharp as a tack. With eyesight and a facile mind at her command, she was able to boldly go where few centenarians had ever gone before: she mastered the arts of email, iPad, and TTY—the trinity of holy technology.

"What is TTY?" Lily expounded proudly, perched on her gold velvet chaise lounge. She was wearing her pale-yellow Japanese silk kimono, looking like an empress, overseeing Andy and me as we unpacked the box on the Napoleonic mahogany night table in her master bedroom.

"TTY stands for teletypewriter," Lily explained. "This is the service for the hard of hearing where a ticker tape of what is being said to me is physically typed by a third party listening to our conversation. If I know word for word what's being asked of me, or what's being said, I can respond appropriately."

Proud as I was of my mother going to the League of Hard of Hearing, being alerted to this groundbreaking piece of technology, and immediately ordering it for the master bedroom, there was one factor I hadn't anticipated.

"There's a third party listening to our conversation?" As the wife and daughter of lawyers, I was concerned.

"Of course, Tovah. That's how it works. The words of whoever's talking to me are typed across this small screen, you see it?" she said, pointing to a small monitor encased in the large plastic body of this state-of-the-art Lily-friendly telephone. "I'll be able to hear with my eyes. You'll no longer have to scream to me, darling! I'm leaping into the twenty-first century."

To tell you this was a G-dsend of technology would be an understatement. Overnight, the shouting into the mouthpiece from Riverside Drive subsided, and the swelling on my right vocal cord finally found some relief. Communications with my mother actually flourished. Before TTY, conversations often had been cryptic to her from my end of the line, which forced me to focus on just bullet points, necessary nouns, verbs, or dates to get them into Lily's ears. Now our conversations, by comparison, were nuanced.

Here's a typical example of speaking to Mom, mindful of not going too quickly for the TTY stenographer:

Operator: Hello, this is TTY, stenographer number 413, are you ready to start your call?

Tovah: Yes, operator. Go ahead. Hi Mom! How are things going at Château Feldshuh?

Lily: *Très bien!* I bet this operator thinks I'm French nobility. Tovah, you are such a celebrity, I keep getting letters with clippings that mention your name!

Tovah: What do they say, Mom?

Lily: I've got one right here. I'm referring to the Emelin Theatre Gala at the Glen Island Harbour Club. You will be receiving "The Emelin Award for Excellence in the Performing Arts!" *Excellence!* So, *nu?* (Yiddish for that's not surprising.) That's N-U, operator!

Tovah: Mom, the operator doesn't have to spell it for me. I can hear you.

Lily: Right, right. Listen, that dinner is quite expensive. If I remember correctly, $500 a seat! What kind of chicken could they be serving that costs $500? Gold-encrusted? *(laughing at her own jokes)* You are the guest of honor, so this will not concern *you*. For me? I would love to be present, but it's a lot of money. Is there any possibility that you might be allowed to have your 96-year-old mother come on a complimentary dinner ticket? Perhaps you can subtly check.

Tovah: *(Subtly?)* I'll get that done.

Lily: Get a gun?

Tovah: Re-type, operator. Done. D as in David o-n-e.

Lily: Five hundred dollars a chicken? You *should* bring a gun. It's robbery! Thank you, darling, or should I say, *merci beaucoup* from Château FeldSHOO! *(leaning into the rhyme)*

Regardless of minor miscommunication hiccups, the miracle of TTY made our connection with Mom infinitely more manageable and meaningful.

My daughter Amanda, Lily's first granddaughter, however, had a different point of view:

"The funniest moments on TTY were when we would tell Gramee important things that were urgent. For example, when I was just thirteen years old, I broke my nose on the soccer field. I called her crying: 'Gramee, Gramee, I broke my nose in twenty-three places! I have a nose cast! What am I gonna do?' I was expecting words of wisdom, but what

I heard back was an operator who needed to transcribe everything, and she's saying in a flat monotone, 'I . . . broke . . . my . . . nose . . . in . . . twenty . . . three . . . places. . . .' I was hoping for immediate assurance from Gramee for my teenage tragedy. Instead, I got some stranger repeating the bad news right back to me like a robot."

I was infinitely more comfortable when I was the typist, which brings us to the iPad. I came up with the perfect plan. I bought my mother an iPad and bought myself a remote keyboard. I would become her personal court stenographer by propping up the iPad in front of her, sitting behind her, and furiously typing verbatim whatever people were saying. To say this was a breakthrough for Mom was an understatement. Now, though virtually deaf, she could toss off her Lily quips in real time and still be the life of the party wherever we went.

It was all going smoothly until one night at the University Club.

Many of our family celebrations are spent at New York's glorious University Club at the corner of West Fifty-Fourth and Fifth Avenue. For this particular fête, we took possession of the seventh-floor Council Room, with its exquisite mahogany-paneled walls, gilt and celadon-green hand-painted moldings, and frescoed ceiling graced with a Greek goddess. There couldn't be a more majestic setting. It was a sit-down dinner for fifty-five relatives seated in a horseshoe table configuration so that all the guests could see and hear the lady of honor: my mother, Lillian Kaplan Feldshuh.

She was in top form, peppering her repartee with some of her gems from Leonard Sorcher's book like: "The optimist sees the bagel, the pessimist sees the hole," and "If you can't say something nice, say it in Yiddish." Imagine, she inhabited a world of silence, deaf even to the voices of those she loved, yet she was able to reach beyond that silence to create laughter, even though she couldn't hear the laughter. Then I realized she had gone silent for twenty minutes. Concerned, I typed: "Mom if you're really bored just tap your glass with your fork twice, and I'll get you out of here."

Suddenly Mom was like Handel's handbell choir. The table fell silent, looking at Mother as if she were about to make a wedding toast.

During this pregnant pause, I typed furiously, "Mom, just say *anything*, and I'll get you out of here."

Glancing at her iPad, Mom stood like royalty, taking in fifty-four pairs of eyes staring at her expectantly, and proceeded to say, "Excuse me, I have to go to the bathroom."

———◆———

MY COUSIN LUCILLE, A PSYCHIATRIC social worker, told me the minute Dad died to give Mom events she could look forward to. And I did. I gave her birthday parties every year, starting with her eighty-sixth, the year after Dad died. That party was at Windows on the World in the Twin Towers. The head catering sales manager of the restaurant was Jay Magazine, a beloved friend. "If food be the music of love, play on," he would say, and I would laugh as he malafoostered the quote from *Twelfth Night*. We flanked each other on Amanda's soccer team; I was coach and he was team manager. He was wonderful on the field and even more so on the 107th floor. He had a face that radiated warmth from every auburn follicle of his mustache, and he excelled in making sure his events sparkled. Like Sidney, he was an unbridled optimist. Jay helped me plan the first bash for my mother, right down to the yellow-and-blue sunrise place cards.

From Windows on the World, you could see the Statue of Liberty that Ada and Gershan had sailed past in 1902, almost a century before. Borrowing a line from *An Affair to Remember*, I wanted Lily's party to be "the nearest thing to heaven," which it was.

Amanda played Chopin on the piano, Brandon played the Bach double on the violin. All the years of Suzuki lessons bloomed at Mom's eighty-sixth. This is a memory that remains wrapped in a tender spot in my heart, given what that location now means to history. It was the last team effort on which Jay Magazine and I joined forces, and he handled everything to perfection. Then, tragically, Jay was taken from us along with his entire staff on 9/11.

"Welcome, Mrs. Feldshuh," he said, waiting to receive us the minute we emerged from the elevator on the 107th floor. "I've got the best seat in the house for you today," he continued, walking us to the table of honor in front of the floor-to-ceiling windows and the dizzying view of the tip of Manhattan and Lady Liberty, her torch held high.

Standing at her place, Lily said, "Thank you, Jay. You're a doll." Then she shouted, "Hello, everyone!" She couldn't hear the rousing applause, but she saw the standing ovation of so many of us who loved her. She raised a glass of water, and Jay immediately replaced it with a glass of champagne. "Are you trying to get me drunk, Jay?" she flirted.

Seizing this moment and inspired by the view, with gravitas she continued, "A century ago, my parents Ada and Gershan first saw the Statue of Liberty as they sailed into New York Harbor. Gershan was twenty-two, Ada was eighteen, and the Statue of Liberty was sixteen! They were children; all babies! From third-class steerage my parents made a life for my sisters and me in the New World. And look where we are standing today."

I was dazzled by my mother, even more so than the view. Here was Lily taking her moment, at her birthday party, elevating it to something profound and regifting it back to us. Lily the sage, no longer so shy.

She continued, "My children have brought me up to this perch today. My mother always used to sing, 'I'm only a bird in a gilded cage.' This is no gilded cage; this is a piece of heaven." Looking toward the ceiling, she shouted, "I only hope Sidney can hear me."

———————

THE NEXT BIG SURPRISE WAS Mom becoming my scene partner at an audition. Well, not literally, but thanks to her, I landed a major role in a gem of a film, *A Walk on the Moon*.

"Mom," I said, visiting her at 47 Penn, "You and I did an audition today."

"Ridiculous. I've been home all day," she replied, leading me into the solarium. "What are you talking about?"

"Well, you've been home, but your diaries were with me."

"You got ahold of my diaries?!"

"Momma, the ones you wrote in 1928. You *gave* them to me for safekeeping."

Joyce came in from the kitchen carrying the usual: decaf Lipton tea in Mother's porcelain yellow-flowered teapot with two matching cups, two napkins, two sterling silver teaspoons, and chocolate-covered graham crackers—bittersweet. Joyce also brought a hug for me.

"Momma, the part I auditioned for was a grandmother. A sage, like you. Her name is Lillian Kantrowitz."

My mother, pouring skim milk into her teacup, perked up and said, "Her name is Lillian? You're going to get the part."

"I *got* the part, Mom. I got it before I even got home, because of you! You were there in the audition room with me. When they asked me to read the scene, I asked first if I could read the backstory I had written for the character. They were surprised, but they said 'yes.' And I started with your diaries, 'I was born on a dining room table in the Bronx, 1534 Charlotte Street—'"

Mother interrupted mid-sip, "*Goniff!*" (Yiddish for robber.) "I should get royalties!" she joked.

"You will. They were gobsmacked."

I took a chocolate-covered graham and before the first bite, gleefully continued, "Then I took off my sweater and flipped the fat under my left arm, the way I used to play with yours—"

"Oh G-d, Tovah, please."

"I had to show them that I could play fifty-seven. I'm still in my forties."

"*Sha!* You're thirty-nine. *Forever* thirty-nine! 'Age is a number—'"

And in unison we finished, "—and mine is unlisted.'"

"Mom, what they loved about my audition was everything that had to do with you!" I said, pointing at her with my second cookie.

"Then you should bring me to auditions more often," she said.

Taking her to every audition would have been impossible, but I did do the next best thing. I got her a part in the movie. This was the first and only time we worked together, and thankfully there was no billing dispute about the size of our names for the credits.

Before this nepotism was even a notion, we were mid-flight to Canada with Joyce in tow.

"Mom," I said, taking her by the shoulders, so she could see my overly articulated diction, "You're going to love St. Agathe. The Laurentians are serving as the location for the Catskills. The movie takes place in the Catskills, but the production couldn't afford to film in New York."

Suddenly grasping that this would be as rustic as the mountainous destination so favored by the vacationers of her generation, Lily barked, "Are we *camping*?"

Now miming directly into her face so as not to be overheard, I mouthed, "Jews don't camp!" which set Mom off with a burst of a laugh.

"We're staying at a lovely hotel on a natural lake," I continued. "*Auberge Hôtel Spa Watel.*" We both peered out the window at the irresistibly inviting greenery far below. It was just mountains of forest. "Mom, we can go swimming every day."

"Can you get into the lake with a walker?" she quipped.

"Mom, Joyce and I will make it happen."

And we did. Mother and I enjoyed the bracingly crisp early-morning waters, an easy walk for us both from the absolutely enchanting hotel nestled in the even more enchanting woods enveloping it. My mother, however, was more enchanted by the beauty of my costars: the worldly Viggo Mortensen, who is half-Danish, half-American, and totally *gawgeous*; and the tall, dark, and brilliant Liev Schreiber. Even my director, Tony Goldwyn, was a visual delight.

On the set, I had to say repeatedly, "Mom, stop flirting with the leading men! You're holding up production!" Then it occurred to me a little bribery might reign her in, so I proffered, "Mom, I'll get you a part as an extra in the movie if you promise to behave!"

That is how my mother indeed was cast as an extra in the Rec Hall scene when the residents of the *kuchelein* (Yiddish for cottages) were all watching a movie. Thanks to that little Lily-bribe, I now have a close-up of her face, preserved forever with me in one of my favorite films.

Is it one of my more glamorous roles? No. I wanted to look chubby and squishy as Bubbe—a look Grandma Ada and my Aunt Nancy had mastered. So designer Jess Goldstein and I picked out costumes that were most unflattering to my figure. I wore stuffing around my waist and enhanced the size of my breasts, and then proceeded to eat whatever I wanted, to achieve the body I needed for the grandmother. Considering the Kaplan obsession with food, this was a happy time.

We were filming on the grounds of Camp Massad, actually, a nearby Jewish camp that was, for the moment, dormant, and looked a hell of a lot like Loch Sheldrake in the Catskills. Like the hotel, the camp too was on a lake, and I took every appropriate opportunity to take off my fat suit and my stuffed breasts, and grab a dip in the water.

Lily loved the Laurentians. It reminded her of a trip to Montreal that we took when I was a little girl—just the three of us, after we visited David in Maine at Camp Androscoggin. She and Joyce spent beautiful days sunning themselves at the hotel lake or on the set. Flirting? Yes, once Lily's scene was in the can, there was no reeling her in.

Viggo Mortensen was another daily dose of cool water. Every morning, he insisted on carrying my scripts, my research, and my props to the set. I soon put them in a wheelie, not wanting to impose, but without fail that young man would come to my room and ask if he could help me with my "luggage." He would never let me pull it on my own. I began to notice Lily was waking up earlier and earlier to make these journeys with us to work. Eighty-eight going on eighteen, she wanted in on the action. Viggo was an absolute prince to both of us.

Here's some scuttlebutt: by the time Liev began filming with us, the buzz on the set was that Viggo and Diane Lane were having a fabulous love affair. In fact, when you watch the film and witness their sizzling chemistry, it's an easy leap to think it might have indeed been happening off-camera, as well. Playing the cuckolded husband, Liev was not going to need a big reach for subtext. Apparently none of them were. Life was imitating art. Was it true? True or not, the set was crackling with heat. It was a *fantastic* shoot.

The movie was released on April 2, 1999. Mom, of course, was at the gala premiere. I remember sitting on Dustin Hoffman's lap in the red taffeta Saks Fifth Avenue dress I had worn to Brandon's Bar Mitzvah. All the cast and particularly the publicity crew, headed by Patrick Harrison and Meryl Katz, greeted Lily with such warmth. After all, she was the senior cast member. After the screening, Viggo leaned over to Mother and said, "I don't care what they say about Tovah's performance, it's *your* picture!"

Lily beamed and looked up to me, "Did you hear that? Next time I want my name above the title!"

1999 passed and we rolled into the next millennium. We survived Y2K and began preparing for Mom's ninetieth birthday in 2001. It started as a bang-up year for the Kaplan-Feldshuhs: Amanda's Bat Mitzvah on February 24, Mom's big "Nine-O" on April 18, a trip to London then Spain in June and July . . . and then the earth stood still on September 11.

In those innocent months preceding 9/11, I was in the midst of planning to celebrate Lily's major milestone on the top floors of another New York landmark, the Russian Tea Room. Opened in 1927 by members of the Russian Imperial Ballet, the fourth floor featured a mechanical diorama of majestic Moscow in four seasons. As we got out of the elevator, the miniature choo-choo train was circling the city.

The Hearth Room, with its walls of hand-inlaid faux wood–carved mirrors, and beautiful paintings that converge on a grand fireplace, was the most elegant setting for the sit-down luncheon in honor of Lily. The room hugged all 160 of us as toasts were topped with shots of top-shelf vodka.

I had a red leather customized guest book made at T. Anthony on Park Avenue that was engraved in gold title case, "Lillian Kaplan Feldshuh Birthday Celebrations." I placed the book on the third floor in the Bear Ballroom, a stunning, soaring space that measures two stories tall. It features etched mirrors of cavorting bears, frolicking rabbits, and silver leaf stag heads. There, the waiters served champagne and blinis with caviar and crème fraîche. I kept thinking, *My grandfather escaped the pogroms of Russia to bring us to this land, to this city, and to this moment.* Today, it was our turn. *We* felt like Russian royalty.

Once Grandpa Gershan's mother was murdered in the Easter pogrom of 1895, Grandpa and his siblings were spirited out of White Russia, across Poland and Germany, to arrive in Britain by 1896. There, he fell madly in love with a British girl named Ada Abrahams and asked her to marry him. From England, Ada and all of his siblings, except for Gershan's sister Fanny, left for America. Fanny married Leon Petrokovski, the butcher on Buress Street off Commercial, in London's East End. Remember the butcher in *Fiddler?* They never went hungry because they always had meat.

Fanny's grandchildren and great-grandchildren all flew in from London to honor Lily. The reunion with the family we left behind in the Motherland almost one hundred years ago was extremely touching. This was the branch of the family who didn't need to cross the waters for a better life.

I made a huge chart of our family tree out of oaktag, Post-it Notes, and magic marker. I felt like I was in sixth grade doing an art project, but the result was oh so helpful. All of the Kaplan clan had escaped the scourge of the Nazis. (The Feldshuhs from Austria were not as lucky.)

My mother's side of the family was huge, warm, beautiful, and always hungry. They didn't have to worry at the Russian Tea Room. Borscht with sour cream, a delicious herring salad, Chicken Kiev, and golubtsi (stuffed cabbage) were served throughout the two-hour repast. For dessert, Lily was the first in the family to receive a photo-image cake. When she saw it, she said, "Stop everything! I'm putting the top of this cake in the freezer for my ninety-first! Look at me, I'm too good to eat."

Ever intrepid, Lily set off into her nineties with her very first computer. David and I, with Lily's nephews and nieces, bought Mother a brand-new Dell computer with a matching printer for her birthday. She loved that they were "coordinated." She was on email in no time.

Perhaps this was the most successful of all of these technological marvels in Lily's unflappable hands. Mother took to the computer like gefilte fish to *chrain*. (Yiddish for horseradish, and make sure to pronounce the uvular fricative *ch*! Remember, Yiddish is Phlegm-ish.) A great typist since her youth, her fingers flew across the computer keyboard like the pianist she once was. Lily's emails kept coming to us in a flurry until just weeks before her death. The list of centenarians who write emails is very short, and I'm proud to say my mother's name is on it. Here are three of my favorites:

FROM: Lilyfeldshuh@aol.com
TO: Tovah Feldshuh
DATE: June 30, 2007
SUBJECT: July Fourth Weekend

DEAREST TOVAH,

JOYCE WANTS TO TAKE OFF JULY FOURTH. YOU WILL BE STUCK WITH ME.

I WILL BRING THE WHEELCHAIR IN THE EVENT WE WANT TO PRANCE AROUND TOWN!

I LOVE YOU!

MOMMA

FROM: Lilyfeldshuh@aol.com
TO: Cousin Karen Shafron in London
DATE: March 29, 2011
Subject: The Birthday Gift!

DEAR KAREN,

THANKS FOR THE CLASSIC LARGE BAILEYS IRISH CREAM . . .

I LOVE THE STUFF.

CHOCOLATE AND LAUGHTER . . . AND BAILEYS ON A DAILY BASIS.

XOXOXO

LILY

And this single email I received after a Lyrics & Lyricists concert I appeared in entitled "Great Jews Singing Great Jews" made up for all the proverbial opening-night telegrams I never got as a child:

FROM: Lilyfeldshuh@aol.com
TO: Tovah Feldshuh
DATE: September 27, 2005

DEAREST TOVAH,

THANK YOU FOR SUCH A SPECIAL, WONDERFUL EVENING.

YOU DID A STUPENDOUS PERFORMANCE AND YOU SURE HAD THE AUDIENCE IN THE PALM OF YOUR HAND, THEY WERE LAUGH-ING THE WHOLE TIME!! THANKS FOR BEING SUCH A TALENTED ACTRESS AND GIVING ME SUCH PLEASURE CONSTANTLY!!

LOVE, LOVE, LOVE YOOOOOOOOOOOOOOOOOOOOOOO OOOOOOOOOOOOOOOOOOOOOOOOOU MOMMA

At over ninety years old, daily she was finding and forwarding web advice such as, "Old age is like a bank account; you withdraw from it what you've put in. So my advice to you would be to deposit a lot of happiness," to which Lily added, "I'm still depositing!" There were also jokes from *Life's Little Instruction Book* by H. Jackson Brown Jr., which was printed the year my father died. On Passover, she quoted, "A bad matzah ball makes a great paperweight." And for her birthday, "Pork is forbidden, but pigs in blankets make great hors d'oeuvres." No day was complete without Lily forwarding funny email jokes she discovered online. Her full engagement in social conversations, through TTY, iPad, and the computer, kept Lily in the game.

———————

LILY WAS ALWAYS READY FOR the sharp, piercing retort. They say when people get older they lose their edit button, so their comments can be mortifying, but still have a morsel of truth in them. For my fiftieth birthday, ever the optimist, I asked Mom if she wanted to come with me to Antarctica. My mother said, "Antarctica? *Mishuganah*, what are you trying to do, show Andy what frigid *really* means? If I want to see penguins, I'll turn on PBS."

When Amanda was Bat Mitzvahed, she wore a shocking pink *very* slinky dress with glitter dots all over it for the evening celebration. She picked it out herself and absolutely loved it. Mom took one look at Amanda in that dress and said, "Amanda! What, are you open for business?"

Amanda looked at me quizzically and said, "Mom, what does that mean?"

Scrambling for a euphemism, "She thinks you look like a manager at Ralph Lauren," I said lamely.

When we were alone, I admonished my mother, "You mean the world to Amanda, so why would you say such a thing?"

Lily replied, "Because that dress makes her look like a streetwalker!"

I snapped back, "Just because she isn't in lace anklets and white gloves doesn't mean she looks like a hooker!" Then, trying to salvage the moment, I offered in my best adult voice, "Come, Your Highness. Let's party."

———————

NOTHING MADE MY MOTHER FEEL more like royalty than the day we were seated together atop a red convertible as the mother/daughter stars in the inaugural parade to celebrate Walt Disney's one hundredth birthday, touted as "100 Years of Magic," at Disney World in Orlando, Florida. Mind you, I had to have Joyce sitting in the back seat to anchor Mother's legs and knees so we didn't lose her off the side of the vehicle. She was alternately waving like Queen Elizabeth and shouting down to Joyce, "Stop it! I'm alright!"

That evening we were invited to the Magic Kingdom Private VIP Dinner Reception, hosted by Michael Eisner and Roy Disney. It was followed by a blur of "Fantasy in the Sky" fireworks, an Animal Kingdom safari breakfast expedition the next morning, and a taping of *Who Wants to Be a Millionaire?* This was a cross between fabulous and a migraine, but the price was right.

Mother cried in disbelief, "You paid *nothing* for all this?"

I replied proudly, "My career paid for this, Mom. That's why we're guests of management and have that gorgeous suite at the Port Orleans Resort."

Our eyes and ears were in overtime, and how my ninety-year-old mother got through all that excitement was a miracle. Perhaps it was because after Dad's death, she had started collecting small stuffed animals to keep her company, and at Disney World, they were everywhere. Maybe these friendly creatures reminded her of when she was a girl, or a young mother. Her love for them made me think of Shakespeare's *Seven Ages of Man* and the return to "second childishness."

———·•·———

IF I HAD TO PICK a moment in my memories of the intersection of our best nights on the town and Lily's best moments as the mother she had become, it would be the night that she accompanied me to the 2004 Tony Awards. I was nominated for my work as Prime Minister Golda Meir in *Golda's Balcony*. It was my fourth nomination. The stakes were high, and the ceremony was at Radio City Music Hall. The play was a tremendous success and by artistic merit, I thought, *Wow, maybe this is my year.* I had already been lucky enough to win the Drama Desk, the Outer Critics Circle, and the Lucille Lortel. And I went on to win the Helen Hayes and the Dramalogue Awards for my portrayal of Golda.

Peers dropped off notes at the Helen Hayes stage door saying, "Darling Tovah, this year it's your turn." My sister-in-law and brother-in-law flew up from Washington, DC, because they felt I had a real shot. Friends flew up from as far as Florida and bought the exorbitantly priced Tony tickets because they were certain I would win. A big party was planned in my honor on Park Avenue after the ceremony. And since this was my sixth nomination for a major award (two Emmys and four Tonys) I thought, *Yes, maybe they're right.*

The award for Best Actress came toward the end of the ceremony. My heart was in my throat. *Could the planets ever be better aligned for me in my career?*

Thinking it would be bad luck to hand my evening purse to Andy in anticipation of them calling my name, I sat like a lady, purse resting in my lap, waiting for them to announce, "Tovah Feldshuh."

Foolish me. It wasn't my turn after all.

I lost to Phylicia Rashad in the Sean Combs–led production of *A Raisin in the Sun.*

My mother was outraged. She turned to the actor next to her and said facetiously, "How do I get ahold of a Tony? I want to buy one for my baby."

Then she said to me privately, "You lost because you were a Jew in a Jewish play."

I thought, *Without Jewish mothers, who would need therapy?*

I reminded her that *Fiddler* had won many Tonys for the Jews in *that* Jewish play. My mother didn't buy it.

I have to admit, that loss was a knife in my artistic, excellence-driven heart, and my mother knew it, and she would have none of it.

"Mom, I just want to go home," I confided.

She replied, "Are you kidding? Tonight's a night to celebrate. There's a party in your honor, so slam a smile on your face like the cream cheese you'd schmear on a bagel."

The Tony party in my honor was at the home of Patricia Askwith Kenner on Park Avenue. Even her lobby was a wow: a huge eighteen-foot-high space, with diamond-shaped black-and-white stone tile, elegant WASP furniture, and a cloak room to "check the furs." You never had to hail a cab from Patti Kenner's building. You simply pushed a special button in the elevator to alert one of the three doormen to hail one for you, and by the time you reached that Park Avenue awning, the taxi was waiting.

Patti did a bang-up job as she always does, and thankfully, we had a blast. She made sure of that. So did Lily. I was asked to climb up on a chair and give the acceptance speech that I had carefully tucked in my chest, should I win. After I thanked the appropriate people, I then ended with the following passage:

> If, in my lifetime, I have seen the Berlin Wall come down, apartheid end in South Africa, and communism collapse in Russia, then in our lifetime, surely we are capable of making a quantum leap as civilized human beings to bring peace in the Middle East between Arab and Jew. And so we must—now more than ever.

My beloved dresser, Trevor McGinnis, surprised me with a handmade Tony out of cardboard and aluminum foil with a picture of me as Golda holding up the award with my right hand extended like Lady Liberty. He presented it to me as I stood next to the custom-made cake with my portrait on it whose headline read, "Tovah Feldshuh, Best Actress." We celebrated the night away with laughs and much gratitude for the friends and allies who were there to cheer me on, win or lose. My mother was there for every second of it. At the tender-hearted age of ninety-three, she never budged from her belief that I was robbed.

She said to me, "Just remember, three-fourths of the nominees at the Tonys walk out without a Tony. So enjoy the cake."

Then she said to all the guests, "I want to toast my marvelous daughter, who is a brilliant actress, and if this were a meritocracy, *she* would be holding the Tony tonight."

I was uplifted. I may not have won the Tony, but I felt like I had just won the Lily. I kept repeating to myself over and over, *I have pleased my mother. I have met my mother's mark. I have pleased my mother!* That was my mantra that evening, and the Tony loss was dwarfed next to her unequivocal approval.

Lily on My Becoming an Actress

"You want to be an actress? Terri Sue, why don't you just go into the kitchen, get my challah knife, stick it in my heart, and twist it!"

You Only Live Twice

M OM COASTED ALONG, WITH CROWN ON HEAD, UNTIL 2006. She had ten years of HLE: Healthy Life Expectancy. In January, I was busy planning her ninety-fifth birthday celebration for April. Brandon graduated from Harvard and was at Oxford University getting a master's in financial economics, Amanda was graduating from Spence to enter MIT as a physics major in the fall, and Momma kept spiraling upward in her *"amazing"* years.

People would say, "You're ninety-four? You're *amazing.* You look fifty!"

She would reply, "Almost ninety-five!"

Her star was ascending and she finally began to give herself top billing on her own marquee. Then I received this email from her at the end of February:

FROM: Lilyfeldshuh@aol.com
TO: Tovah Feldshuh
DATE: FEBRUARY 20, 2006

MY DARLING:

DAVID JUST CALLED ME AND HE SPOKE TO DR. PECHMAN (mom's gerontologist) AND ASKED HIM FOR MY OLD RECORDS. AORTIC STENOSIS WAS ON THEM, SO IT COULDN'T HAVE BEEN VERY SERIOUS OR ELSE HE WOULD HAVE TOLD ME. IT IS THE FIRST TIME I'VE HEARD OF IT. ANYWAY, LET US JUST FORGET ABOUT IT UNTIL I SEE DR. RAIZES ON MONDAY. HE IS MY CARDIOLOGIST.

I AM GOING TO THE BEAUTY PARLOR AT 12:30 P.M. TOMORROW AND I WILL SEE HOW I FEEL ABOUT GOING OUT TOMORROW NIGHT. DON'T WORRY, I ALWAYS LOVE A PARTY.

OH, ABOUT MY BIRTHDAY PARTY—I DON'T WANT TO DEPRIVE YOU OF THE PLEASURE OF MAKING A PARTY FOR ME, SO WE'LL GO AHEAD WITH IT. IT DOESN'T HAVE TO BE SUPER ELEGANT, JUST NICE AND HOMEY—WITH A GOOD VIEW.

I LOVE YOU MY DARLING.

YOUR LOVING MOMMA

Mom's morning cheer was wrapped around two words that were new to me, "aortic stenosis." I toggled from her email immediately to an Internet search. There I learned the following: stenosis, wherever we get it, means "narrowing of." In aortic stenosis, the narrowing is around the aorta, one of the heart's primary highways for pumping fresh, oxygenated blood around the body. A person can go along with this condition for years without having symptoms. As the stenosis of the aorta slowly builds up, symptoms manifest, and it signals that the aortic heart valve is becoming so calcified that it is having trouble functioning. It can't contract and expand properly to push fresh blood back into the body. The result is chest pain, fatigue, and shortness of breath. The heart starts to labor overtime. The condition is eventually fatal.

I reread the words "eventually fatal" and immediately swept the laptop up and set off to find Andy. He was at his home office in what was once Brandon's bedroom at the immense desk that was once my father's, sipping his morning coffee.

"Darling, 'aortic stenosis.' Have you heard of it?"

Looking up from the digital *New York Times*, Andy paused then answered, "No. Why do you ask?"

"Mother's been diagnosed with this condition of the narrowing of her aortic valve. It's reducing the blood flow to her body and making her heart work harder and harder. Andy, it's ultimately fatal."

"Now slow down," Andy said, beckoning me to sit next to him. "Is she having symptoms? How did she find out?"

"It showed up in her medical reports. She was unaware of it till today."

Unable to sit, I opened my computer to share Mother's email. As I waited impatiently for the screen to find the Wi-Fi, I continued. "Andy this can't be happening. Mom is my Rock of Gibraltar."

Andy looked up skeptically.

"My Lily-Gibraltar. My Olympian of common sense, my wise stone mountain."

Andy said, "I get it, I get it!"

Giving up on the computer, I sat on his lap. "She's finally become the softer, more empathetic, open-minded, even supportive mother I dreamed of having all my life. She cannot be dying."

Andy, ever rational, assured me, "Sweetheart, she's showing no signs of slowing down. If this is the diagnosis, and she's presently asymptomatic, maybe we can manage her care accordingly and arrest this condition."

Andy's brilliant logic had just pulled the "Stop" lever to the carousel of catastrophizing swirling inside of me. He continued, "Let's call Doctor Dave. He'll guide us. And remember: she's doing fine today, right? She's writing emails at 9:00 a.m.? Sounds pretty good to me at ninety-five years old."

I hugged him around the neck and laid my head on his strong, broad right shoulder. "Andy, I know you've been through decades of hearing about my conflicts with Lily. The deep, dirty secret is that ever since Dad died, and my mother's personality has started to alter, or perhaps return to its original joy, I've come to adore my mother. I can barely reconcile these new feelings within myself, but I am G-ddamn grateful for them. I know I've been given a gift. Have you noticed that as she has softened, she's strengthened?"

Andy just looked at me.

"It sounds like an oxymoron," I mused, trying to convince him, "but it's true. I've been given this gift, Andy. Very few people have the gift of a challenging, hard-to-please parent, especially one of her generation, actually evolving over time, becoming more flexible, not more rigid. Oh, Andy," I said, the words seemed to be pulling themselves literally from my heart, not my lungs, "now we need the gift of time."

What was so especially true about this honeymoon Mother and I were enjoying is that we had finally vaulted over the remaining hurdle between us: our conflicts about how to raise my children. Mother was so afraid that by not following *her* rules, I could screw up the children—and thus my marriage.

Our disagreements over Brandon and Amanda were the last vestiges of her judgmental eye that lingered after Daddy's passing. Now we were "home free," pun intended, and she and I were able to connect with a buoyancy we never had before. Incidentally we both agreed, if you marry for love, the empty nest is highly underrated.

In fact, the entire family was flying high. Andrew was a senior partner at Gibson Dunn, one of the great American international law firms. I had finished my run as Golda, not only on Broadway, but in Los Angeles, and San Francisco, and was planning to open in London. The children were soaring academically and emotionally.

It was Saturday night, April 15 (and we had paid our taxes on time!). We were walking out of the three-star restaurant Daniel on Sixty-Fifth between Madison and Park. It was a wedding reception for my cousin

Wendy, and Mother had been a trouper, leaping at the opportunity to attend even with her big birthday party the following day.

Knowing that she would never turn down an invitation, I questioned her as to whether it might be too much on the eve of her ninety-fifth birthday celebration.

"Nonsense!" she had retorted. "If there's a bell I want to ring it. Besides, I have a new Anne Klein cocktail dress that's looking forward to a night out on the town."

Walking the half block on Sixty-Fifth Street to Park Avenue where the recently rehired Milton and the silver Chevy were awaiting, I noticed Mother's breathing was unusually labored. Getting into the car from her walker was a particular ordeal.

"Mom," I said, aware she was struggling, "take your time, and breathe deep. You've had a big night."

She turned to me with a scolding look and said, "Tovah, you're not my mother. I'm *your* mother! And I'm fine. *Sha!*" (Yiddish for hush.)

As she looked up at me, the harsh light from the street lamp caught her face. I gasped. Her typically pink porcelain skin had turned a pale yellow. Now I was not concerned, I was alarmed.

"Andy look!" I said to my husband, motioning him to come round to Mom's side of the car. "Mother, are you OK?" I said. "You don't look right. Your breathing . . ."

"Stop it, Tovah," she interrupted, her words lacking the bark that would normally propel them like a dart, "I'm just catching my breath. I'm fine."

Her "I'm fine's" had become an irritant between us, and she knew it. Just the week before I had told her, "I want you to put a quarter in the *pushke* (Yiddish for charity box) every time you say 'I'm fine.' *Caching!* 'I'm fine' is not an answer, it's denial, and it's unacceptable. I don't want to hear it. I'm *fine*-ing you twenty-five cents for every 'I'm fine.' Got it?!"

Here she was tossing off an "I'm fine" when all the evidence was saying otherwise.

Our eyes met and she saw my disapproval. She smiled, "Got it. *Ca-ching.*"

"Mom, it's just that I've never seen you look like this. You seem to be struggling for air. Do you think we should go to a hospital?"

Andy then backed me up, "Lily dear, you're looking pale. Are you sure you're OK?"

"A hospital? Absolutely not," she said, proving her mettle as she slid into the passenger seat. It's not that she was so anxious to sit near Milton; she would get carsick when she sat in the back seat. "What I need is a good night's sleep . . . and for you two to stop worrying. *Genug!*" (Yiddish for enough.)

It's odd looking back that I chose to obey her wishes rather than trust my instincts and my eyes, but even at fifty-seven years old, I did as she asked. After all, she was my mother. As I closed the door, I said, "Don't aggravate yourself if Milton drives slowly. Just stay calm." Then I went to Milton's window and said under my breath, "Milton, please, step on it."

I suddenly realized, thank G-d before they pulled away: What if something were truly wrong, and G-d forbid, what if this were the last time I'd see my mother? Had I said the right words to her that I could live with going forward? What *were* the right words?

I rapped on the glass and motioned to Mother to roll down her window. She proceeded to push all the wrong buttons on the central console, opening every window but her own. Finally, Milton gently intervened and calmly pushed the proper button for her. I said, "You were dazzling tonight, Mom. Andrew was so proud to have you on his arm; you and your Anne Klein dress made such a splash. You are truly *amazing,* Mother. I know you hear that plenty from everyone else, but I'm your only daughter and, therefore, I claim authority. Daddy may have been the *greatest* . . . but you're the queen of *amazing.*"

"Tovah, I can't hear a damn thing. I *think* what you said was a compliment."

Then I stuck my head through the window, six inches from her face so she could lip-read, and I articulated, "I love you. You are the best mother in the world. I am the luckiest daughter in the world."

"*Now* I hear you. You're such a good egg. But *please* let me go." She stopped suddenly, trying to draw in a big breath, then added, "I've got to get my beauty sleep. After all, I've got a show to do tomorrow!" We laughed.

———◆———

RELIEF DIDN'T REALLY COME UNTIL the next morning when there was an email awaiting me from Mother, sent at 9:00 a.m.:

FROM: Lilyfeldshuh@aol.com
TO: Tovah Feldshuh
DATE: APRIL 16, 2006

MY DARLING FABULOUS DAUGHTER;

YOU DO NOT HAVE TO CONCERN YOURSELF ABOUT MY HEALTH. I LAUGH ABOUT EVERYTHING NOWADAYS LIKE AN IDIOT WITH A GOOD BRAIN. NOW DON'T YOU GET YOURSELF EXCITED EITHER. YOU HEAR ME? DON'T GET YOURSELF UPSET.

I'M FINE!—CA-CHING!

AND TODAY IS MY BIRTHDAY PARTY. WHOO WHOO!

XOX

THE OLE LADY! AKA MOMMY AKA THE MATRIARCH OF THE KAPLAN-FELDSHUH CLAN

A wave of peace washed over me, and I read the missive to Andy, who was shaving. He called back, "Great update!" And it was.

It was, until the phone rang two hours later. It was my brother David. He was calling from his home in Ithaca, where he is a tenured professor in theater at Cornell University, as well as the artistic director of Theater Cornell. The pertinent detail at this moment was: David was also an MD in emergency room medicine. I call him Dr. *Doctor* Dave. My mother calls him G-d.

"Tovah, where are you?" came his voice, steady but clearly energized by something alarming.

"I'm home, Dovey. I'm confirming the deliveries for Mom's party this afternoon. Why aren't you in the car?"

"Because I've been on the phone for the last hour with the doctors." My heart pounded.

"Mom collapsed while she was getting dressed. Joyce called 911. Mother's already in the ambulance to White Plains Hospital. They gave her oxygen immediately. I need you to get to White Plains Hospital now, and of course, cancel the party."

I thought to myself, *Please G-d, let my mother live.*

Meanwhile, cancelling the party was no small task. I asked my razor-sharp assistant to organize all the phone numbers of the guests then divide them amongst Mom's best (and youngest) friends, hoping that word would get out in time.

David from Ithaca and I from New York drove with a fury to Flanzer Pavilion, the same wing where my father had died ten years before. Then I discovered Mother was assigned to room 1318. For a Jewish person, 1318 is the luckiest number in the world. Thirteen signifies the transition from childhood to adulthood, and eighteen signifies chai for life.

I knocked on her door, quietly went in, and there was Lily, with an oxygen mask, an IV, a digital monitor . . . and a stunning pale-pink satin Dior bed jacket with matching lipstick. Joyce was there by her side. I said, "Joycie, how is she?"

She replied, "Well enough to have commanded me, 'Joyce, grab my Dior night jacket and my makeup!' as the paramedics were carrying her out."

"I'm amazed she didn't ask for her evening purse and white gloves," I joked.

We tried to chuckle.

When Mom woke up, she said, "Where am I? Where are the guests?" Looking around the room, "Am I in Flanzer? Do we still have time to get to the party? How late are we?"

I assured her, "Mom, no worries, no pressure. We've postponed the party till May and they didn't even charge me cancellation fees!"

But it was not meant to be. Mom was simply not getting better. She was in and out of the hospital all month, and two days before the party, as much as they'd rather bring me good news, the doctors insisted that leaving Flanzer for a birthday party was out of the question—her condition was that tenuous.

My British family had already flown in for the celebration and were staying with me on Central Park West. I woke up May 19 like a lightning bolt and ran to the library, where I found cousins Karen and Philippa and said, "Here's the plan. If Lily can't get to the party, we're going to bring the party to her. Cuzzies, my adrenaline's kicked in, and I have to admit, I love when it does. I will reorganize the catering. You two, if you don't mind, get on the phones to the fifty-six guests. (This was the second time I had a date with Alexander Graham Bell to alter Mom's party.) You don't need to use your British mobiles, I've got two landlines. Tell each guest that the party venue has been changed from the Heathcote Tavern to, wait for it . . . the staff cafeteria of White Plains Hospital."

Barreling on, because I could not waste a moment on truly absorbing the larger truth, I narrowed my focus to the pinspot center of what I could control: making this party happen in time. I said to Karen and Philippa, "While you make those phone calls, I'll get the caterer to work some magic, even if I have to rent them a truck."

What the University Club and the staff cafeteria at the White Plains Hospital have in common is that visitors are not allowed unless accompanied by members of the former and nurses of the latter. And there the similarities stop. Unlike the University Club, the decor in the staff cafeteria, to put it mildly, was stark. White walls, beige linoleum floor, white Formica tables with industrial plastic chairs, two steel sinks with antibacterial soap and paper towels, topped off by a prominent red fire alarm—all of it made more vividly clear by fluorescent lighting bright enough to perform an emergency appendectomy.

At the appointed hour, less than twenty-four hours after the calls were made, the grateful guests assembled in the White Plains Hospital staff cafeteria, waiting to see their beloved Lily. I had Bloody Marys served, pigs in blankets and spanakopita paraded on trays, and I had hired a ragtime band to play all the tunes of the '20s and '30s that Mom adored.

Sixty minutes passed, and still no Lily.

Here's a riddle: how many drinks do you think you can serve a Jew? Barely one.

The hors d'oeuvres, of course, were devoured.

To fill this now gaping hole in the party schedule, I showed a video interview of Mother talking from her solarium. In the video she says, "You know, here we're making this video, and wouldn't it be wild if I died before the party?" then she laughs with abandon. We, the party guests who were watching the video, dropped our jaws and turned green. I felt like I had entered Salvador Dali's melting clocks. I quickly asked the caterers to serve another round of Bloody Marys and pour it down those Jewish throats if necessary. If the guests were drunk enough, maybe they wouldn't notice Lily's absence. I leaned over to the ragtime band, and said, "Hit it! Play some peppy Gershwin." They did, but no one wanted to dance.

I ran up to room 1318.

Unexpectedly, a young resident on rounds met me outside Mother's door. She said, "I'm sorry Ms. Feldshuh, I can't even allow your mother to leave her room to go down to her birthday party for fear that her heart couldn't handle it. She could die right there."

I was stunned. "Are you sure, doctor?" I stuttered, thinking I was in a bad dream.

"Very sure," replied the doctor.

"Would it be possible to bring the guests up here?" I asked.

The doctor said, "You may, but they need to line up outside the room and be allowed in, at the most, two at a time. And the *minute* your mother gets tired, we stop."

I went down to the cafeteria, and with false gaiety, I said, "Stop the music, maestro! We have a Plan B, ladies and gentlemen. As you may have noticed, our guest of honor has not yet graced our presence. Since the theme of this day is 'if Lily can't come to the party, we'll bring the party to her,' the doctors have invited us to visit Lily right up in her room. Isn't that fabulous? How exclusive!"

Seeing the news land with a thud, I gave it my best two punch: "Taking a page from Noah, we're going to do it two by two. Each of you will have a short private visit with Momma Lily to wish her well."

And thus began the solemn processional up the elevator to room 1318, our formation clearly reminiscent of the animals entering Noah's Ark. The only thing missing was the forty days and forty nights of rain, but one only had to look at the concern on everyone's faces to feel the emotional downpour of the occasion. If only Lily could be saved the way Noah saved those animals. We needed a miracle.

Mother was the color of her pale-yellow, ivory satin Japanese robe, the one she wore so proudly when TTY was installed in her bedroom at 47 Penn. No pink in her face, her porcelain skin was sallow. Her cheeks were dull white on top of which she put some rouge in an effort to look healthy. Instead she looked like a painted doll. I was growing increasingly nervous and started to bite my cuticles, a childhood habit born from anxiety. *Stop it*, I said to myself, and painted that cream-cheese-schmear smile across my face, which I knew Mother liked.

"Mom? You're a star. There are so many of your fans waiting to see you. They're in a line just outside your door. I'm going to escort them in two by two."

She said, "Here, take my legal pad and write me exactly whom you are bringing in. I'm afraid I won't know who's who."

"Of course you will, Momma," I assured her as she gathered herself together and took her silver-plated hand mirror to check her lipstick. How wonderful that she was still vain. It showed a will to live.

Soon, the young resident asked to speak to me out of earshot of our guests and said, "Ms. Feldshuh, your mother's condition cannot go on much longer." The panicked little girl inside was hearing the unspeakable. I kept trying to push her down so that the adult in me could dominate and take hold. "I suggest you transfer her immediately to Milstein Heart Hospital. They're doing cutting-edge experiments that may be able to help your mom." One part of my mind leapt into action, while the other part was shouting, *There's hope, there's hope!* Within forty-eight hours, by the grace of the Milstein family, my mother was ambulanced down to Allan Schwartz, chief of cardiology.

After examining her papers, Dr. Schwartz looked up and said to my mother, "Mrs. Feldshuh, if you had come to me ninety days ago, we couldn't have helped you, but we are doing a new procedure that is in stage-one experimentation and we think we have an 80 percent chance of saving your life. You would, in fact, be the oldest person in the world we have tried this on—patient number thirteen."

Again, lucky number thirteen.

"Mrs. Feldshuh," he continued, "This is our shot. Without this procedure, your medical condition is fatal."

My mother paused, then looked up at Dr. Schwartz and said, "Death?" extending her left hand, "Experiment?" extending her right. "I'll take experiment!"

My mother was a woman with uncommon courage and, in the eleventh hour, a sense of humor.

She asked to be immediately admitted to Columbia Presbyterian at 168th Street. It was the end of May 2006, and I had begun rehearsals to play Dolly in *Hello, Dolly!* at the fabled Paper Mill Playhouse just over the George Washington Bridge.

Every day after rehearsal, I took the number one train from the 42nd Street Studios to 168th Street to see my mother. *Dolly* opened on June 10, and thereafter, every night the actors' van would take me from a rousing curtain call in a twelve-hundred-seat theater to a hospital room. From the most extravagant, pure-white wedding gown with matching hat, gloves, and parasol, I would take my final bow then quickly strip down to my Lululemons and tank top, grab my zippered *Golda's Balcony* sweatshirt, and hop into the company van that dropped me off at Columbia Presbyterian Milstein Hospital.

Bathed in the fluorescent light of her hospital room, my mother slept, looking so delicate and pale. I would tiptoe in and lie down on the small, rust-colored foam chair that unfolded into a floor cot, parallel to her bed. I had brought it there from our apartment. This was the "mountain bed" that Brandon slept on as a toddler in our bedroom when he wanted to be near his mommy and daddy. Once again it was nestling a child who needed to be near her mother.

On her door chart, my mother's billing read "Patient #13: stage-one experimentation for a percutaneous aortic valve replacement." She was a pioneer for this procedure, a test case for replacing a part of the heart *without* an operation. She was ninety-five years old and still grabbing at the ring of life.

"We need to put five stents into your heart, Mrs. Feldshuh," Dr. Leon said.

"What's a stent?" Mom asked.

"A tiny tube inserted into your aorta to keep it open. The minute the stents stabilize, we will replace your aortic valve with the valve of a pony."

"Pony?!" Mother said, her interest piqued.

Dr. Leon replied, "Well, we were deliberating between a pony and a pig."

Mother said, "Forget the pig. It's high treif."

"Mommy," I offered, "Daddy was always riding in on his horse to show you how great he was. This is a sign."

"You and your signs. *Mishuganah!*"

"Mrs. Feldshuh," Dr. Leon continued, "we've slated the procedure for June 28."

But on the evening of June 13, I received a call from Dr. Schwartz saying, "Your mother is dying and we have to go in immediately." June 14 was the chosen moment.

My first call was to Brandon in England. I asked him to fly home right away to see his Gramee for what could possibly be the last time. June 14 also happened to be his little sister Amanda's graduation from Spence. I alerted my entire extended family that Lily would be in the OR in just a few hours, and all those relatives came a-runnin' to see my mother off: my husband Andy, my brother David, his wife Martha, their son Noah, first cousins Peter and Joan, caretaker Joyce, and our beloved children Brandon direct from JFK and Amanda, one hour before her commencement ceremony.

At dawn on June 14, David and I were with Mom in the pre-op room, where she had to sign papers. She suddenly said, "I've changed my mind, I'm not doing this."

I said, "Momma, if you don't try this experiment, you will die by drowning to death at one point or another. And if you *do* try this experiment, you will make medical history. And G-d forbid, if it doesn't work out, you will die in your sleep while daring greatly and having served a cause bigger than yourself. *Tikkun olam*, Momma. The Talmudic principle states, 'Every person is put on this earth for the purpose of healing the world.' This is your opportunity."

She looked at me, she looked at the papers, and she said, "*Fuck it! I'll sign.*"

At that moment, Dr. Martin Leon came out to take the gurney from us with his protégé, the surgeon whose hands would actually perform the intricate replacement of Mom's aortic valve through her vascular system.

"Tovah, David, I'd like to introduce you to the man whose hands are going to save your mother's life. This is Dr. Susheel Kodali."

I looked up, and there was this handsome, young Indian doctor staring me in the face. I shot a glance at David. Not one month ago, David told me he kept having dreams of taking Mommy to India where he knew the doctors would take a chance at operating on her heart. And here was Dr. Susheel Kodali. It felt like the whole universe was aligning.

As the doctors took the gurney from us we suddenly heard, in a bellowing fortissimo, the singular voice of the intrepid adventurer Lily belting out:

> *Come on and hear, come on and hear,*
> *Alexander's Ragtime Band.*
> *Come on and hear, come on and hear,*
> *It's the best band in the land!*

Lily sang her way into this stage-one experiment with Irving Berlin's rousing Broadway anthem. She was probably thinking, *It ain't over till the fat lady sings—well, I'm the fat lady, so I'm going out singin'!*

Nervously, I attended Amanda's high school graduation and was determined not to give our daughter short shrift on this turning point in her life. My sweet Andrew was with me, and though I was concerned about not being in the hospital waiting room, we chose not to sit in the back of the Church of the Heavenly Rest on Fifth Avenue and Ninetieth Street, where the graduation took place. Nor did we rush out at the end of the ceremony. This was the only day our only daughter would graduate from the beloved school she attended for the prior thirteen years, and I was not about to reburden her with Gramee's critical condition. She had come to the hospital at the crack of dawn to be with her Gramee, for better or for worse, and with this weight, went on to her graduation. When she and her friends were settled in at their own private post-ceremony luncheon, I sprinted back to the hospital.

To my great surprise, Mother was still on the table.

Hours passed, and from the look on David's face, he knew this was not a good sign. "Tov," he started, "I'm worried. This doesn't feel right."

I said, "David, nonsense. Listen to this. This procedure was supposed to take place on June 28. I remember that date vividly because

June 28 is the date that Andy asked me to marry him, and I believe that date, had Mom been able to reach it, would've been a positive and lucky one. It has four sevens in it and lies exactly one month before Brandon's July 28 birthday, which was also Dad's Bar Mitzvah date in 1923."

David looked at me incredulous, uncertain where I was going with this line of thinking, and knowing I was never very good at math.

Undeterred, I pressed on: "Do you believe in divine intervention? At this moment, I do, because when Dr. Schwartz said that Mom's surgery needed to be today, bells went off. *This* is the day our parents were married publicly on the rooftop of the St. Moritz in 1935. It was their shout to the world that they were man and wife. Today is Columbia Presbyterian's shout to the world that a percutaneous aortic valve replacement, without an operation, is not just a dream. It's a concrete possibility. P.S. Dovey, you just had a dream about an Indian doctor successfully operating on our mother! Isn't Dr. Susheel Kodali in there right now with Mom? What's more, Daddy has been gone now for eighteen years. I can't help but think that he has a hand in this. Eighteen, chai for life, Dovey! Buck up, there's hope!"

I must've sounded insane to my brother, who was, after all, a doctor. But I have to admit, the coincidence of numbers was acute.

Very late that afternoon, after what seemed to us an eternity, Doctor Leon came out of the OR, still in his scrubs. Pulling down his mask, he revealed a big smile. "Lillian has made it through. The procedure is a success."

Our tension balloon burst at that point, and we started to weep with relief. We were elated. I started hugging everyone, the whole family, the doctors, and when Allan Schwartz came by, I got down on my knees and kissed the top of his hand and said, "I can't thank you enough."

He said, "Don't be so dramatic."

"But I'm an actress. That's what I do."

On July Fourth, *Hello, Dolly!* was dark. Having spent the day with Mother, I left the hospital for a moment and walked to the middle of the

George Washington Bridge. I was alone at night—right in its center—watching fireworks in the distance to the north and south over the Hudson River, somewhere so far away you could only see them and not hear them. As the firecrackers silently popped, I thought to myself, *This is the way my mother hears fireworks. And she never complains.* I imagined that this celebration of America was also a celebration that Lily was still alive and would pull through. I also kept repeating what gave me a chuckle: "Death? Experiment? I'll take experiment."

Her aortic stenosis had completely disappeared. She now had the heart of a fifteen-year-old and we would bask in the wit and wisdom of Lillian Kaplan Feldshuh for as long as we could. From her hospital bed, she said, "I've got the valve of a pony? Well, I guess I'm as strong as a horse!"

By the end of my run in *Hello, Dolly!* my mother made enough progress to come to the last matinee at the Paper Mill Playhouse. She came by ambulance with a bevy of staff attendants from Sarah Neuman Rehabilitation who were eager to see the show.

That afternoon after an exceptionally exhilarating performance, I made a curtain speech to stop the conveyor belt of life on this precious moment. I said: "Only five weeks ago at Columbia Presbyterian Hospital, in an experimental procedure, my mother became the first ninety-five-year-old in the history of the world to receive a percutaneous aortic valve replacement. She now has the valve of a pony and has started to gallop around the rehab facility in Mamaroneck. On the day of the operation, as I held her, I said to her: 'If you make it through this operation, you will have your life back, and if you don't, you will have died while daring greatly—while contributing to and advancing medical history.'

"Well, this afternoon she is here to tell the tale. Ladies and gentlemen: my most beloved mother, Lillian Kaplan Feldshuh."

The audience roared and came to their feet, and together twelve hundred people spontaneously sang "Hello, *Lily*," to the tune of "Hello, Dolly."

It was as if a spotlight were behind us shining directly on Mother's radiantly beaming face. I extended my arms toward her and she miraculously hoisted herself to her feet. A second roar erupted.

Hoping she could hear me, I belted out my very own lyrics to the final lines:

Lily will never go away
Lily, my mom, is here to stay
Lily don't ever go away again!

Tovah on Visiting the White House

Whenever I enter a new room, a new job, or a new meeting, people find me very elegant . . . until they see me eat.

When I was invited to the White House by President and First Lady Obama, I said to myself, *I know it's Hanukkah, but whatever you do, Tovah, DON'T EAT.*

It was really hard for me to restrain myself when the Marine Band played "I Have a Little Dreidel" and the waiters served latkes, those delicious potato pancakes that I adore—with a choice of sour cream or applesauce, my favorite food groups: carbs, grease, and sugar. Very dangerous to my outfit—and my waistline.

With the strength of Goliath, I controlled my obsession for food and shouted over the crowd to the waiter, "Latkes? No, thank you!" The President entered, and the room halted to a hush, but I was still screaming, "YOU MIGHT AS WELL JUST SLAM THEM ON MY THIGHS."

Oops! How elegant was *that*?

The Great Encore

I F *CARPE DIEM* MEANS TO SEIZE THE DAY, THEN HOW DOES ONE SAY *carpe* minute or *carpe* second? That was the life force behind the bonus years of Lily's return from the brink of death. It wasn't just Lily who got the wake-up call; it was a wake-up call for all of us. It brought to mind the words of Mahatma Gandhi: "Live as if you were to die tomorrow, learn as if you were to live forever."

Lily didn't mean to be so self-effacing all those decades from 1928 to 1996, but, as she explained it to me, "Your father took up the spotlight. . . . Perhaps he needed it." As the era in which she was born dictated, Lily let him do it. The pattern was probably formed early in her life. Being the third of four girls, there was nothing special about her position in the pecking order of her family. Somewhere genetically or psychologically, she was given the message that to be quiet was best. Nonetheless, underneath her silence, it turned out she had a will of iron.

Launching into this new gift of time, Mom began to attend classes at the synagogue on a biweekly basis. She was the only one in the class who could not hear. Wonderful Rabbi Tucker would pin the lavalier of Lily's hearing device on his lapel so she could supposedly discern what he was saying. He also sat her in the front of the class so she could read his lips. In other words, at ninety-five, she was studying Torah and Talmud without even being able to hear! Now our calls went from talking about Lord & Taylor to talking about the Lord and Talmud.

"Did you know that in the *Parshat Va'etchanan*—"

I interrupted, "Impressive, Mother!"

She continued, ". . . that the word *shamah* is used over ninety times? *Shamah* means 'hear.' And Moses felt people weren't listening. Remember Tovah, G-d gave us one mouth and two ears."

It was refreshing to hear a woman with *no* ears make such brilliant use of her mouth. I was thrilled by Lily's hunger to learn. Nothing makes us younger than our joy of rediscovering the world—at any age. That's what I learned raising my children, and now I was relearning it, this time from my mother.

My mother taught me well that an older person cannot afford to fall. "Tovah, I saw Dr. Pechman today and he said I'm doing *great*. And I quote, 'There is absolutely nothing wrong with you Mrs. Feldshuh. I only have two words of advice about staying healthy: *don't fall!*'" she said, imitating the doctor. On the other hand, she also taught me not to succumb to a wheelchair. The walker was the perfect assist to keep Lily moving.

When she wasn't ambulating, I saw my mother lying in her nineteenth-century Napoleonic bed from the French Empire doing her now *horizontal* interpretation of Jack LaLanne. She commanded herself, "Flex those feet!"—which now suffered hammertoes and were warped from so many years of chic high heels.

"Wave those arms!" Hers, still alabaster white.

"Pull in your gut!" Hers was herniated beyond recognition.

"Increase your pecs!" Is she still trying to lift up her size-C breasts?

"Slide those hands up and down . . . up and down . . . like a flying angel."

I saw her do this routine every day before she got out of bed in the morning.

If I arrived early for a visit and went to greet her in the master bedroom, she would always say, "Don't interrupt me. I have to finish my aerobics. If I can't have Dad, at least I can have endorphins. And flex, and point . . . and flex, and point."

My mother had the discipline of Jane Fonda, if not the Oscars and the rap sheet.

—•—

NOT TAKING ANYTHING FOR GRANTED, I gave her yearly birthday parties that would put Anna Wintour to shame.

I looked at gorgeous venues for her 103rd: the River Cafe, NYU's Kimmel Center—my mom was the class of 1931—the Harvard Club, The Harmonie Club, and finally, just as an exercise, the astronomically expensive Metropolitan Club at Sixtieth and Fifth Avenue. Built in 1891 by J. P. Morgan and twenty-five of his millionaire friends, the Metropolitan Club was constructed in response to the Knickerbocker Club and other social institutions, which did not allow the upstart nouveau riche J. P. Morgan and his family membership. The Great Hall was a forty-five-foot-high, gold-coffered ceiling with a huge Venetian lantern purchased at the Chicago World's Fair of 1893, hanging down from the middle. A grand double staircase on the north side framed a set of five opalescent stained glass windows facing the immense marble fireplace to the south. It made Tara in *Gone With the Wind* look like a cottage. I knew it would be unaffordable. *But what the heck*, I figured. *Make the call.*

I spoke to the events planner, Deidre Curran. I said we wanted the party to be on Friday, April 18, right in the middle of Passover. When she told me how much it would cost per head, I thought she had made a mistake. I said, "The Metropolitan Club is actually this affordable?"

She replied, "On a Friday night it is." Good Shabbos indeed! Preparations began.

Cocktails would be served in the President's Foyer, with its vaulted ceilings, stained glass, and extensive gilding. At our first meeting with Deidre and catering, Mom said, "For the hors d'oeuvres, I've got to have pigs in blankets."

I said, "Mom, we're in the middle of Passover, and the blanket on the pig is leavened."

She said, "If it's a blanket, how can it be leavened? Look, I'm 103 and G-d will forgive me." Then turning to Ms. Curran, she said "Listen, Deidre, at the cocktail hour, gimme those little piggies—and at dinner, serve matzah. No one will notice."

"Not much," I muttered.

Mother quickly retorted, "We can only do the best we can," calling over her shoulder as she sallied forth with her walker, looking at the decor.

"This place is gorgeous, Tovah! *Gawgeous!*"

I quietly whispered to Vincent, the head chef, "Just make sure the mini franks are kosher."

The President's Ballroom had tree-lined views of Central Park, Renaissance-style ceiling murals, and two showstopping Baccarat crystal chandeliers. There were marble fireplaces, rich burgundy upholstery, and extensive gold panel work. I wanted Little Lily from 1534 Charlotte Street to feel like she was attending her own coronation.

The one caveat was that Lily was no longer able to shop at her beloved Saks Fifth Avenue for her outfit. She had to order her beautiful beaded and embroidered jacket from the catalog, and I told her, "It's not a defeat Mom, it's a great alternative, and it's still from Saks."

"Well, it sounds to me like the mailman's having all the fun."

The day of April 18 arrived. Chai for life! Mom was 103! The President's Ballroom filled up with loved ones. Unique to this guest list were the "Four Musketeers" from Columbia Presbyterian: the doctors whose procedure eight years ago brought Lily to this triumphant day. She had broken all records by living longer than any previous patient who had a percutaneous aortic valve replacement, and she was in the first group of experiments!

At the party, my mother made the following toast, reading what she had written in her familiar size sixteen, all caps Arial font:

HOW THRILLED I AM TO CELEBRATE MY 103RD BIRTHDAY WITH YOU.

WHAT MORE CAN I SAY EXCEPT THAT THE DATE WOULD BE COMPLETE IF ONLY SIDNEY WERE PRESENT.

I MISS MY BOYFRIEND!

AND IF HE WERE HERE, HE'D LOVE THE FOOD.

I LOOK FORWARD TO CELEBRATING THE 104TH AT A MCDONALD'S SOMEWHERE IN THE NEIGHBORHOOD UNLESS TOVAH WINS THE LOTTERY.

TOVAH, YOU'VE OUTDONE YOURSELF. THIS YEAR SHE HAS HOSTED US IN A PALACE.

THANK YOU DARLING TOVAH WITH DAVID, ANDREW, AND MARTHA.

I KNEW I WAS THE MATRIARCH OF THE FAMILY, I DIDN'T REALIZE I WAS THE QUEEN. WATCH OUT ELIZABETH, I AM GIVING YOU A RUN FOR YOUR MONEY!

I'M IN MY PALACE TODAY—NOT JUST THE METROPOLITAN CLUB, BUT A PALACE OF THE HEART.

G-D BLESS YOU ALL AND I WISH YOU AS LONG AND AS HEALTHY A LIFE AS I HAVE HAD.

MY SECRET?

Anticipating her familiar mantra, the room joined her in unison:

"CHOCOLATE AND LAUGHTER ON A DAILY BASIS!"

Then Mom reached into a large gift bag I held next to her, and as if we were at a wedding, instead of throwing rice, she pelted her guests with handfuls of Hershey kisses. Our guests were startled and delighted.

As the final topper, she actually did a Vaudeville act. David and his son Zach fed her the setups, and she delivered the punchlines. All of these jokes were taken from actual incidents and quotes from Lily. Here's one of them:

David and Zach: Do you want a boyfriend?
Mom: Do I want a boyfriend? Another man? He'd be one hundred, he'd be crotchety, decrepit, and I'd be a nurse with a purse. I wouldn't be caught dead with him.
Ba-dum-bum!

Riding on the wave of her own euphoria, at the end of the evening, she said to my brother and me, "I should have been an actress. I had so much fun up there, and I was not afraid of anything." She repeated emphatically, "I was not afraid." This new level of fearlessness thrilled my mother. She was shattering her own glass ceiling.

Before Dad's death, what I had witnessed were decades of Lily's silent courage and unexpressed feelings. When he died, and it pains me to say this, she bloomed. At ninety-five, she became a medical pioneer. At one hundred, she traveled five hours down in a car to receive the Courageous Patient Award at the Washington Convention Center from over five thousand cardiologists who came in from around the world. She spoke to all of them saying, "You did such a great job with my heart! I don't know how I'm gonna die. You got any suggestions?"

At 103 years old, this once quiet mother of mine had emerged not merely as the matriarch of the Kaplan clan, but as a queen on the throne of her own life.

As time rolled on, and more and more of her contemporaries were dying, she would joke, "Ah, the good old days . . . when people were *alive*! Now, there's only one guy left from Sid's class, but he's got no teeth—*unkissable!*"

Mom just kept moving. In 2013 and 2014, she met me every Wednesday between matinee and evening shows of *Pippin* so we could have dinner together at Kodama, the nearby Japanese restaurant on Eighth Avenue between Forty-Fifth and Forty-Sixth Streets. She called me from the car. "Preorder me the shrimp tempura and that soup. What is that soup called?"

"Miso soup, Mother."

"Alright, one order of miso soup—without the salt!"

I said, "It doesn't come without the salt."

She said, "Get me a cup of boiling water. I'll *dilute*."

Getting in the car to come down to Manhattan beautifully dressed, properly driven, eating dinner, getting back in the car, and going home was wonderfully exhausting for her, and it broke up the day. I loved seeing her devour that tempura! At the end of the meal, she would cackle, "Oh my G-d, I out-ate myself!" Often we invited her friend Fran Bigman to join us with her daughter, Linda Adams; Fran was only eighty-eight. Mother would say, "Eighty-eight? You're a *youngster!*"

She was one of the last of her generation, and without her coterie of contemporaries, I realized that Lily had less and less physical contact with other human beings. Nobody dropped by because they had all dropped dead. I started to buy her massages so she would at least feel human touch. She preferred male masseurs. I wonder why?

On one rare occasion, she said, "What used to take me ten minutes now takes me two hours. Have you seen me try to tie my shoe lately? It's pathetic. I'm ready to die."

I reminded her, "You can't die now, Mom. You have a party at The Plaza, a luncheon at The Pierre, and a wedding at the Metropolitan Club!"

"Wait a minute!" she said. "Let me get my book!"

She was not afraid to be silly; the hundreds of stuffed animals she had accrued she would rearrange daily and knew by name. 47 Penn was a very big house in which to grow old all by yourself with just one loyal, wonderful caretaker, Joyce. Oh, there was also Socorro, who worked Saturdays and Sundays and only spoke Spanish, a language my mother didn't speak. Not that it mattered, because my mother was stone deaf. I assume they communicated through sign language. Mother must've been a fabulous Marcel Marceau because there was one command Socorro always got right. How do I know? Because Mother raved, "Oh, that Socorro, she's marvelous! She massages my feet."

When asked about her longevity, my mother would say, "When you pick your angel of death, make sure he's a slow walker. Well, mine is a *really* slow walker." She knew she was living on borrowed time.

In early June, Mom was invited to dinner at the home of Dr. Mehmet Oz, the famous TV doctor. He wanted to honor her success as a survivor of the breakthrough medical experiment. Once again, her brave cardiology team, the Four Musketeers, were present to celebrate. Eight years after their procedure, Lily was still thriving.

Joyce drove Mom into Manhattan, and Andrew then drove the four of us over the George Washington Bridge, to Cliffside Park, New Jersey. The street on which the Ozes lived did not look particularly distinguished. And then we took a left turn into their winding driveway and were greeted by the most incredible views of the Hudson River and the full skyline of Manhattan from north to south. Dr. Oz's majestic compound sat proudly on this hillside. The main house was beige stucco with a terracotta roof, a Mediterranean mansion. It sat just below a sparkling swimming pool. Perched above both was a large guest house you'd have to pry me out of.

We had cocktails in the main house, then Dr. Oz pointed up the hill to the guest house pavilion where dinner would be served. I saw there was no elevator, no ramps, no stairlifts. I looked at Mehmet and he said, "No worries, Tovah! Here's what we're gonna do." Now calling Mother's surgical team, "Martin, Matt, Susheel, Jeffrey, let's put Lily on this gold armchair and carry her up the hill like the royalty she is. And fellas, I'm talking about the stone stairway as well," he said pointing to the steep, uneven granite steps that some contractor had gone to great lengths to create. The five doctors plus my valiant husband Andrew grabbed the four legs and the back of the chair and hoisted Lily to carry her up the incline. Five doctors and a lawyer; it was a Jewish mother's dream.

Her arrival at the top of the stairs could have been mistaken for a scene out of Verdi's *Aida*. At 103 years old, Lily looked like the Queen of Sheba or a Maharana of India arriving on her palanquin.

The view from the poolside dinner table was breathtaking. Doctor Oz stood up and explained, "When I saw this piece of property I had to have it because it overlooked the vast Hudson going north, and reminded me of the beautiful Bosporus and our home in Turkey when I was a child." Mehmet, like many of us, sought to re-create the best moments of his childhood. Sometimes every heart beats the same. I looked over at Mother and imagined her looking over the fields of wildflowers in the Bronx in 1914. It brought me great satisfaction to see her one hundred years later peering over the Hudson with a marvelous view of Lilyville.

Lily lived to see the Bar and Bat Mitzvahs of all of her grandchildren. Her life was saved on the day Amanda graduated from the Spence School, and she lived to see Amanda graduate from MIT with a major in physics. Can you imagine what a proud moment that was for a woman who was born before women's suffrage? She lived to see Brandon graduate from Harvard, Oxford, and Harvard Business School. She lived to see Amanda's engagement to the amazing Joel and lived to meet the incredible Jami, who later became Brandon's beautiful wife.

She lived from one Shabbos dinner to another at our home, and she lived to take trips to Cornell to visit David and his family. I don't ever remember her turning down a party or a platter.

She *lived*!

How I wish this chapter could be longer.

Tovah on Golda Meir

Prime Minister Golda Meir had a great sense of humor. One thing I learned during the sixteen months I played her on Broadway at the Helen Hayes was that the audience expected pure drama. Maybe it was the way Golda looked—her size-sixteen dresses, her black Oxfords, her omnipresent cigarette, her phlebitis legs, and her serious countenance.

But when Henry Kissinger was balking at sending her the US Airlift that could save Israel in the 1973 Yom Kippur War, Secretary Kissinger said to her: "First of all I am an American. Secondly, I am Secretary of State of the United States. Lastly, I am a Jew."

Golda replied, "That's fine, Henry—we read from right to left."

Taking the Final Bow

T HE SECOND TIME THAT DEATH CAME KNOCKING FOR LILY WAS June 10, 2014. She had gone out for an early dinner with one of her five grandchildren, my brother's oldest son, Noah Feldshuh. Before he dropped her off at home, they called me together from his car and left me a voicemail. In the message, Lily's Bronx accent sounded even thicker than usual. By now, she knew how terrified I was at the prospect that each exchange could be our last. She knew because I ended all our phone conversations with, "I'm the luckiest daughter in the world because you're the best mother in the world."

So her voice message was a wonderful spin on my mantra, "Hello, darling! Noah and I ate up a storm. I guess I'm getting your voicemail. So let me say, I'm the luckiest mother in the world because you're the best daughter in the world. How do ya like that?! I love you, bye bye!"

At 5:00 a.m. the next morning, David called.

"This is it," he said.

I instantly understood the subtext of those three words.

In her sleep, Lily had cried out for Joyce, then started babbling, then moaning, then went silent. She was rushed to White Plains Hospital. Her doctors said that she had suffered a massive cerebral hemorrhage on the left side of her brain—she was in a coma and she would never recover. For all intents and purposes, Mom was gone.

David arrived, and we knew that our next task was to get Mom home immediately. At 47 Penn, we talked about how long it might take for Mom's body to shut down. The only sustenance she'd be getting was ice chips, which we gently slid into her mouth. I imagined that at this rate, the end would be fairly quick.

I was wildly wrong: Lily survived for fourteen days without food, water, or extra oxygen.

We filled those fourteen days with a bedside vigil that included a parade of family and friends from across the country and the Atlantic—all the denizens of Lilyville. We cried, we laughed, we watched the World Cup! The family formed an emotional campfire around her deathbed, never leaving. We slept on the floor in a circle like paramecia and amoebas facing the dimming light.

There's no dress rehearsal for the final moments. At 12:51 a.m. on June 23, Death got tired of waiting. For forty-five minutes, her body was at war with the Angel of Death. You could hear her flesh and bone screaming, *I'm healthy! I've got the heart of a fifteen-year-old. Don't take me! Please, don't take me!*

At 1:36 a.m., Lily died on an inhale, blood visibly draining from her face, her skin going from rose to pale-yellow alabaster in a millisecond. Observing her, I understood for the first time what it truly means to be stone still. I understood why Michelangelo carved the dead out of pale, unmovable marble.

For me, seeing the life float out of Lily was miraculous. The only thing I can compare it to is giving birth to our children; it was like surfing on a giant wave and being taken in the direction of nature's desire. Death, this much-anticipated caller, wasn't something to fear. It was miraculous, otherworldly, and so much bigger than I was—it was also a relief and release for my mother.

Confronting death wasn't scary, as I'd always assumed it would be. It was merely the other side of the golden coin of life. Whereas birth pushes one forth into the world, death sucks one away from it, both with relentless, majestic power.

To die at 1:36 a.m. could be interpreted as a religious omen. As you know, eighteen—chai—is a magical and mystical number in the Jewish religion. Mother died at the moment of double chai, double life. We can interpret this several ways: as the two lives my mother was given from ages 1 to 95 and then from ages 95 to over 103—her medical miracle. We could also interpret it as the two lives I had with my mother that were polar opposites: the cold, vacant one for the first twenty-seven years of my life, and the warm, inextricably intertwined one in the last eighteen years of her life. We can even interpret the eighteen years she lived as a widow as a lifetime in itself. To die on the dot of double chai could also be a message about life after life, one that exists in an imperceivable dimension where hopefully, she may be experiencing eternity.

LILYVILLE. WHAT HAPPENS TO A town when its namesake passes away? What happens when the mayor has left office? Where are the monuments and where are the plaques? One thing I can tell you: a ghost town Lilyville is not. It is a thriving metropolis, the height of Manhattan and the breadth of the universe. Andy and I, David and Martha, stand as the great bridges, linking the island of family to its past. Our children stand as skyscrapers and their children as super-highways, still under construction, going out into the world. The thousands of photographs are the billboards, liberally peppered above every street, in every direction you look, ever reminding the future generations to look at who was here, look at what they did, and look at their legacy.

And if you happen to walk through the heart of town and notice a gorgeous, majestic theater with a sparkling marquee, there in electric lights ever and always will shine *Lillian Kaplan Feldshuh* above the title of the long-running, now-and-forever generational hit, *LILYVILLE*.

Curtain

Curtain Call

RATHER THAN USE THIS CURTAIN CALL TO BRING TO THE STAGE the resplendent cast of characters that have and continue to people Lilyville, I would like to share three visitations I've had. Two are from my father, one from my mother, each returning, as it were, for an unexpected encore, spectacularly breaking the wall of the fourth dimension.

I

The day before what would have been my father's eighty-sixth birthday, we were invited to stay at Rabbi Marc Schneier's house in Westhampton. The rabbi and his wife were kind enough to extend the invitation not only to my husband and me, but also to my mother, a new widow. It was a very generous offer and deeply appreciated.

We arrived on the afternoon of July 31. I took Mom out for a drink at the Crazy Dog Diner in Westhampton and said, "Tomorrow is Dad's birthday. He would've been eighty-six, and he promised me he would live till eighty-six. Would you like to ask for a sign that he's still here?"

She looked up from her vodka gimlet and snapped, "*Mishuganah.*"

Undeterred, I lifted my glass of Baileys Irish Cream, Mother's other favorite drink, and toasted. "Here's to Dad. Happy birthday tomorrow! Show us a sign that you're still here."

"Ridiculous," toasted Lily.

We returned to the rabbi's house, and I went back to reading my book, *Life After Death,* which consisted of two hundred case studies about people who heard from loved ones who had passed away. The book stated that there were two common elements in the signs: the message would be transmitted to a messenger who was open to receiving it, and the message would be an obscure detail that would be significant only to that messenger and other intimates of the deceased.

As the clock struck twelve, I said to Andrew, "It's August 1. I'm going to celebrate my father's birthday."

I went to the rabbi's kitchen. I opened the freezer door. Staring me in the face, front and center, was butter pecan ice cream. Incredulously, I said to myself, "This is wild. Dad's favorite ice cream was butter pecan! He ate it every day."

I proceeded to go from the rabbi, to the *rebbetzin* (Yiddish for rabbi's wife), to the housekeeper, sharing the delight of this coincidence. None of them could explain how the ice cream even got into the freezer because it wasn't kosher. To my eyes, this coincidence was morphing into a miracle.

I proceeded to break the seal and open the brand-new quart of Blue Bell Butter Pecan in front of the three of them, and lo and behold, one scoop was clearly taken out. This miracle had become a visitation.

From the corner of the living room, Lily was observing all of this. Triumphantly I crowed, "Dad sent us a sign. He said he would live till eight-six. Today is his birthday. I'm telling you, he's here tonight."

She quipped, "If Sid's having a scoop, I'll have two!"

II

During the summer of 1996, when I could barely sing a note, I was forced to take constant medication to get through the first theatrical run of my one-woman show *Tovah: Out of Her Mind!* Summer passed, the show closed, the High Holidays were upon us, and still no voice. Rosh Hashanah? No voice. Yom Kippur? No voice.

On the Day of Atonement, I had been given the honor of carrying the Torah throughout the congregation. That honor was a long time coming for women, and I remember vividly how I was denied that opportunity in 1961 at my Bat Mitzvah, but the privilege was here today.

Because the ceiling collapsed in our synagogue on West Eighty-Eighth Street, the gracious pastors at St. Andrew and St. Paul on Eighty-Sixth Street had generously offered us their sanctuary. To accommodate our services, all church icons were covered except for the sculpted angels that couldn't be reached on top of their stalwart cement pillars.

I was holding the Torah, and I could have sworn that as I turned the corner to return to the bimah, an angel was moving on the top pillar. And not just any angel—it was my father. I could see my father! He was robed in white, but the tips of his toes were black. Were those his transgressions?

When we got to *Yizkor*, the memorial service for the dead—a service of gratitude that encourages dialogue between the living and the souls who have left this earth—I whispered up to the angel, "Dad, Dad, I can't sing. I feel as if I've been shot in the throat."

I shut my eyes. I could sense my father coming toward me. His arms were now pristine white wings. As he inched closer, I could see that feathers covered his hands, extending past his fingers. He placed those hands on either side of each vocal cord, gently moving up and down, up and down, again and again as if to soothe my swollen cords with his touch, a touch that was light as gossamer. Then, without a word, just as quickly as he came, he was gone.

I opened my mouth, and unexpectedly, I could sing. *I could sing!* A renewed life energy started to flow in me once more. Was this a miracle? Did this really happen? Had I been Christian, I guess I would have been born again. Instead, having been touched by Sidney's spirit, I sang out in growing crescendo.

III

On the fifth anniversary of my mother's death, I went to East Hampton's Guild Hall to view a documentary called *Witness Theater,* produced and directed by my friend Oren Rudavsky. The film shined a light on the Holocaust Survivor Program (HSP), which paired Holocaust survivors in their nineties with high school students. The survivors narrated their truth, and the teenagers enacted their stories. The senior citizens had made young friends for life who would carry their testimony far into the future like a bright torch in a starless night.

When I watched this film, all I could think about was my mother, as I realized I too was chronicling the story of an elder so that her wisdom and experience could live forever. I too was creating a record to honor a survivor of gender inequality, which brought with it corsets, no women's suffrage, no women's liberation, no major profession, no financial power, and no way to get there except after the death of her husband.

As I left this daytime screening, I met the head of Self Help, the organization that sponsors HSP, which created the theater pieces that are presented all over the country now, culminating in this documentary. I said to him, "Mr. Friedman, I was extremely moved today by your program, and I have the honor of seeing this documentary on the very day my mother died five years ago."

He asked, "What was your mother's name?"

I said, "Lily. Lily Kaplan."

Mr. Friedman blanched and said, "Lily Kaplan? That's *my* mother's name." We just stood and looked at each other, two strangers with an inexorable connection, experiencing a perfectly timed revelation.

I wished him well, and I got in my car to follow my close friend, Julie Ratner, to her East Hampton home for an impromptu cup of tea. As we sat on her veranda overlooking the verdant backyard, we peered into her blue-bottomed pool. I talked again about Mr. Friedman and the Lily Kaplan coincidence. I also talked about how much I longed for my mother and how I had wailed the night before at the hour of her death, keening like a wounded animal. The fifth anniversary of anything usually marks the time for a reunion, not a separation.

At that very moment, my attention was caught by a specter of white in the far-left corner of the pool. There at the bottom was the soft shape of a human being. I thought maybe the sun was playing tricks on us, but Julie's backyard was surrounded by high trees. Seeing it as well, Julie ran to grab her skimmer to check if some large object was lying in the depths of her pool. There was nothing, yet the specter remained in the loose form of swirling energy.

I instinctively yelled out, "Mom. Mom is that you?" Miraculously, the light started to move toward the stairs of the pool. I immediately waded into the water toward the light and sat with my feet dangling where I felt my mother's feet now were. The water was warm and calm, vaguely reminiscent of the bathtub water in which my mother invited me to join her when I was a little girl.

I had not heard from my mother since she left her body. I truly feel that somehow, in the transmigration of energy, which we are taught can neither be created nor destroyed, she was approaching us. I remember what my brother David said, "The way Mom showed her love is that she was always there." Well, on June 23, 2019, my mother was there.

My mother's visit created the hope of a future for us and illuminated wondrous possibilities for me. Perhaps she would return, or, come my turn, as my life force leaves my body—so it would join forever with my mother's.

I always used to think the Catholics had death cornered; all those saints and little figures waiting for them when they popped off. The Jews? Forget it. So when it's my time to go, I may not have Jesus, Mary, and Joseph on the other side of my rainbow, but I may very well have Lily. And under the dome of Lilyville, all my precious forebears and beloved Sidney too.

Exit Music

AS I WRITE THIS BOOK, THERE'S A TWO-YEAR-OLD CURTAIN riser tugging at my toes, a four-month-old who has just learned to laugh, and a newborn cradled in my arms. These are my three grandchildren, Rafael (Hebrew for the Angel of Healing), Sidney Mei (whose Hebrew name, Simcha Meira, means happiness and creator of light), and Camille Willa (whose Hebrew name is Lila Malka—Lila for Lily and Malka meaning Queen).

Witnessing these babies sprout and grow gives me a joyous pathway to *non-aging*. My knees are bone on bone from forty years of running, my spine is slightly curved from holding books and babies on my right hip for decades, and my size has shrunk from five feet two-and-a-half inches to five feet *nothin'*. My face is increasingly wrinkled and may one day resemble a road map of Manhattan. Even so, being with Rafael, Sidney, and Camille as they gaze into my eyes, fully engaged in wonder, brings *me* to a place of wonder.

Mother always said that being a grandmother was better than being a mother because you get "the icing on the cake." You get the smiles, the gurgles, the burps, and the farts, but you don't have to change the diapers. You get the sleeping, the waking, the crying, the laughter, but only during the day because you're home by nightfall. Nonetheless, I can't wait until my babysitting duties are in full swing.

I am now entering my seventies. Many of my close relatives were gone by the time they finished this decade of life. So, as the possibility of leaving this earth comes closer, focusing on new life becomes an essential gift to my vitality.

As Margaret Mead said, "Children find their place in the universe not through their parents but through their grandparents."

Rafi, Sidney, and Camille, I will be your intimate forebear as Gershan and Ada were mine. I will be your storyteller, the one who gives you that extra knowledge of where you came from and thus who you are—knowledge that will feel like a light beam of strength going through your body down into the earth. I will carry you back more than one hundred years to your great-grandparents and teach you how to be a mensch, how to give life your best shot no matter what, how to strive for excellence because excellence leads to self-respect and self-respect leads to happiness. How to have self-compassion when your best simply doesn't make it.

I have finally learned self-compassion very late in my own life. It's the one area of my development I wish I could redo. I should have developed self-forgiveness long ago, for from there comes true forgiveness of others. In the last decades of her life, Gramee Lily had this virtue in abundance.

Before we go, I want to thank you for being excellent scene partners with me as you turned these pages. (Remember turning pages?) You've been whisper quiet and attentive, the supreme gift to any artist. And as you exit from this time we've shared, I invite you to look at the theater piece *you* are living. Is it a musical, a comedy, or G-d forbid, *Long Day's Journey Into Night?* Just remember what Lily used to tell me: "Happiness is a choice." So choose wisely. Audition your company carefully, collaborate generously, celebrate the successes, and share the sorrows collectively. And please look around you. Is there a Lily in your life who might be your best producer? *That*, dear ones, is my wish for you.

Thank you for visiting Lilyville.

Cast Party

THANK YOU FOR COMING INTO THE THEATER OF MY MEMORIES. I was blessed with a brilliant original cast, and I wouldn't change a single player in my original production: Gershan, Ada, Rose, Nancy, May, their mates and children; Sidney (ז״ל); my brother David, husband Andrew, children Brandon and Amanda; nephews Noah, Zach, and niece Hannah; cherished in-laws Martha, Joel, and Jami; radiant footlights Rafael, Sidney Mei, and Camille; and finally, the megastar and my original producer, Lillian Kaplan Feldshuh.

Lily, who now that she has left me, is always with me. I want to make sure my children understand this, and my grandchildren as well. Lily will be in them, in their heads, in their hearts, in their bones, as will I. My mother Lily's voice was muted by the era in which she was born. Now, with *Lilyville*, her clarion call will be heard aloud and forever.

When her breast was put away in an airtight brassiere six weeks after my birth, and warmth was then dominated by a shyness that no infant could comprehend, there were consequences.

But then, aren't consequences, challenges, setbacks, and triumphs all part of the dramatic action of any production worth the price of admission?

But a show is judged not by its star alone. The essential corners of the production must shine for the piece to succeed. You, listed below, have focused your superlative klieg light wattage on *Lilyville*.

You, who are my guests at this cast party, have seen me through generations of family—births, deaths, laughter, sorrow, and even that *bris!* You have helped me represent myself in my best writer's voice, as I spent time with people in my life who made deep impressions on me, for better or for worse.

Even my mother would be impressed by your support and wisdom, which helped bring this saga of *Lilyville* to fruition.

And now I'd like to thank you.

This piece would not have been possible without:

The ever brilliant Jeff Harnar

My wonderful editor Lauren Marino

The intellectual overview of Kate Buford

My incredible assistants: Oliver Shoulson, Firozah Najmi, Kailey Marshall, Gabi Nail, Nicola Saffron, and Hayley Pace

Holocaust producer, Robert "Buzz" Berger

Patrick Byrnes of the Passaic Historical Society

Photographers Julio Gaggia, Anita and Steven Shevett, Eric Stephen Jacobs, Barry Polyak, Laura Pettibone, Arnold Weissberger, Aaron Epstein, and photographer and critic Stephen Mosher

Professor Ilja Wachs of Sarah Lawrence College, *the first one to believe I had a writer's voice*

My friend Albert Lee

My agent, Lane Zachary

Consultant Bev West and theater treasure Peter Filichia

Cousins Jonathan Silbermann, Lucille and Cathryn Lewis

Cousin Karen Shafron from London

And those who deserve another round of applause, my co-stars: beloved Andrew Harris Levy, cherished Amanda Claire Levy Ryzowy and Garson Brandon Levy, irreplaceable Dr. David Feldshuh, and my treasured grandchildren, Rafael Levi Ryzowy, Sidney Mei Kirk Levy, and Camille Willa Ryzowy *for every cup of sunshine they brought me as I wrote.*

———❖———

LET ME CONCLUDE WITH ONE of Leading Lady Lily's last emails to me.

TO MY LOVELY DAUGHTER;

YOU KNOW . . . YOU WRITE VERY WELL.

I CAN NOW SEE WHERE I INHERIT MY EXPERTISE.

HA! HA!

I AM A REGULAR CRACKERJACK!!!

I FEEL SAFE IN GIVING MYSELF COMPLIMENTS BECAUSE I GET SO MANY THESE DAYS.

LOVE YOU.

MOMMY